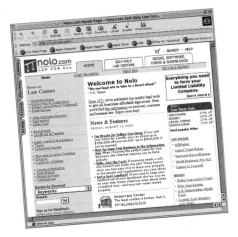

LEGAL INFORMATION ONLINE ANYTIME

24 hours a day

www.nolo.com

AT THE NOLO.COM SELF-HELP LAW CENTER, YOU'LL FIND

- **Nolo's comprehensive Legal Encyclopedia** filled with plain-English information on a variety of legal topics
- **Nolo's Law Dictionary**—legal terms without the legalese
- **Auntie Nolo**—if you've got questions, Auntie's got answers
- **The Law Store**—over 250 self-help legal products including: Downloadable Software, Books, Form Kits and eGuides
- **Legal and product updates**
- **Frequently Asked Questions**
- **NoloBriefs, our free monthly email newsletter**
- **Legal Research Center,** for access to state and federal statutes
- **Our ever-popular lawyer jokes**

Quality LAW BOOKS & SOFTWARE FOR EVERYONE

Nolo's user-friendly products are consistently first-rate. Here's why:

- A dozen in-house legal editors, working with highly skilled authors, ensure that our products are accurate, up-to-date and easy to use
- We continually update every book and software program to keep up with changes in the law
- Our commitment to a more democratic legal system informs all of our work
- We appreciate & listen to your feedback. Please fill out and return the card at the back of this book.

OUR "NO-HASSLE" GUARANTEE

Return anything you buy directly from Nolo for any reason and we'll cheerfully refund your purchase price. No ifs, ands or buts.

Read This First

The information in this book is as up to date and accurate as we can make it. But it's important to realize that the law changes frequently, as do fees, forms and procedures. If you handle your own legal matters, it's up to you to be sure that all information you use—including the information in this book—is accurate. Here are some suggestions to help you:

First, make sure you've got the most recent edition of this book. To learn whether a later edition is available, check the edition number on the book's spine and then go to Nolo's online Law Store at www.nolo.com or call Nolo's Customer Service Department at 800-728-3555.

Next, even if you have a current edition, you need to be sure it's fully up to date. The law can change overnight. At *www.nolo.com*, we post notices of major legal and practical changes that affect the latest edition of a book. To check for updates, find your book in the Law Store on Nolo's website (you can use the "A to Z Product List" and click the book's title). If you see an "Updates" link on the left side of the page, click it. If you don't see a link, that means we haven't posted any updates. (But check back regularly.)

Finally, we believe accurate and current legal information should help you solve many of your own legal problems on a cost-efficient basis. But this text is not a substitute for personalized advice from a knowledgeable lawyer. If you want the help of a trained professional, consult an attorney licensed to practice in your state.

4th edition

Choose the Right Long-Term Care:

Home Care, Assisted Living and Nursing Homes

by Joseph L. Matthews

FOURTH EDITION

Second Printing   AUGUST 2003
Editor   DIANA FITZPATRICK
Book Design   JACKIE MANCUSO
Cover Design   TONI IHARA
Proofreading   JOE SADUSKY
Index   PATRICIA DEMINNA
Printing   CONSOLIDATED PRINTERS, INC.

Matthews, Joseph L.
    Choose the right long-term care : home care, assisted living and nursing homes / by
Joseph Matthews. -- 4th ed.
    p. cm.
    Includes index.
    ISBN 0-87337-824-5
    1. Aged—Long term care--Evaluation. 2. Long-term care of the sick--Evaluation. 3.
Aged--Long-term care--Finance. 4. Long-term care of the sick--Finance. 5. Consumer
education. I. Title.

RA644.5 .M38 2002
362.1'6--dc21   2002018833

Quantity sales: For information on bulk purchases or corporate premium sales, please contact
the Special Sales department. For academic sales or textbook adoptions, ask for Academic
Sales. 800-955-4775, Nolo, 950 Parker St., Berkeley, CA 94710.

Acknowledgments

Many thanks go to Ralph Warner, who saw immediately the value of a book such as this and who gave the project its birth.

Special thanks go to Peter Yedidia, President of Geriatric Health Systems of San Francisco, who gave generously of his time and vast professional experience in matters of health care programs for the elderly. His corrective commentaries greatly strengthened the manuscript.

Special thanks also to Diane Arnold-Driver, Coordinator of the Center on Aging at the University of California, Berkeley. She shared readily her great expertise in geriatric care matters and tactfully made a number of suggestions which redounded to the significant benefit of the text.

Thank you also to Lora Connolly and Sandra Pierce-Miller of the California Department of Health Services, who took the time to clarify a number of matters pertaining to state partnership long-term care insurance programs.

And many thanks to Stan Jacobsen, whose thorough research has not only helped keep this book up-to-date, but has also provided readers with valuable new information.

Also, my thanks to Spencer Sherman for updating the third edition.

A final and most exuberant thanks goes to my editor, Barbara Kate Repa, whose perspicacity and skill are matched only by her patience and good humor. She needed all of them with me. The quality of this book is in large measure due to her talents.

Contents

1
Making Decisions About Long-Term Care

2

At-Home Care

3

Organized Senior Residences

4

Long-Term Care Facilities

5   Care for Elders With Alzheimer's Disease

6
Medicare and Veterans' Benefits

7

Medicaid Coverage for Long-Term Care

8

Medicaid and Asset Protection

9.

Protecting Choices About Medical Care and Finances

10

Estate Planning: Controlling Your Money and Property

11

Long-Term Care Insurance

Appendix

Resource Directory

Making Decisions About Long-Term Care

A ll of us have to face the uncomfortable fact that, one day, we or our family members may need some kind of expensive long-term care. Most older people, even if they remain basically healthy, develop physical or mental frailties or impairments that at some point prevent them from living completely independent lives.

More than five million older people in the United States receive some form of daily care at home, provided by someone from outside the family. Millions more receive regular care, though not on a daily basis. And still more millions receive at-home care entirely from family members—who may not be able to continue that care indefinitely. Nearly two million people over age 65 live full-time in some type of nursing facility or other residential care facility, at a cost of between $30,000 and $150,000 per year. Of people over 65 in nursing facilities, about 25% will live there for longer than a year and about 10% for more than three years.

Medicare, which some believe pays for medical care for everyone over 65, in fact pays for only about 10% of all nursing facility costs, a smaller fraction of all home care costs and nothing at all for long-term care. Medicaid, the federal government program which pays medical costs for the financially needy, pays for about half of all nursing facility costs, but you have to spend most of your personal assets before you become eligible for coverage. And while Medicaid pays for residence in a few assisted living, shelter care or residential care facilities, most of this cost must be paid with private funds.

These statistics convey an urgent, unsettling message: Many of us will need long-term care—and the government is not going to foot much of the bill. This book can help you prepare for what the future might bring by presenting the alternatives you need to consider. The more physically, emotionally and financially prepared you are, and the more in control of your own life, the better off you and your family will be.

A. What Is Long-Term Care?

As used in this book, "long-term care" means regular assistance with medical care (nursing, medicating, physical therapy) or personal needs (eating, dressing, bathing, moving around) provided by someone outside an older person's family. There are many varieties of long-term care—ranging from part-time home care and adult daycare, to independent living and assisted living residential communities, to personal care residences and nursing facilities. Some long-term care is temporary—for example, just long enough to help an older person recover from a broken hip or a stroke. Often, though, once begun it lasts for the remainder of an older person's life.

B. Complex Questions of Long-Term Care

An older person's debilitating condition may be only partial—such as failing hearing or eyesight, memory loss or weakness in arms or legs. Or it may be extreme—the effects of a major stroke or heart ailment, overall frailty, the later stages of Alzheimer's disease. Whatever the specific nature of the impairment, you will have to face a number of difficult questions:

- What kind of care is needed?
- Who will provide it?
- Where will it be provided?
- How much will it cost?
- Who will pay for it?

Attempting to answer these questions will require you to negotiate a number of minefields: finding the right level and amount of care, avoiding unnecessary institutionalization, understanding complicated Medicare and Medicaid rules, considering private long-term care insurance—and importantly, paying for the high cost of care without losing every cent you have.

If the elder is unable to arrange for the care needed, or is not fully aware of the need for care, the burden of providing care may fall heavily on other family members. Spouses and grown children often must take on major if not total responsibility for organizing and paying for long-term care. This book, then, is a guide not just for the elder who needs long-term care, but for all those who will participate in organizing, providing and paying for that care. The book explains financial planning for long-term care: what Medicare and Medicaid pay, whether to buy long-term care insurance and how some of an elder's assets might be protected from long-term care costs. The book emphasizes the need to explore the many available care alternatives and guides you in choosing home care, a residential care facility or a nursing facility if that becomes necessary.

The book also explains legal devices and documents that can help ensure that the elder's wishes for medical procedures and property management are followed if he or she can no longer make decisions alone.

LONG-TERM CARE BY ANY OTHER NAME: A GLOSSARY

Long-term care comes in many varieties and settings. Some types of care are services that can be provided in a senior's own home; others are residential care options. This book covers all of the following types of long-term care in detail. Here we provide brief definitions of various care options, to help you keep the terms straight as you use this book. Bear in mind that most of these are not formal or technical terms—what people mean when they use these terms may differ slightly from place to place, or from facility to facility.

Adult Daycare: services such as meals, social activities and exercise programs, plus companionship, provided for free or low cost at senior centers or special adult daycare centers. For seniors who live independently, either at home or with relatives. See Chapter 2, Section J.

Assisted Living: private apartment in a seniors-only residential facility that offers meals, assistance with personal care and housekeeping and close monitoring of residents' health and safety, but not nursing or other medical care. See Chapter 3, Section B.

Board and Care Facility/Home: a long-term care residence facility—often small, sometimes in a private home—in which a resident is provided a room (often shared), meals, assistance with personal care, activities and health and safety monitoring, but not nursing or other medical care. Also called a Residential Care Facility for the Elderly, a Personal Care Facility or a Sheltered Care Facility. See Chapter 4, Section A.

Continuing Care Retirement Community: a multi-level facility which permits a resident to remain in the facility while moving among Independent Living, Assisted Living and Nursing Facility care, as the resident's needs require. See Chapter 3, Section C.

Convalescent Home: a general term that could describe either a Nursing Facility or a Board and Care or Sheltered Care home. Like "Rest Home," the term is being used less and less.

Custodial Care Facility: any long-term care residential facility—including Nursing Facility, Board and Care Home, Residential Care Facility for the Elderly, Personal Care Facility and Sheltered Care Facility—in which residents get a private or shared room, meals, assistance with personal care, physical and social activities and round-the-clock monitoring. Depending on the level of the facility, residents may also receive regular nursing or other medical care. See Chapter 4, Section A.

Extended Care Facility: a long-term care residence offering more than one level of care within the same facility. It may combine Independent Living with Assisted Living, Assisted Living with a Custodial Care Facility, a Custodial Care Facility with Skilled Nursing Care or some other combination of these. It does not necessarily offer all levels of care, as a Continuing Care Retirement Community does. See Chapter 3, Section C.

Geriatric Care Manager: someone who assists in locating and arranging short-term or long-term care for an elder, either at home or in a residential setting. See Chapter 1, Section G.

Home Care/Home Health Care: short-term or long-term care at a senior's residence. It can include nursing, some medical and therapeutic services, assistance with personal care and the activities of daily life, housekeeping and meal preparation. Home care can be provided in a private residence or an Independent or Assisted Living facility, either by a licensed Home Health Care Agency or by individual paid providers. See Chapter 2.

Home Health Care Agency: certified by each state and by Medicare, these agencies can provide everything from skilled nursing care and therapy to assistance with grocery shopping and personal paperwork. See Chapter 2, Sections D and E.

Independent Living Residence/Community: a building or community specially designed for and restricted to seniors, offering a rented or purchased apartment or house. They provide on-site common facilities and services, but not personal or health care. See Chapter 3, Section A.

Intermediate Care Nursing Facility: a residential facility that provides some nursing and other medical care, but not as much as a Skilled Nursing Facility provides. These facilities provide long-term care of the chronically ill or disabled, or short-term care until a patient/resident can be moved to a Custodial Care Facility. See Chapter 4, Section A.

Long-Term Care: an extended period—either permanent or during recovery from a serious illness or injury—of assistance with basic activities of daily living (sometimes called personal care), such as bathing, eating, dressing and moving around. It includes monitoring of health and safety and may also include nursing care and physical or other therapy, meals, social activities and housekeeping. Long-term care can be provided in a private home, organized senior residence or nursing facility.

Long-Term Care Facility: any of several types of residences designed and operated to provide on-site assistance with basic activities of daily living and to monitor health and safety. See Chapter 4.

Multi-Level Facility: same as Extended Care Facility, above.

Nursing Facility/Home: a residential care facility that provides long-term custodial care. Depending on the type of facility, it may also provide more or less extensive nursing care and physical or other therapy. See Chapter 4.

Personal Care Facility: same as Board and Care Home, above.

Residential Care Facility for the Elderly (RCFE): another name for a Personal Care Facility or Board and Care Home.

Respite Care: temporary, part-time company for a dependent elder intended to give the primary caregiver (usually a spouse or other family member) some time off. See Chapter 2, Section J.

Rest Home: an old-fashioned term, not used much any longer, for a Long-Term Care Facility.

Senior Residence: a residential building or community that is designed for and limited to seniors. This term is often used to refer to Independent Living or Assisted Living. See Chapter 3.

Sheltered Care: usually refers to a Board and Care Home (see above) but sometimes refers to Assisted Living (see above).

Skilled Nursing Facility: a residential facility that provides round-the-clock medical monitoring and daily, intensive nursing and therapy, as well as all necessary personal care. Usually limited to short-term stays following serious injury, illness or surgery. See Chapter 4, Section A.

1. Finding the Information You Need

Many people, at many different stages in the process of deciding how and where to get long-term care, will find guidance in this book.

- *If your parent, grandparent or other older relative is no longer able to live a fully independent life, and you have to figure out where additional care will come from, where your elder relative will live to receive that care, who will pay for it and how*

Section G of this chapter explains how a geriatric care manager can organize a program of care for your relative. This may be particularly helpful to you, especially if the elder lives in a different city or state from you. In addition, Chapters 3 and 4 discuss in detail how to choose the right kind and level of elder housing or nursing facility for your relative, and how to make sure the facility will provide a comfortable and humane residential setting. Chapter 5 provides information on meeting the special needs of those who have Alzheimer's Disease and similar conditions.

Chapters 6 through 8 explain how much you can expect Medicare, Medicaid and other government programs to pay for long-term care, and how much income or other property your relative will be able to retain or transfer to others. Throughout the book, you will also find referrals to agencies and organizations that can provide detailed information and assistance about specific long-term care needs; this information is also collected in a Resource Directory in the Appendix of the book.

- *If you or a family member is over fifty and wants to begin planning to protect their home and other assets from the potential financial disaster of future long-term care*

In addition to the chapters on Medicare and Medicaid financing, you will find several other chapters particularly valuable. Chapter 8 explains how to make long-range plans that will protect some of your assets from future long-term care costs. Chapter 9 explores ways to preserve your dignity and retain some control over your life and property when you are no longer physically or mentally able to handle all your own affairs. Chapter 10 gives an overview of estate planning techniques that can be used to protect an elder's money and property. And Chapter 11 describes in detail the definite risks and potential benefits of private long-term care insurance—and the most important policy terms to consider.

- *If your spouse or partner has personal or medical needs that the two of you are no longer able to handle without outside help, whether or not your spouse or partner has recognized the need*

In Chapter 2, you will learn about how home care may permit you both to remain at home and get the care you need. Chapter 3 discusses the kinds of residential alternatives in which you might both live and receive the care you need with more comfort, but at much less cost than a nursing facility. Chapter 5 addresses the particular problems faced by those whose spouse or partner has Alzheimer's Disease or a similar form of cognitive impairment. Chapters 7 and 8 describe how the Medicaid government assistance program might help pay for one spouse's care while leaving the other spouse with some income and assets.

- *If you increasingly find that you cannot manage all your own personal or medical needs without outside assistance and you face an immediate need to organize long-term personal assistance or medical care*

Chapter 2 introduces the many kinds of care available to you at home as alternatives to entering a nursing facility. Chapter 3 discusses the kinds of housing available for seniors that might provide the right level of assistance for you without the tremendous expense and unnecessary restrictions of a nursing facility. And Section G of this chapter explains how a geriatric care manager can help you start making care arrangements.

C. Exploring Long-Term Care Options

Although the sudden onset of an illness or disability does not always permit much advanced planning for long-term care, this book encourages you to be the best comparison shopper possible. If you are able to explore alternatives before rushing to move into a nursing facility, you improve your chances of obtaining the level of care you need—and perhaps saving a great deal of money.

Being prepared and researching alternatives when choosing long-term care allows you to realistically assess what is needed, and to choose only the kind of care that is actually required. In this way, you can avoid the loss of independence and great cost that come with taking on more care than necessary. This is particularly true when some combination of home health care and personal assistance would be sufficient to permit a person to remain at home instead of entering a residential nursing facility. Or when an assisted living or residential care facility can provide sufficient care to allow a person to avoid entering a nursing facility. When time permits, doing some financial planning *before* residence in a long-term care facility becomes necessary may permit you to protect some of the value of your home or life's savings.

Finally, but not least important, the more thorough you are, the greater the opportunity for everyone concerned to participate—particularly if the person who needs care is not easily able to investigate and make decisions on his or her own. With more alternatives, everyone involved will have greater emotional room to come to terms with the decisions that have to be made.

D. Recognizing and Discussing the Situation

If you need care, you may find it a hard topic to raise with others because it seems like a blow to your self-esteem, a subject that means you are really "old." You may also be reluctant to begin a process of giving up some of your independence or surrendering full control over your life. And when you know you need the help of your family, you may be fearful of becoming a burden.

If you believe that someone else—a family member or other loved one—is in need of care, you may be reluctant to bring up the subject because it may seem like a challenge or an insult. And within the family there may be anxiety, guilt and wide differences of opinion about what care is needed and who should provide it. Remember, the first step in getting necessary care is to overcome your reluctance to talk about it. Once the discussion has begun, you can use the information in this book to organize and choose the right kinds of care.

1. Getting Help From Others

To get the discussion underway and keep it on the right track, it is often best to look outside the family. An unrelated person can sometimes soothe ruffled family feathers, present a neutral opinion and offer solutions the family might not know about. Also, you may find it easier to reveal fears and other feelings to an outsider than to an involved family member.

Here are some of the people you can turn to for help in beginning to evaluate long-term care needs:

- Your personal physician is often a good place to start, not necessarily to moderate discussions but to define your medical needs and refer you to others who may be helpful in making arrangements.

- Traditional word-of-mouth is still one of the best ways to begin tackling any new problem. Friends and neighbors whose opinions you trust, and who may have already faced similar situations, are often a good source of information. The people at your local senior center may know of sources for long-term care assistance. These word-of-mouth sources often let you know of "unofficial" personal care aides who would not be available through more formal channels.
- A clergy member may be able to help directly or to refer you and your family to professionals who can introduce alternatives and coordinate planning.
- County family service agencies, Area Agencies on Aging or other senior information and referral services are experienced sources that can provide direct access to specific care providers and help you develop an overall care plan. These agencies can direct you to a counselor or social worker who specializes in long-term care for elders and can help you begin your discussions and planning. (See the Resource Directory in the Appendix of this book.)
- If residence in a nursing facility is not absolutely necessary, many people make use of the services of a professional geriatric care manager to see what at-home and other supportive services are available and to organize care from different providers. (Geriatric care managers are discussed in detail in Section G.)
- If you or your loved one has Alzheimer's Disease or a similar mental impairment, you can turn to organizations that specialize in providing information and referrals to people facing these difficult situations. (See the listing for "Alzheimer's Disease Organizations" in the Resource Directory in this book's Appendix).

INVOLVE THE CARE RECEIVER

If you are a family member helping to plan for someone else's care, bear in mind that the most essential participant in planning long-term care is the person whose care is being considered.

---

2. Assessing Medical Needs

Because a specific physical or mental condition often leads to the need for long-term care, one of the first things you should do is get professional advice both about the need for immediate care and about likely changes in the condition over time. Talk with your primary care physician first; he or she may refer you to a geriatric specialist for further consultation.

An additional resource to help you assess medical and personal care needs is a geriatric screening program. Local hospitals have them, as do community and county health centers. If you have trouble finding a geriatric screening program, check with your county social service agency or local or Area Agency on Aging, or call the senior referral number in the white pages of the phone book.

Some important things to consider when assessing an older person's need for medical care are:

- **Specific medical requirements.** The doctor or other health screening personnel can discuss the elder's specific medical needs (such as monitoring and administering drugs or providing physical therapy), explain how they can be met and let you know who can do it. The doctor or health care worker can also discuss the level of ongoing care that would be required to deliver those medical services: family members supplemented by occasional visits from home care aides, a more sophisticated home care program or various levels of residential nursing facility care, for example.

- **Changes in care over time.** The doctor or other health care worker can also discuss the medical prognosis—that is, what the future is likely to hold: whether to anticipate a short or long recovery period, whether a condition is likely to stabilize over a long period or whether it will become worse over a short or long period. Knowing of likely developments in the medical condition will help you plan the right level of care and allow for these changes.

- **Mental impairment.** A thorough geriatric screening and evaluation are particularly important when the elder seems to have a mental impairment. An older person's physical problems may become much more difficult to manage because of added symptoms of forgetfulness, disorientation or general listlessness.

Such changes are often the beginnings of a permanent loss of mental faculties: the early stages of Alzheimer's disease or other forms of dementia, which will require careful long-term care planning. (See Chapter 5 for a detailed discussion of care options for those suffering from Alzheimer's disease or similar impairments.)

Sometimes, though, what looks like an irreversible loss of mental facilities may really be the result of some specific and treatable problem such as improper or over-medication, poor nutrition, depression over the loss of a spouse or a friend or a subtle medical condition that has not been diagnosed and treated. It is very important not to mistake a temporary and treatable loss of mental capacities for a permanent condition.

In determining the true nature and cause of any loss of mental faculties, family members and friends can be particularly helpful to physicians and other health workers. The people who see an older person frequently are in the best position to know what factors may be contributing to diminished mental capabilities.

3. Assessing Personal Needs and Capabilities

You will also have to figure out what sort of personal, nonmedical care is needed and what aspects of daily life a person can still manage without outside assistance. The need and ability to care for oneself is not simply a matter of physical competence. Often, it depends just as much on personality and emotional state. So, don't just consider what kind of care is needed and whether providers are available and affordable. The ultimate decision should also depend on how important it is to the elder to remain in control of his or her own life.

Some people fiercely hold on to personal independence and privacy. For these people (if they also have the ability to organize, manage and pay for individual programs to meet their specific needs), it may be possible—and important— to stay at home and receive only minimal outside assistance.

Others may be willing to have an outside agency organize a more comprehensive care program, as long as they or their family members remain in primary control of daily life. For these people, an agency-directed program of home care in a family residence or in secured housing, perhaps combined with adult daycare, may be the best option, especially if family members are willing to give additional assistance.

Still other people prefer the security and ease of complete care organized and provided by others. For them, a residential care facility may be best, even though they may not physically require the high level of care offered there.

4. Laws Providing for Family Leave

The days and weeks when a family member's need for long-term care becomes apparent can be extremely difficult and stressful. Balancing your work responsibilities with your efforts to understand, locate and arrange care can be overwhelming.

In recent years, many states and the federal government have tried to help solve this problem by requiring employers to provide some unpaid leave when a family member needs attention because of a health crisis. The federal Family and Medical Leave Act (FMLA) provides some needed help by requiring the following:

- Companies with 50 or more employees must give workers up to 12 weeks per year of unpaid leave to care for a child, spouse or parent with a serious health condition.
- Companies must allow employees to return to their old jobs, or equivalent jobs at the same pay, when they return to work.
- Companies must continue providing the same health benefits as when the employees are being paid.

However, the law does not apply to all employees—or to all care-giving situations. You are entitled to FMLA leave only if you have worked for your employer for at least a year and have worked at least 1,250 hours (about 25 hours per week) during that time. Also, you are entitled to FMLA leave only to provide care to a parent, spouse or child—if you need time off to care for another close family member, such as a sibling, parent-in-law or domestic partner, you can't use FMLA leave.

Some state laws give workers more rights, apply to businesses with fewer than 50 employees or provide longer leave periods. Some large companies also have their own leave policies which are more generous than state or federal laws require.

If some unpaid time off work would help you organize long-term care for a spouse or parent, check your employer's policy and make sure it complies with the FMLA and the law of your state. And if, when you return to work after unpaid leave, you find that your job has been changed for the worse, you may have a legal claim under the FMLA or similar state laws.

For more information on the FMLA, contact the Department of Labor at 202-219-8776, or visit its website at www.dol.gov, where you will find lots of helpful fact sheets on your rights under the law. For information on your state's laws, contact your state labor department. The National Partnership for Women and Families in Washington, DC has lots of free information available on your rights under the FMLA, including a question-and-answer guide to the law's provisions and information on state leave laws. Call them at 202-986-2600, or check out their website at www.nationalpartnership.org.

Finally, if the family member who needs care has long-term care insurance, check the policy to see if it provides for respite care. Respite care pays for home care aides who give short-term breaks to family members who care for an elder. (See Chapter 11 for a discussion of long-term care insurance.)

E. Making a Realistic Family Commitment

Whether older people have the option to receive long-term care while maintaining their independence often depends on the extent to which family members are able and willing to help. But family situations vary widely in terms of whether relatives are willing and able to provide care, transportation, companionship or financial support to an elder. Before any long-term care program is organized—particularly when the elder is to remain at home without a spouse—family members must get together and discuss what each of them will do to help meet needs that cannot be met by outside care or would be prohibitively expensive if provided by paid caregivers.

Some arrangements that may require family involvement are:

1. Staying at Home

An older person's ability to stay at home while receiving long-term care may depend on several kinds of family help. The elder may need daily or weekly assistance with personal or medical care that is not provided by a home care or other outside agency. Help with house-keeping, shopping and home maintenance may also be necessary. And there will certainly be a need for regular visits and transportation to allow the elder to maintain contact with the outside world. The elder may also need help to plan, coordinate and oversee outside care programs and to plan and administer financial matters.

2. Moving in With Family

If older people are unable to maintain themselves in their own homes, they may still be able to avoid the cost and loss of independence a residential care facility requires by moving in with willing family members and receiving long-term home care there. This kind of arrangement may permit family members to supplement home care provided by outside agencies with direct care of their own, which can help keep down costs while allowing the elder more personal control.

But such an arrangement is obviously not for every family. It requires physical space and financial resources. And both the elder and the relatives with whom the elder lives must be willing to make it work. Everyone involved has to give up some room and some privacy and make adjustments in daily habits and expectations. Relatives with whom the elder does not live must also be willing to share the re-sponsibilities by visiting, taking the elder on outings and providing financial assistance. Obviously, all this takes a lot of talking, planning and ongoing cooperation among all family members.

3. Entering a Residential Facility

Recent surveys of nursing facility residents have shown that contact with the world outside—leaving the facility for visits and outings and receiving visits, phone calls and mail from family and friends—is their single greatest concern. So even when an elder moves into an organized residential setting that provides personal care and social activities, or into a long-term care facility that provides complete care, family participation remains of the utmost importance.

To prepare for any residential care setting, family members must be willing to discuss how much each is *realistically* able and willing to help. But most important, family members must discuss the future directly with the loved one who needs care.

F.   What Can You Afford?

Most communities have a wide variety of home care programs and residential facilities, but almost all of them are quite costly. Home care is often much less expensive than residential care; part-time home care may run between $3,000 and $10,000 per year. But as more frequent and extensive home care is needed, it also becomes very costly: 24-hour home care with nursing may cost more than $100,000 per year.

Residential facilities also vary greatly in cost—independent living facilities begin at around $20,000 per year, and the least expensive assisted living and personal care facilities run about $30,000. The average cost of a nursing facility is about $50,000 per year. And prices for each of these types of facilities may reach $100,000 per year in more expensive urban areas.

Unfortunately, government programs and private insurance pay a much smaller chunk of these costs than most people think. Medicare pays only about 10% of all nursing facility costs,—and this all goes to short-term skilled nursing care, not long-term residential care. Similarly, Medicare pays only for short-term home care for people who need actual nursing—it pays nothing for long-term care at home. (See Chapter 6 for a discussion of Medicare, medi-gap insurance and veterans' benefits.) Medicaid (or Medi-Cal in California)—the federal program for low-income people—does pay about half of all long-term nursing facility costs and a significant amount of home care charges. But Medicaid will pay for these only after you have used up almost all your savings to pay for your own care. And Medicaid might not pay anything at all for assisted living or some residential care facilities. (See Chapters 7 and 8.) Private long-term care insurance may pay some portion of nursing facility and home care costs, but it usually doesn't pay for everything—and it pays nothing at all for many types of residential care facilities.

A BRIEF LOOK AT MEDICARE, MEDICAID AND INSURANCE

Medicare. A federal government program for which virtually everyone 65 and over is eligible. It provides for the following coverage:

Home Care: Short-term only; skilled nursing and therapy but not custodial care

Senior residences (independent living): None

Personal care facilities: None

Nursing facilities: Skilled nursing facility only, following a hospital stay; full payment for only 20 days, partial payment for up to 100 days; only in facilities certified by Medicare

Medi-gap Insurance. Private insurance policies that can be purchased by individuals 65 or over. They provide the following coverage:

Home Care: Some policies provide limited coverage for short-term care if Medicare also covers it; no coverage for long-term care

Senior residences (independent living): None

Personal care facilities: None

Nursing facilities: Many policies cover short-term stays in skilled nursing facilities if Medicare also covers them, paying the amount Medicare does not; no coverage for long-term custodial care

Managed Care (with Medicare). HMOs or other managed care plans specifically for people on Medicare. They provide the following coverage:

Home Care: Limited coverage for short-term care under Medicare rules; for extra premium, some plans offer extra home care coverage under easier rules than Medicare's; no coverage for long-term care

Senior residences (independent living): None

Personal care facilities: None

Nursing facilities: Short-term stays in skilled nursing facilities under rules similar to Medicare; no coverage for long-term custodial care

Medicaid (called Medi-Cal in California). Varies in each state; to be eligible, you must have very low income and few assets, not counting your home, car and household goods. It provides the following coverage:

Home care: Personal as well as medical care; usually limited in amount

Senior residences (independent living): Usually no coverage

Personal care facilities: Coverage in some states for Medicaid-certified assisted living and shelter care facilities; if covered, unlimited duration

Nursing facilities: Extensive coverage in facilities certified by Medicaid: no time limit

Long-Term Care Insurance. Private insurance policies; they vary greatly in coverage and amount of benefits. They provide the following coverage:

Home care: Some policies cover only home care; more expensive comprehensive policies cover both home care and residential care; amount of coverage depends on amount of premium paid

Senior residences (independent living): None

Personal care facilities: Some policies cover long-term care in residential care (shelter care) or assisted living facilities if policyholder is unable to perform certain amount of activities of daily living

Nursing facilities: Coverage in licensed nursing and board and care facilities for custodial care if medically necessary or if elder is unable to perform activities of daily living; benefits depend on cost of policy and rarely cover full cost of care

1. Help With Paying

Throughout this book, you will see references to coverage, and lack of coverage, of long-term care costs by Medicare, Medicaid and private insurance. Chapter 6 is devoted entirely to Medicare, Medicare managed care and private medi-gap insurance coverage of long-term care; Chapter 7 covers Medicaid eligibility and coverage; Chapter 8 discusses how to protect personal assets and still qualify for Medicaid coverage; and Chapter 11 covers long-term care insurance.

The chart we've provided gives a brief introduction to each of these subjects so that you will be familiar with them as you read through the first few chapters on long-term care alternatives.

2. Determining Income and Assets

The first step in figuring out what money is realistically available for long-term care is to add up all income and available assets. For guidance, use the list that follows. Consider the last category—Liabilities—as a set-off to be subtracted from available financial resources. Because this list is only for your own reference, you don't have to use precise figures.

Once you have a complete picture of your income and assets, you may be able to take certain steps to protect some of those assets from long-term care costs. (See Chapter 8.)

When regular outside care does become necessary, determine which services and facilities are available at low or no cost and which might be at least partially covered by government programs or private insurance.

Finally, family members must begin to think about their own financial contributions. While there may be no immediate need for money from relatives, the decisions you make now about long-term care may determine if and when money from beyond the elder's own resources will be required. The earlier this is discussed, the easier it will be to plan and provide for it.

Here are the most common items (and some that you might overlook) to factor in as you try to get a complete picture of your income and assets—an essential first step in making long-term care decisions.

GETTING AND STAYING ORGANIZED

As you fill out this list, you may discover that your financial and ownership documents are located in a number of different places. If so, this is a good time to gather them together and put them in one safe place, then give a list of the documents and their location to family members or others you trust. *Nolo's Personal Recordkeeper* (Nolo) is a computer program and manual that will help you gather and organize this information.

INCOME AND ASSETS

I. Estimated Income

Ongoing business income _____

Social Security retirement or disability benefits _____

Pension benefits _____

Income from rental property _____

Income from patents or royalties _____

Other income _____

II. Liquid Assets

Cash _____

Savings and money market accounts _____

Checking accounts _____

Certificates of deposit _____

U.S. savings and other bonds _____

Gold, silver, rare coins and other precious metals _____

III. Personal Property Assets

Interest in ongoing business (ownership, stock option, profit-sharing) _____

Value of any patents or copyrights _____

Brokerage accounts and other stocks _____

Money owed to you _____

Automobiles, boats, other vehicles _____

Antiques and works of art _____

Valuable jewelry _____

Face value of life insurance _____

Miscellaneous _____

IV. Real Estate (full or partial interest)

Property #1 (principal residence) _____

Property #2 _____

Property #3 _____

V. Liabilities (what you owe)

Mortgage debts (all money you owe on real property listed above) _____

Personal property debts (loans) _____

Miscellaneous debts _____

G. Help Getting Started: Geriatric Care Managers

Geriatric care managers (also known as private care managers for the aging) are professional counselors or guides who, on a one-time or ongoing basis, help assess long-term care needs and organize services to meet those needs. They can be particularly useful when family members don't live in the same city as the person who needs the care.

Geriatric care managers can assist with placing elders in different types of assisted living, residential care and nursing facilities. And they can be invaluable in guiding you through the maze of home health care and supporting services needed for long-term care in the home. Care managers are generally familiar with residential facilities and can help find a facility that meets the elder's care needs and ability to pay. They can evaluate home care agencies. They may also know of difficult-to-find services that may supplement care provided by an agency or of individual caregivers who can fill gaps in home care. And they can help you set up a coordinated program of care among several providers. They also follow up, monitoring ongoing care and helping make changes as necessary.

However, despite a care manager's expertise, decisions about long-term care are too important to leave solely in the hands of any one advisor. You and other family members should consider and evaluate what a care manager recommends, meeting with all caregivers and visiting any residence the care manager suggests. You know best the abilities, needs and personality of the elder who requires care; the more you learn about long-term care choices and participate in the decision-making process, the better able you will be to choose among the alternatives a care manager may offer.

1. Where to Find Geriatric Care Managers

As with other long-term care resources, your personal physician, a local senior citizens center or friends and neighbors might be able to refer you to a geriatric care manager.

You can also find geriatric care managers in the white pages of the telephone directory under "Geriatric Care," "Geriatric Management," "Older Adults Care Managers" or something similar. Your local senior information or senior referral directory—usually listed separately in the white pages (sometimes under county or city offices or public health department)—can also make referrals. Several national organizations, including Aging Network Services, can help locate care managers in your area. (Addresses and telephone numbers for these organizations can be found in the Resource Directory in the Appendix of this book.) A national directory is available from the National Association of Private Geriatric Care Managers, 1604 North Country Club Road, Tucson, AZ 85716, 520-881-8008, www.caremanager.org.

2. Evaluating a Geriatric Care Manager

There is no easy way to know in advance whether a particular geriatric care manager is likely to be effective. Some care managers are connected to organizations dedicated to elder care; other excellent care managers work on their own. Unfortunately, there are no firm guidelines and no state certifications yet for this relatively new field. Here are some ideas on what to ask before hiring a geriatric care manager:

- Where has the care manager worked before? Experience with a local public agency that deals with the elderly is a good sign, as is work at a local nursing facility or home health care agency. Whatever the form, some public health experience is essential. The care manager should provide you with references from previous employment if you ask for them.

- What is the care manager's professional training? Normally, a care manager should have a license or degree in public health nursing, public health management, social work or gerontology. If not, be very sure that the person has an extensive work history you can check personally.

- Does the care manager belong to any state or national professional organizations? Membership in a professional organization such as the National Association of Social Workers, Visiting Nurse Association or National Association of Private Geriatric Care Managers does not guarantee quality of work, but it may indicate a professional attitude and a willingness to have credentials verified.

- How does the care manager structure fees? Find out in advance exactly how much you will have to pay—and what you will get for your money. Some organizations with public or philanthropic support offer free or low-cost services to low-income individuals and families. Many private care managers charge a flat fee ($100 to $250) for the initial family visit and evaluation, then an hourly fee ($15 to $100) for making arrangements and for follow-up visits. Whatever the terms, make sure to get them in writing.

- How extensive is the follow-up? After initial arrangements have been made, to what extent is the care manager available for personal or telephone consultations? For emergencies? What are the charges? Are there continuing services available, such as weekly or monthly reviews or visits, either by phone or in person? And what happens if a service or provider the care manager has arranged for does not work out? On what terms will the care manager arrange for replacement services?

- Does the care manager have a business contract of any kind with a particular home care agency or residential facility? If so, you must be somewhat cautious about accepting the care manager's recommendation of that agency or facility; the care manager has a motive to steer business there. Make sure that the care manager presents you with some alternatives.

- Does the care manager have any clients or former clients who can give a personal recommendation? Speaking with someone who has used the care manager's services may give you confidence in the care manager and a better idea of what to expect.

OTHER RESOURCES

Even if you rely on a care manager, you should also check with friends, relatives and any other potential sources of information about the kind of care you want. We offer some good leads on finding home care in Chapter 2, choosing an organized senior residence or assisted living facility in Chapter 3 and locating long-term care facilities in Chapter 4.

There are two good general resources you can use to find out about home care and residential care in your area. Although these services cannot tell you which option or facility would be best for you, they can give you a list of choices to investigate, either on your own or with the help of a geriatric care manager. Eldercare Locator, 800-677-1116, is a nonprofit, government-sponsored service run by the National Association of Area Agencies on Aging. Its services are free, and are available Monday through Friday, from 9:00 a.m. to 11:00 p.m. (Eastern Time). A similar commercial service, Total Living Choices, is available on the Internet at www.tlchoices.com.

H. Additional Considerations

When you consider long-term care needs, you should also review other legal and financial matters. A person who needs long-term care may have increasing difficulty taking care of personal matters—so now is a good time to review legal and financial documents and arrangements. These issues are discussed more fully in Chapters 8, 9 and 10.)

1. Health Care Directives

When long-term care becomes necessary, you should start preparing to make decisions about future health care choices. In particular, you need to think about what kind of medical treatments you would like to receive if you become terminally ill or are no longer able to communicate your wishes about your medical care.

To make sure that your medical choices are respected, you can create two basic legal documents:

- a medical directive (sometimes referred to as a living will or advanced healthcare directive), which sets forth the type of care you wish to receive if you become incapacitated, and
- a durable power of attorney for healthcare, in which you name someone you trust to make sure that you get the kind of medical care you want—and, in some states, to make decisions about your medical care if you are unable to do so.

We discuss these documents in detail in Chapter 9, Section A.

2. Durable Powers of Attorney for Finances

As you grow older, you will want to make sure that someone will make financial decisions in accordance with your wishes if you are no longer able to handle your financial matters on your own. A durable power of attorney for finances, which can take effect right away or only if and when you become legally incompetent to handle your own financial decisions, can help ensure that your finances are handled as you wish, by someone you trust, without the expensive, cumbersome and time-consuming process of going to court. (See Chapter 9, Section B.)

3. Wills

Although an elder's need for long-term care certainly does not mean that death is imminent, it may be a signal of decreasing competence to make decisions about income, assets and estate. It is a good idea to review any existing will—which may be years old and out of date—and to make a new will that meets with the current wishes of the elder. (See Chapter 10, Section A.)

However, if there is any question about an older person's mental competence to make a new will, or about whether the elder's decisions about leaving property to others might be unduly influenced by another person, be sure to consult with a lawyer who specializes in wills and probate matters before taking action.

4. Living Trusts

A living trust is a legal document that allows you to retain control over your property during your lifetime and arrange for that property to be transferred, at your death, to beneficiaries you name—all without going through probate. You designate what property goes into the trust and who gets it when you die. During your lifetime, you act as the trustee—and you have the right to change the trust property, change the beneficiary or revoke the trust altogether. On your death, the trust property is distributed directly to the named beneficiaries, without going through probate or any other legal proceeding.

Some people have the misconception that living trusts can also permit you to qualify for Medicaid coverage of long-term care, by sheltering assets that the government would otherwise consider in determining your eligibility. This is wrong, however—when the government looks at your financial situation, it will include any property in your living trust in its calculations. ■

Trusts do not shelter Medi-Cal attachable assets.

At-Home Care

Until recently, older Americans and their families had few choices for elder care. The options were either family care at home or residence in a nursing facility or "rest home." Family care often placed an overwhelming burden on adult children and grandchildren and seriously strained family relations. Care in a nursing facility, on the other hand, often created guilty feelings, drained family finances and restricted the elder's comfort and independence.

Fortunately, the number and kinds of home care services have increased substantially in recent years. And new technologies have made many medical treatments—such as oxygen and intravenous therapy—mobile enough for home administration. As a result, more elders who need care can remain at home or live with relatives without putting undue stress on the family.

Another impetus toward using home care is the rapidly rising cost of residential nursing facility care, which has made consumers of medical care more interested in finding cost-effective alternatives. And in response to the larger number of people receiving medical care at home, agencies and programs have increased the kinds of therapeutic, nutrition, homemaking and other personal care services they offer for home care.

This trend toward home care is particularly welcome in light of public health surveys indicating that up to half of all nursing facility residents could live independently if they had adequate and affordable home care services. And other studies have shown that the longer people remain independent from institutional care, the better their overall physical and emotional health.

Unfortunately, though, long-term home care is not always a practical solution. Home care may be adequate and affordable if the elder needs help with some physical movements around the home—bathing and getting meals, for example—or with exercise or physical therapy or monitoring a chronic health condition. But if the elder needs extensive medical treatment or close monitoring for many hours each day, the difficulty of arranging different types of care may make home care impractical—and the cost may become prohibitive. In most cases, long-term home care also requires family members to fill in gaps that the outside care services do not cover. For many people without such family assistance, long-term home care is simply not an option.

HOME CARE NOW MAY STILL MEAN RESIDENTIAL CARE LATER

Even if home care is a workable alternative, it may not remain so. Your physical needs will change over time; home care that now works well may later become impractical. For this reason, you may want to begin planning for the possibility of residential care at some later date. This is particularly true if you or your family member is facing Alzheimer's Disease (a progressive condition) or some other form of dementia. (See Chapter 5.)

Your planning should take two forms. First, get to know the kinds of residential facilities in your area. (Elder residences are discussed in Chapter 3, long-term care facilities in Chapter 4.)

Also, begin to consider how you might pay for residential care. If it appears that Medicaid may be an option, explore ways to protect some of your assets while still qualifying for Medicaid coverage. (Medicaid is explained in Chapter 7, asset protection in Chapter 8.)

A. What Is Home Care?

The term "home care" encompasses a multitude of medical and personal services provided at home to a partially or fully dependent elder (although home care is available for people of any age who require long-term care, we focus on the needs of older people). These services often make it possible for an older person to remain at home, or with a relative, rather than enter a residential facility for extended recovery or long-term care. In this book, the terms "home" and "home care" refer to the private house or apartment where the elder lives alone, with a spouse or with other family members or friends.

Depending on what is available in your community, home care and related supplemental services can include:

- health care—nursing, physical and other rehabilitative therapy, medicating, monitoring and medical equipment
- personal care—assistance with personal hygiene, dressing, getting in and out of a bed or chair, bathing and exercise
- nutrition—meal planning, cooking, meal delivery or meals at outside meal sites
- homemaking—housekeeping, shopping, home repair services and household paperwork, and
- social and safety needs—escort and transportation services, companions, telephone check, overall planning and program coordination service.

(See Sections C and D, below, for a complete discussion of the home care services.)

Not everyone using home care will need all of the services available. Not every community will offer every possible service, and a single program or agency might not provide everything that the elder requires. An elder's additional needs may have to be filled by community agencies or organizations, adult daycare or senior centers, individuals hired through informal networks, family and friends. Geriatric care managers can help establish a home care program for elders who require a mix of care—different services from different providers. (See Chapter 1, Section G.)

1. Independence

One of the great advantages of home care is that it permits an older person to maintain a feeling of independence and comfort in familiar surroundings. Also, you and your family may be better able to control the care received—and to avoid care that isn't necessary or desired.

On the other hand, for home care to work well, you and your family must take the initiative to find services, coordinate different programs and personnel, monitor home care needs and performance, figure costs and budgets and make changes when required. And the family will be making all these decisions without a professional institution to help. This decision-making responsibility can add an extra burden to the daily task of meeting the elder's needs for physical care.

isolation

Remaining at home isolates some people from social activity and limits mental stimulation. Although friends and family often intend to provide lots of companionship, too many elders wind up spending their days in bed asleep or watching television. An organized elder residence, on the other hand, offers both a community of people and a constant stream of activities.

2. Financial Savings

In addition to the physical and emotional advantages of remaining at home, there can also be significant financial savings if the care you need is not too complicated or frequent and family and friends help out. While residential care facilities average $30,000 to $100,000 a year, home care can average from 25% to 90% less, depending on what care is required. You save by not paying for unnecessary services or institutional overhead. The things you provide yourself at home—food, drugs and supplies—come without any nursing facility mark-up.

However, home care often becomes more expensive over time. Home care needs may become more extensive or complicated and family members may not be able to pick up the slack, which could require additional paid care and services.

Sometimes, hidden expenses make the true cost of home care too high. Families often fail to calculate peripheral expenses: the continued or expanded cost of running a home (such as taxes, utilities, insurance and maintenance), the cost to family members of transportation and missed work (to help care for the elder) and the cost of temporary care workers to fill in when family members can't make it or regular care falls through.

3. Quality of Care

While the comfort and financial advantages of home care sound attractive, you may have some doubts about whether the quality of care at home compares to the care provided in a nursing facility or other elder residence.

a. Medical and Nursing Care.

The American Medical Association, the American Hospital Association, the American Nurses' Association and the U.S. Department of Health and Human Services all stand behind the quality of medical and nursing care delivered by home care agencies that are certified by both Medicare and your state's home care licensing agency. So, when medical or nursing care—as compared with assistance with the nonmedical activities of daily living—is a significant part of the home care you need, you should seek help from certified agencies rather than independent caregivers. (See Section D.) Also ask your doctor whether the medical or nursing care you require can be safely and adequately delivered at home.

b. Nonmedical Care.

The care people need at home is not primarily medical or nursing care, but help with what are called the activities of daily living (ADLs). These include bathing, using the toilet, dressing, eating, getting in and out of bed or a chair and walking around. For people with Alzheimer's or other cognitive impairments, home care may consist primarily of making sure that the person does not become lost, disoriented or injured. For these kinds of nonmedical assistance, home care is often better than residential care. Home care is provided one-on-one, whereas residential facilities have staff-to-resident ratios of one-to-ten or more. And by choosing and monitoring a home care agency or individual home care providers, you may be better able to control the quality of care you receive. On the other hand, tracking the effectiveness of home care is primarily up to the family, whereas residential facilities have professional staff members who are supposed to check regularly on the quality of nonmedical care provided.

B. How to Find Home Care Services

As you've probably gathered by now, arranging a program of home care involves some searching and organizing, and often requires you to use services from more than one source. To do this, you need to learn where to find these services and how to locate recommended agencies and individuals.

Much of home care—particularly nursing and other medical services—can be provided by a home care or home health care agency. (The services such agencies provide are discussed below, in Section C.)

There are a number of ways to find a good agency:

1. Friends and Relatives

While the opinions of professionals are often helpful, you should start your search by talking to friends and relatives who have had home care experiences. Friends may know of a program or person unfamiliar to an agency or professional, or warn you about providers to avoid despite their apparently sound credentials. Call a few friends or relatives and tell them the kind of help you think you need. They may be able to tell you of other people they know who have arranged for similar help. This kind of networking can snowball, with each phone call leading you to others to contact for information or services. Don't be shy. Call around and start the snowball rolling.

2. Hospital Personnel

If you are looking for home care following a stay in a medical facility, most have a "discharge planner" or "social services" administrator who can refer you to a home care agency capable of meeting your needs. Many hospitals and skilled nursing facilities operate their own home health care units. Although you should not automatically sign up with the hospital or nursing facility's home care unit, it is a good place to start comparison shopping.

3. Physicians

Your own physician may have worked with a good home care agency. Your doctor may also be willing to put you in contact with other patients who use the agency, so you can ask them about their experiences.

4. Nursing Registries

If you need at-home nursing, contact your local hospital—many have a registry of visiting nurses. The local chapter of the Visiting Nurses' Association provides visiting nurses and may also be a good source of referrals for other care.

5. National, State and Local Agencies and Organizations

If you need home care because of a particular illness or disability, ask for referrals from the local chapter of a volunteer organization that focuses on that illness or disability, such as the American Heart Association, American Cancer Society, American Diabetes Association or Alzheimer's Foundation.

Public agencies that specialize in the needs of older people can also refer you to home care agencies in your area. The federal government has set up Area Agencies on Aging, which operate some federally funded programs that might help. The area agencies can also refer you to Medicare-approved home care agencies.

Most states have their own Agencies on Aging—and there may be local offices of the state agency in your own community. Check the state government listings in the white pages of the telephone book.

City and county Agencies on Aging may offer low-cost programs of their own. They can also refer you to reputable home care agencies.

You can find referral services in your phone book under listings for Senior Referral, Department of Social Services, Family Service Agency or Information and Referral. Often these services have a social worker or public health worker who specializes in referrals for older people.

FOR MORE INFORMATION

You can find addresses, telephone numbers and websites for many of these organizations and agencies in the Resource Directory in the Appendix of this book.

---

6. Senior Centers

Because it is part of the job of local senior centers to provide information for seniors, they are usually happy to help with referrals to agencies and individual services. Home care providers know that senior centers supply this information, so they often make their services known at the centers. You can also get personal recommendations and opinions from other older people at the centers.

7. Volunteer Organizations

A number of community volunteer organizations not only provide referrals, but also administer their own home care programs. Your local United Way, for example, is a good clearinghouse for different services. Churches or synagogues, and local religious, ethnic or fraternal agencies and organizations are often very helpful in coordinating home care services, usually free of charge, and in helping you make informal care arrangements.

OLDER PEOPLE HELPING OLDER PEOPLE

The Retired Senior Volunteer Program (RSVP) is a federally funded program through which retired older people volunteer to help other less mobile elders. RSVP, together with the Senior Companion Program, provides all sorts of general assistance with nonmedical daily needs, free of charge. And if RSVP is not equipped to help you directly, it may be able to refer you to a program or agency that can. To find your local RSVP, look in the white pages of the phone book under Retired Senior Volunteer Program or contact the national office of Senior Corps at 800-424-8867 or at its website, www.seniorcorps.org. The national office will help connect you with the branch nearest you.

C. Services Provided Through Home Care

Home care services range from highly skilled medical care, nursing and therapy to simple household tasks such as cleaning and cooking. Home care agencies can also provide what is called respite care, care from a stand-in home care provider who visits with an elder while a regular caregiver—usually a family member—takes a break.

1. Medical Services

Most home care agencies and Visiting Nurses' Associations can provide or arrange for a number of medical services, including skilled and basic nursing, rehabilitation therapies and dietary services.

a. Nursing

With a physician overseeing the course of treatment, a home care agency or nursing registry can provide geriatric nurse practitioners, registered nurses and licensed vocational or practical nurses. These highly skilled nurses plan and monitor health care, give injections and intravenous medication and instruct you on self-administered medications, injections and treatments.

More routine nursing care is provided by vocational and practical nurses and by aides who work under the nurses' supervision. They monitor pulse, blood pressure and temperature; administer simple diagnostic procedures, such as drawing blood and other samples for the laboratory; and instruct home patients on how to use portable testing equipment.

b. Therapies

Most home care agencies provide a physical therapist, respiratory therapist, speech therapist or occupational therapist. These specialists give short-term assistance to people recovering from an illness or injury and ongoing therapy to those with permanent disabilities.

c. Nutrition

Most agencies either have someone on staff or can arrange for someone to help plan a diet and show how to prepare foods that provide proper nutrition and meet special dietary needs. You may also be able to get help in shopping for and preparing meals or have prepared meals brought to your home.

2. Medical and Safety Equipment and Supplies

Home care agencies can provide medical equipment and supplies such as a hospital bed, wheelchair, walker, oxygen equipment and various home testing and monitoring equipment and supplies for incontinence and other conditions. You can buy or rent the equipment from the agency or from a medical equipment company with which the agency does business.

Some home care agencies will also inspect your home for safety needs and arrange to install any necessary equipment, such as support railings, access ramps or an emergency response system.

ON SAVING MONEY

Find out whether you are required to buy or rent all medical equipment and supplies from any home care agency you are considering. If so, and if you need substantial medical equipment or supplies, make sure their prices are competitive with what you would pay if you purchased the equipment or supplies on your own. Always comparison shop before buying equipment or having any work done through an agency.

---

3. Nonmedical Personal Care

a. Home Health Aides

Most people who consider home care do not need skilled medical care as much as they need assistance with personal tasks that have become difficult because of frailty or other physical debility. This type of care is provided not by skilled medical personnel, but by "home health aides" or "home care aides."

Aides are the people who spend the most time with you. Their tasks vary, depending on your needs, the rules of the agency and the willingness of the individual aide, but in general they include:

- assistance with personal care such as bathing, grooming, toilet needs and eating
- help with movement or exercise, such as getting in and out of a bed or chair, getting around the house, stretching or taking a walk
- simple health tasks, such as taking blood pressure and temperature and helping with self-administered medications, salves and breathing equipment, and
- minimal homemaking, such as helping to plan and cook simple meals.

More general homemaking services (grocery shopping, meal preparation and clean-up, light housecleaning and laundry) are often available through home care agencies. Not every home care agency provides homemaking services, however, and you may need to make separate arrangements through informal networks of friends, relatives and neighbors or with an independent home care provider.

REMEMBER TO ASK

Just because something is not on a home care agency's or individual aide's list of offered services does not mean it is not available. Depending on how flexible your home care aide is, any light task around the house might be included. If the aide will not help, or is not allowed by an agency to assist with certain needed tasks, the agency may be able to provide someone who can.

b. Respite Care

With home care, the primary responsibility for care and companion-ship often still rests with family members. Particularly if an elder requires extensive monitoring, it can become a substantial burden on family members to always stay around the house. Some agencies provide temporary respite care—a companion for the elder, whose presence allows a family member to leave the house and go to work, attend to other business or simply have a break. Obviously, you can also make private arrangements for someone to fill this need.

Respite companions are often volunteers, organized through a community group. If your agency does not have respite care, it should be able to refer you to a community group or organization that does. (See Section J, Supplements to Home Care, below.)

D. Kinds of Home Care Providers

Home care providers range from hospitals or other high-tech organi-zations with highly trained medical staffs to full-service home care agencies to the ten-year-old kid down the block who takes out your trash. Getting the most sophisticated and well-equipped home care provider is not the point. The goal is to find providers who can give you the specific care you need, for the best price.

1. Full-Service Home Care Agencies

Most home care agencies, whether their name refers to home care in general or to home *health* care, provide a great variety of services. Some agencies offer more services than others, although a few will supply all the services mentioned below. Some will help you find outside services they don't provide; others will leave it to you to fill in the gaps. In any case, if there is a service you need that the agency does not mention, be sure to ask about it. If an agency cannot provide the service, it may know someone who can.

full plan

Many home care agencies will create a written care plan and include a written estimate of costs as part of any contract you sign for their services. Review the care plan and contract carefully to make sure you are not obligated to buy, rent or pay for any services or equipment in the future.

Home care agencies are often affiliated with hospitals, nursing facilities and nursing organizations. But since most home care is *not* direct medical care, the fact that an agency is connected with a medical institution does not necessarily mean it will provide better overall personal care.

On the whole, full-service agencies tend to be more expensive than independent providers or support-care agencies that do not provide nursing or medical therapies. Despite their higher cost, full-service agencies can be extremely useful in coordinating different levels of care and when no family members are available to organize and oversee separate independent providers.

2. Support-Care Agencies

Support-care agencies provide personal, household and respite care, but not skilled nursing or medical therapies. They are often sponsored by community or charitable organizations. Because they do not maintain highly skilled medical staffs, some can provide home aides at lower rates than full-service agencies. (In choosing a support-care agency, refer to the criteria discussed in Section E, What to Look for in a Home Care Agency.)

3. Independent and Informal Arrangements

As emphasized throughout this chapter, not all care has to come through a formal agency. More important, not all *good* care comes from an agency. Independent home care workers are often more flexible in the tasks they will perform—and less expensive—than agency personnel.

a. Finding Independent Aides

Some communities have what are called In-Home Support Services that refer home attendants and aides for nonmedical home care. And many public agencies, community or charitable organizations and churches, while not sponsoring a home care agency, offer a referral list of independent home care aides that the organization or agency has referred successfully in the past.

informal

You can also find professional nurses and nonprofessional aides through informal networks. Friends and relatives may know of an individual who suits your needs but does not work through an agency and may not have any formal certification or training. Many people have found that "unofficial" aides provide very personal, flexible and competent assistance and charge considerably less than certified nurses or aides.

Keep in mind, though, that the range and quality of care you get depends entirely on the knowledge, skill and attitude of one care-giver. There is no outside supervision, no one to make sure you are getting high quality care. Also, no agency has done a background check on the person who will be spending a considerable amount of time in your home. And while agencies routinely post a "bond" for their aides to protect the consumer from theft or damage by the home care aide, most independent aides are not bonded.

Finally, independent aides sometimes get sick or are otherwise unavailable—which can pose significant problems if you depend on their care. If you will need an independent aide regularly, it is a good idea to have a back-up to call on short notice.

b. Home Care Personnel

Home care agency workers go by different titles—and offer different types of services and skills. Knowing what these titles mean can help you make the best use of the services an agency has to offer. Because fees are higher for more skilled workers, understanding the different options available can also help you avoid paying for an *overqualified*, and therefore overly expensive, home care provider when a less skilled but equally effective provider would do.

Supervisors and Planning Coordinators. Probably the first person you will have contact with, the planner assesses your needs and capabilities and develops an overall plan for care. The planner may also oversee personnel assignments and assist you in making changes in services or personnel after your care has begun.

Clinical or Nursing Supervisors. A clinical supervisor, usually a public health or geriatric nurse, monitors your direct home medical care, including diet and nutrition. This is the person with whom you, your family or your doctor should speak if you have a question or problem with the skilled medical care you receive.

Social Workers. The agency's social worker, resource manager or caseworker can help coordinate your care with other programs and services not provided by the agency and can help with financial and insurance planning and paperwork.

Nurses. Every home health care agency should have at least one nurse practitioner or registered nurse (RN) on call at all times to monitor patient nursing needs. Nurse practitioners generally supervise other nurses, and can prescribe some medicines, give injections and diagnose routine medical problems. Registered nurses handle complex nursing functions, including administering intravenous medication, drawing blood, making an overall assessment of patient needs and creating a nursing care plan to meet those needs.

A Licensed Vocational Nurse (LVN) or Licensed Practical Nurse (LPN) handles the more routine nursing tasks, such as monitoring blood pressure and pulse, checking fluids, administering oxygen and some medications and doing some basic physical rehabilitation.

If you require a special physical rehabilitation program—after a hip injury or a stroke, for example—a Certified Rehabilitative Nurse (CRN) may plan the program, begin you on it and monitor your progress, sometimes in conjunction with a rehabilitation therapist.

Rehabilitation Therapists. Physical, occupational, speech and respiratory therapists plan and carry out a program of rehabilitative therapy. Once you are on a regular program, routine therapy assistance is often handled by trained assistants or technicians.

Home Care Aides. The home care aide is the foot soldier of home care. The aide handles simple, everyday health and personal care tasks: bathing; grooming; moving around; exercising; helping with self-administered medications, creams and therapies; and monitoring blood pressure and temperature. The aide may also help you with minimal homemaking—planning and preparing simple meals, for example. But the home care aide is not a housekeeper or house cleaner; these services may or may not be available through your home care agency. An independent home care aide, on the other hand, may be more flexible about doing a certain amount of household work.

Companions. Your greatest need, particularly if you are housebound, may simply be company. Some home care agencies provide, often through a community group, people known as "companions," who will spend time with you in the home or go for a small outing— shopping, to the library, to the park or just for a walk—to give you some company and conversation. Companions may also help with personal paperwork, make phone calls and organize slightly more complicated outings.

E. What to Look for in a Home Care Agency

You may find good quality and less expensive care without using a home care agency. If you do choose to use one, however, here are some things to look for:

1. Certification

Although it's not necessarily a guarantee of quality care, a full-service agency should be approved by both Medicare and your state's Medicaid program. The government checks to make sure certain staff, supervision and basic training requirements are met. If your state licenses home care agencies, make sure your agency has a state license as well. To find out, call your area or local Agency on Aging. (See the Resource Directory in the Appendix.)

Some agencies are also accredited by national health care organizations. For example, the Joint Commission for Accreditation of Health Care Organizations is an umbrella organization that accredits home health care agencies.

2. Reputation

Here are some questions you can ask to find out about an agency's reputation:

• How long has the agency been in business? Look for an agency that has stood the test of time.

- Does the agency belong to the National Association for Home Care or to a state home care association? Membership may indicate adherence to certain standards of care.
- Can the agency give references to doctors, public health workers and clients who have worked with or used the agency? Talk directly with the references. If you will need medical care, ask your doctor to do so, too.

ALZHEIMER'S CARE REQUIRES SPECIAL SKILLS

If you are looking for a home care agency to provide care for someone with Alzheimer's Disease, make sure that both the agency and the specific personnel it plans to send to your home have experience with the disease. Chapter 5 discusses the particular problems faced by those who must find or provide home care to an Alzheimer's patient.

---

3. Services and Flexibility

No matter how many services an agency claims to offer in its brochure, the important thing is to match its services with your needs. If you have any special scheduling needs, make sure the agency will accommodate you. Also, find out if there is any extra cost for night or weekend services.

Flexibility in care is also very important. An agency may be able to meet your needs now, but what if your needs change? Can the agency also provide different, more specialized medical services, a more unusual schedule or some help with household work? It is not necessary that the agency *directly* provide every service you might need in the future, as long as it has the capacity to arrange the service through coordination with other providers.

Before choosing an agency, ask the planning coordinator about the availability of services through other providers. What are their regular arrangements with other programs or agencies? What is the extra charge for such services? Can they arrange for services that they do not already have on call?

4. Personnel Standards

Find out about an agency's personnel before you begin to receive care. What are the skill levels of both in-home and planning personnel on staff? What training and experience are required for different positions? Even nonmedical home care aides should have completed some formal training.

Because home care workers will be spending a significant amount of time in your home, often with no one else present, you should find out how the agency screens an employee's background.

5. What Does Not Matter in Choosing an Agency

Although these might seem like important factors to consider when choosing an agency, they don't mean that much in practice.

a. Nonprofit, Church-Related or Charitable Organization

If an agency is "nonprofit," will it be less expensive? If the agency is sponsored or owned by a church or a charitable organization, will it have the client rather than money or reputation foremost in mind?

The answer to both questions is: not necessarily. Some organizations that operate home care agencies acquire nonprofit tax status by associating with a larger nonprofit group. This means they pay less in taxes, but it does not mean that the rates they charge will be cheaper;

only comparing their rates with those charged by other agencies can answer that question.

Nor does nonprofit status mean the quality of care is any better. Just because a church or charitable organization sponsors an agency does not mean it is involved in the agency's daily operations. These are usually handled by independent administrators—and it is their work that determines the quality of care.

b. National Chain

An agency that is part of a large nationwide organization may seem like a safer bet than a small, independent agency. In certain respects that may be true—for example, standardized personnel duties or computerized billing may make some aspects of home care easier to manage. But gains in paper efficiency may be lost in personalized care. The quality of care you receive from any agency, national chain or small independent, depends on the skill and attention of the people who will be in your home every day.

c. Hospital-Connected

An agency affiliated with a hospital may seem better able to provide medical care than other agencies. But keep in mind that most home care does not involve complicated medical treatment. An agency that focuses on high technology health care may be giving too little attention to what most home care recipients need most—thoughtful human attention.

F. Getting Started With Home Care

Whether or not you use the services of an agency, settling on a home care plan is an important first step. You may also have to supervise the care and update the care plan as needed.

1. Developing a Care Plan

If you are using an agency, personnel there should consult with you and your family in developing a care plan, rather than imposing a standard package on you. Some agencies automatically deliver more care than is needed, partly because the more services they provide, the more money they make. This raises costs unnecessarily and, for many people, stops them from doing things for themselves, which can be an important part of continued psychological well-being. Agency or not, since your family will probably be providing additional care, family members should be directly involved in the planning.

If you have special needs—rehabilitative therapy, a restricted diet or Alzheimer's Disease (see Chapter 5), for example—then specialists in those areas should also participate in planning. And consultations with your doctor should also play a role. A home care plan must take into account your overall comfort and need for human contact as well as specific medical care—for example, it may be important to you for your aides to speak a language you are comfortable speaking or to not smoke. In search of such a match, an agency planner should make at least one extensive visit to the home where you will be receiving care *before* finalizing a plan. And although you will certainly be keeping an eye on your own financial limits, an agency planner should also take your finances into account.

If you are making up your own care plan, using a checklist like the one below can help you keep track of your care. Be sure to include family members and friends who will help with care as well as paid or volunteer outside aides.

CHECKLIST FOR HOME CARE PLAN

1.　Medical and Rehabilitation Care:
　　　Service:
　　　　— Provider:
　　　　— When provided:
　　　　— Additional nonprofessional:
　　　　— Follow-up care (who & when):
　　　Service:
　　　　— Provider:
　　　　— When provided:
　　　　— Additional nonprofessional:
　　　　— Follow-up care (who & when):
　　　Service:
　　　　— Provider:
　　　　— When provided:
　　　　— Additional nonprofessional:
　　　　— Follow-up care (who & when):
2.　Nonmedical Care (including personal assistance, meals, homemaking, escort, companion, transportation, phone check):
　　　Service:
　　　　— Provider:
　　　　— When provided:
　　　Service:
　　　　— Provider:
　　　　— When provided:

---

2. Getting Regular Providers

A home care plan is only as good as the people who carry it out. In addition to the training and experience of home care personnel, how well you get along is also important—and harder to evaluate. It helps to meet and interview home care aides before they begin to provide care. Be warned, however, that some agencies discourage advance selection to prevent clients from overshopping for the "perfect" aide.

Continuity of caregivers is also important. Once you have developed a relationship with caregivers who understand your needs, you want to be able to count on them regularly. On occasion, there are legitimate reasons, such as illness or vacation, for a temporary substitute. But even in these instances, substitute care should be provided only by an aide regularly employed by the agency and not by an independent or "freelance" caregiver—unless that person's qualifications and background have been subjected to the same scrutiny as regular employees.

3. Supervising and Reviewing Your Care

If you use the services of a home care agency, that agency should regularly review the care plan to make sure your needs are being met. The original plan may not have addressed your needs adequately, your needs may have changed over time or the people actually giving you care may not be doing their jobs properly.

A staff member skilled in the specific care you require should regularly supervise and review your care. A certified therapist should be checking on your therapy aide, and a registered nurse should be checking on health care aides. The frequency of reviews should depend on how much care you receive. Medicare, for example, requires that a supervisor visit the home *at least every two weeks* to check on care for a chronic or acute illness. If no skilled medical care is involved, home visits by supervisors can be less frequent—every four to eight weeks, perhaps—but a supervisor should talk with a caregiver at least once a week.

The agency should provide an easy way for you to complain to a supervisor about the care you are receiving. You should have frequent telephone contact with a supervisor and regular visits from a supervisor to review your care—with your family members present, if you wish.

G. Costs of Home Care

As discussed in Chapter 6, you cannot count on Medicare, medi-gap health insurance or managed care to pay for much of the cost of long-term home care. Medicaid (Medi-Cal in California) will pay for long-term home care, but only if you have little income and few assets. (See Chapter 7.) Even if you have long-term care insurance coverage for home care, it will probably pay only a portion of your total home care costs. (See Chapter 11).

Because you will probably have to pay most long-term home care costs out of your own pocket, you should take a close look at the way a provider—particularly a home care agency—calculates its charges. Many agencies will give you a written estimate of charges based on the care plan they develop with you. Before signing up, read the estimate carefully, making sure it does not include charges for services you do not need or want. After you have been receiving home care for a while, check the agency's bills against the estimate to make sure you are actually receiving everything you have paid for.

> ## GOVERNMENT-CERTIFIED PROVIDERS
>
> **Medicare and Medicaid approved.** Even if the care you receive initially is not covered by Medicare or Medicaid, or you are not eligible for Medicaid, make sure the agency you use is certified for both. Your physical situation may change, making your care eligible for Medicare coverage. (See Chapter 6.) Or your financial situation may change, making you eligible for Medicaid. (See Chapter 7.) If the agency is certified, you will have continuity in your home care.
>
> **State licensed.** Some states have minimum quality standards and issue home care licenses or certificates only to those agencies or individual providers that qualify. If you have private medi-gap insurance, Medicare managed care or long-term care insurance that covers home health care, you will probably have to use a state-licensed provider. (Medi-gap and managed care coverage of home care is discussed in Chapter 6, long-term care insurance in Chapter 11.)

1. Sliding Scale (Income-Based) Fee Policy

Many public agency, community, church and philanthropic organization home care providers base eligibility and fees on the care recipient's income. In other words, you only qualify if your income is below a certain level—and the lower your income, the lower the charge. These are not always full-service home care agencies, but they may offer significant savings if they can meet your needs.

2. Cost Varies With Service and Skill Level

Most agencies and individual providers charge by the hour or by the visit. Agencies sometimes also impose a minimum daily or weekly charge. Generally, the amount charged reflects the skill level of the provider. Therefore, you shouldn't receive simple care from a highly skilled provider when someone less skilled can provide it just as well. You can expect to pay rates in these ranges:

- nurse practitioners and registered nurses, $50 to $100 per hour
- practical and vocational nurses, licensed rehabilitative therapists and geriatric social workers, $35 to $75 per hour
- home health aides, $10 to $20 per hour
- homemakers, home workers and companions, $7 to $15 per hour

   Note. The rates charged by independent care givers are usually lower than those charged by agencies. Rates also vary in different parts of the country.

3. Beware the Hidden Charges

When you discuss rates with a prospective home care agency or other provider, make sure to find out about possible hidden charges. For example, there is sometimes a minimum charge per visit, per week or per month. There may also be higher rates for night and weekend visits, which could mean a significant cost increase if you require such care. Some agencies also charge extra for in-home assessments, evaluations and visits by supervisors. These are necessary elements of overall home care planning and service, however, and should *not* be charged as "extras."

HELP WITH HOME CARE COSTS

Medicare, Medicaid, medi-gap insurance, managed care coverage and long-term care insurance all may pay some of the costs of home care. Unfortunately, only Medicaid pays the full cost of long-term care. Here is what you can expect:

- **Medicare.** Pays for short-term home health care—one week up to a couple of months—but not for long-term care. Pays for home care only if you need skilled nursing or rehabilitation. (See Chapter 6.)

- **Medi-gap insurance & Medicare managed care plans.** Medi-gap policies pay nothing for long-term home care. The same is generally true for Medicare managed care plans, although a few managed care plans offer some home care coverage for an extra premium. (See Chapter 6.)

- **Medicaid.** Pays for long-term home care by certified providers. You will qualify only if you have very low income and few assets. (See Chapter 7.)

- **Long-term care insurance.** Some long-term care insurance policies cover home care. Payments begin only when you meet their benefit standards—meaning that, according to their rules, you need the care. (See Chapter 11.)

H. Financing Home Care Through Reverse Mortgages

An older person who has very low income and few assets may qualify for Medicaid, which may pay for the entire cost of home care. (See Chapter 7.) Or an elder may have a long-term care insurance policy that will pay a portion of home care costs. (See Chapter 11.) However, many older people are caught in the middle. They have no long-term home care insurance coverage and they do not have enough income or liquid assets to pay for the long-term home care they need, but they do not qualify for Medicaid coverage.

However, many of these same people own their own homes or condominiums outright, or have considerable equity in them. By using a reverse mortgage, elders can convert home equity into cash while continuing to live at home as long as they are physically able to do so. A reverse mortgage is a loan against the value of a home paid as a lump sum, monthly amount, line of credit or some combination, which does not have to be repaid until the borrower sells or otherwise permanently leaves the home.

Reverse mortgages also have a side benefit. Because the money they provide is a loan, it is not taxable as income, nor does it count as income against Social Security benefits if you haven't yet reached full retirement age. The interest you accumulate on the loan, however, is not tax-deductible until the loan is paid off.

When the borrower sells the home, he or she must pay back the loan out of the proceeds. If the borrower permanently leaves the home—moves in with relatives or to a nursing facility or other location—or dies, the lender must be repaid within a certain time, usually one year to eighteen months. This often means that the borrower or the estate will have to sell the house to repay the reverse mortgage. The final repayment amount is determined by the size of the loan, the interest rate, the cost of insurance and the length of time the loan is outstanding.

If the property is sold for more than the amount of the mortgage, then the owner or owner's survivors keep the difference. On the other hand, if the property receives more under the reverse mortgage than the home is eventually sold for, neither the owner nor the survivors owe the mortgage company anything more; the mortgage company has to take the loss.

There are several types of reverse loans and mortgages, each with somewhat different terms and purposes.

- **Property tax deferral programs.** On a small scale, there are publicly funded and operated property tax deferral programs available in many states. These programs, available to low-income elders, defer the cost of the owner's property tax and take a lien for that amount against the property, payable when the home is sold. Although these deferrals are for relatively small yearly amounts, they free up some cash for home care or other needs. For information about whether such a program is in place where you live, contact your county property tax collector or your Area Agency on Aging, or call your local Senior Information and Referral number (look in the white pages of the telephone directory).

- **Deferred home improvement loans.** Some state and local government agencies also make loans to low-income elders to repair or improve their homes, deferring repayment as long as the elder continues to live in the home. Although these loans are for limited amounts and specific purposes, they can help finance necessary improvements on a home, either to fit it specially for assisted living or merely to repair it so it remains livable. And the money an elder borrows to make home improvements can free up other money for use on home care services.

- **Reverse mortgages insured by the federal government.** The Federal Housing Administration (FHA) insures some reverse mortgage loans through its Home Equity Conversion Mortgage (HECM) program; the loans are processed through private lenders and are available to any homeowner age 62 or older, regardless of his or her income. The loans are available to any owner or occupant of a single-family primary residence including condominiums (but not co-ops and motor homes). A home owner can usually borrow 40–60% of a home's value. Larger, higher-interest reverse mortgages (called "Home Keepers") may be available through the government-sponsored Fannie Mae program.

- **Privately insured reverse mortgages.** In addition to government-insured loans, certain private mortgage holding companies also insure reverse mortgages administered by local lending institutions. These loans have less stringent qualifying standards and higher equity limits than government-insured loans, but they also charge higher fees and interest rates.

1. Drawbacks of Reverse Mortgages

Although reverse mortgages have some attractive features, they also have some serious drawbacks. They often have high initial fees such as appraisal fees, credit checks, insurance, closing costs, origination costs and service charges. So if you die or move out of the home before you have drawn much on the mortgage, you wind up paying a very high cost for what will have turned out to be a short-term loan.

And there are continuing fees and interest payments each year, which may take a serious bite out of the money you actually receive. When considering any reverse mortgage, have the lender show you in writing exactly what these Total Annual Loan Costs (TALCs) will be—not just for the initial year, but for the entire life of the loan.

Even more significantly, interest under a reverse mortgage loan compounds; in other words, you wind up paying interest on interest as the loan period goes on. In addition, as you borrow more monthly or under a line of credit, the principal also goes up. The combination of these two spiraling debt factors means that over a period of years, a modest initial reverse mortgage can cost considerably more than conventional forms of borrowing and can eat up all the equity in the property. An elder who wants to preserve some equity to pass on to heirs or to use in some other way after selling the house may instead wind up with a piece of property that has no residual value.

A reverse mortgage also ties the borrower to the house. Most reverse mortgages require that the loan be repaid when the borrower no longer lives in the house. If the borrower moves in with relatives, moves to another area or enters a nursing home to receive better care, monthly payments and any line of credit stop—and the borrower must repay the loan within a certain time. Elders who borrow under reverse mortgages may one day find themselves faced with the unhappy choice of paying off the loan in order to move to a more comfortable, healthy or secure setting, or staying put to continue receiving the mortgage benefits.

2. Protecting Your Interests

There are several things that people who shop for a reverse mortgage should insist upon to protect themselves and their home equity.

First, the mortgage must have a "nonrecourse" clause. This means that the lender cannot go after any source of debt repayment other than the house. This limits the debt—no matter how long the borrower lives, how high the interest payments pile up or how many other assets the borrower has—to the value of the house.

Second, do not consider any reverse mortgage that requires you to transfer title to your property or transfer title out of your name. A reputable reverse mortgage is a loan with an interest in your equity, not a transfer of title.

Third, never pay any application or processing fees until you have actually decided to apply for a specific loan. If a company tries to get you to pay before you even try to enter a contract with them, you can be sure it will try to squeeze money from you all the way down the line.

All government-insured loans require potential borrowers to receive counseling from a financial advisor unconnected to the lending institution. This advisor can explain all aspects of the loan and highlight its advantages and disadvantages. If you are considering a nongovernment loan, follow the same procedures. Consult with an independent financial advisor unconnected with the institution offering you the reverse mortgage, to find out all of the mortgage's benefits and risks.

For information on where to locate reverse mortgages and how to evaluate the ones being offered, see the Resource Directory in the Appendix at the end of the book.

I. Cashing In a Life Insurance Policy

Life insurance policies offer another source of funds for seniors who are terminally ill. By cashing in a life insurance policy, an elder can get a substantial amount of money relatively quickly—and without having to worry about how the money will get paid back.

However, there are potential drawbacks to cashing in a life insurance policy that may make the option somewhat less attractive than it first appears. First and most obviously, the policy benefits will no longer go to the original beneficiaries. And the amount you receive will be considerably lower than the policy's face value (the amount that would be paid after your death). Also, the payments may be subject to state capital gains tax; although the federal government exempts these amounts from taxes, some states consider them taxable income. Because of this potential tax consequence, plus the complicated terms of the settlements themselves, you should consult with a financial advisor before entering an accelerated benefit or viatical settlement agreement. (See Section 12, below.)

Perhaps most significantly, the amount you receive may disqualify you from receiving Medicaid coverage for home or nursing facility care. (See Chapter 7.) Medicaid does not consider the face value of a life insurance policy as an asset, or require a Medicaid applicant to cash in a policy. But if a policy is cashed in, Medicaid will count the money received as an asset. And if the benefits push the elder over the Medicaid eligibility limits, cashing in the policy will have created a double loss: The elder won't qualify for Medicaid coverage and will receive much less than the policy's face value.

For many terminally ill people, however, the benefits of getting the cash clearly outweigh these negatives. If getting the money before death seems worth it to you, there are two avenues for selling or exchanging a life insurance policy: accelerated or living benefits and viatical settlements.

1. Accelerated or Living Benefits

Some life insurance policies may be cashed in directly with the insurance company itself—a procedure known as collecting accelerated or living benefits. The amount of these benefits runs between 60% and 80% of the face value of the policy, depending on its terms. If the policy provides for accelerated benefits, it usually requires the treating physician to declare the policyholder terminally ill—meaning that he or she has less than two years to live.

The procedures you have to follow to claim accelerated benefits depend on the terms of the individual policy. To learn whether a policy may be cashed in for accelerated benefits and how that process works, check the terms of the policy and speak with a representative of the insurance company that issued it. Do not rely on an insurance agent to explain the details; ask to be referred to staff that specializes in accelerated benefits.

2. Viatical Settlements

Even if a life insurance policy does not provide for accelerated benefits, you can achieve a similar result by selling the policy to a viatical settlement company. These companies take over as beneficiaries under the policy, meaning they get to collect the full face value when the policyholder dies. In exchange for that right to collect later, the settlement company provides cash up front: 60% to 80% of the policy's face value, depending on the length of the policyholder's life expectancy. The longer the life expectancy, the less they pay.

As with accelerated benefits, a policyholder must have been diagnosed as terminally ill to qualify for a viatical settlement. But unlike accelerated benefits, the policyholder must also obtain written permission from the existing beneficiaries.

To shop for the best viatical settlement, compare at least two or three companies. Begin with your own insurance agent or one of the organizations that monitor viatical companies. (See the Appendix at the end of this book for listings.) Regardless of how you find a viatical settlement company, check with your state's Department of Insurance to make sure the company is licensed to do business in your state. A state license means that the company's business practices are subject to some official oversight.

HURRY UP AND WAIT

Most people cash in a life insurance policy because they need the money immediately. But make sure you take the time to consider several companies, compare all the options offered and carefully review all the paperwork before deciding on a settlement. It might also be a good idea to consult with an accountant, lawyer or other financial advisor. Because the insurance and viatical settlement companies also take their time considering your application and plowing through their bureaucratic steps before any money actually changes hands, you shouldn't expect to see your money for two to four months.

J. Supplements to Home Care

A number of free or low-cost programs now provide older people with certain services not offered by most home care agencies. These programs supplement home care services, keep costs down and often make the difference between being able to stay at home and having to enter a nursing facility. Most of all, many of these services give the person receiving care a break in the routine—and give family members some relief from their responsibilities.

1. Meals-on-Wheels

Meals-on-Wheels is perhaps the best known supplement to home care. Although good nutrition is essential to health, many older people begin to neglect their diets when shopping, cooking and cleaning become difficult, or when dietary problems restrict their food choices. Meals-on-Wheels brings easily affordable food that is hot, tasty, nutritious and ready to eat. It also provides daily, friendly human contact that is a welcome diversion in a long day at home.

Almost all communities now have some kind of low-cost meal delivery system for housebound elders, although in some areas there is a waiting list for this service. Funding for Meals-on-Wheels varies, and the service often depends heavily on volunteers, but all of the programs work essentially the same way. For a very small fee, Meals-on-Wheels delivers a hot, nutritional meal once a day, usually around lunchtime. Often, for a slight extra charge, you can also get a snack or another meal, either cold or easily heated, for later in the day.

2. Adult Daycare and Respite Care

Adult daycare can supplement home care or substitute for it. In general, adult daycare centers operate during daytime work hours and provide a meal, monitoring and companionship for people who need some care but are not seriously ill or disabled. Respite care provides a few hours a week of low-cost or free companionship without any active care services. Daycare centers and respite care are often funded by nonprofit organizations. The programs that do not provide medical care tend to be less expensive than home care.

a. Adult Daycare Centers

Adult daycare centers provide meals, companionship, social and physical activities and social services. Some centers also offer limited medical care and monitoring. And they give family caregivers an alternative to full-time home care. These centers can often make it possible for an elder to continue living at home rather than entering a long-term care residential facility.

A few centers affiliated with a hospital or skilled nursing facility offer medical care—including administering medications and treatments, physical and other rehabilitative therapies, health testing, monitoring and screening—as part of a personalized, written health care plan. At centers run by community or public service organizations, more modest levels of medical care may be available.

All daycare centers offer meals, personal care assistance, exercise, recreation and social and educational programs. Social services, including referrals to other agencies and programs, are also usually available. But above all, adult daycare centers offer companionship for elders who might otherwise be housebound—and a little time off for their family members.

Adult daycare centers may offer half-day or full-day programs, one to five days a week. Some require scheduled attendance, while others permit drop-in visits. Some centers also provide or arrange for transportation. Prices depend on the range of services offered and the nature of the sponsoring organization. Many centers charge according to the elder's ability to pay.

FINDING ADULT DAYCARE

To get a referral and references for a center nearby, contact:

National Adult Day Services Association
409 Third St, NW
Washington, DC 20024
202-479-6682
www.ncoa.org/nadsa

---

b. Respite Care

Like adult daycare, respite care serves as a break in routine for both those who give and those who receive care. Unlike adult daycare centers, however, respite care does not involve organized activities or services. It provides companionship and monitoring, often by volunteers, for short periods of time on a regular or occasional basis—a few times a week, one weekend a month or for a full weekend or week when primary caregivers are unavailable. Respite care can be provided at home (yours or the caregiver's), at a church or community center or in a nursing facility. It is often sponsored by a community organization. Unless it is provided at a medical facility, it is usually low-cost or even free.

If your home care agency or geriatric care manager cannot direct you to organizations that provide respite care, you can find referrals through your State Agency on Aging (see the Resource Directory in this book's Appendix), the government-sponsored Eldercare Locator (run by the National Association of Area Agencies on Aging) at 800-677-1116, or the volunteers of Senior Corps at 800-424-8867 (or on the Web at www.seniorcorps.org).

3. Senior Centers

Most senior centers provide free social and recreational activities, education, information and exercise programs and a hot meal on a drop-in basis to physically self-sufficient elders. Generally, there is no fixed schedule required for participation, although elders may have to sign up for meals and some programs in advance.

While senior centers do not offer personal assistance care, they do provide some respite care, nutrition, organized activities and informal companionship for an elder who does not need monitoring. Senior centers often arrange for transportation to and from the center and sometimes organize outings to places of interest. They are excellent sources of information about services available to seniors, particularly about the individual, independent care givers who can be reliable and less expensive alternatives to agency care.

4. County Health Screening

One of the functions of skilled home health care is to monitor the health of the elder receiving care. If you require less extensive care, however, you may be missing regular health monitoring and screening. As a supplement to doctor visits, many city or county health clinics regularly offer free or low-cost health screening and testing.

These clinics can provide adequate general health monitoring if used as part of an ongoing care plan. The public health nurses at these clinics can help schedule a regular program of screening and testing.

5. Family Education Programs

A number of public agencies and community organizations—United Way, Red Cross, Visiting Nurses' Association and many hospitals—offer instruction for elders and their families on various aspects of home health care: personal care assistance (such as bathing and movement techniques), exercise, nutrition for special dietary needs and monitoring health conditions and vital signs. Learning these techniques helps assure the safety and well-being of the elder and permits family members to assist with a wider range of home care—and avoid some of the dependence on professional providers. A family education program can also be a good source of information about other available programs, as well as a chance to share information and experiences with other elders and their families.

6. Additional Services

In addition to the programs discussed above, there are other specific services available free or at very low cost which can help lighten the burdens of home care.

You can find services to supplement home care in much the same way that you find home care itself. With supplemental care, however, the referrals are more likely to come from local rather than state or regional agencies, and from volunteer and community organizations rather than from institutions or medical sources. The local senior center is usually an excellent source of information, as is the Senior Referral telephone service listed in the white pages of your phone directory. Geriatric case managers can be particularly helpful in finding the small, independent or little-known extra services not provided by home care agencies.

Some of the supplemental services available in many communities are:

a. Senior Escort Service

Some people can get around on their own or with minimum assistance, for short trips to the store or the bank or the park, for example. However, they may be concerned about their safety on the streets. Escort services provide someone to accompany you on short trips; they're often available on fairly short notice.

b. Transportation Service

Many people would love to go to a senior center, the library, a park or organized activities if only they could get there. There are a number of public agencies and community groups that provide free transportation, often with wheelchair access.

c. Companion Service

Similar to respite care, a companion service can send someone for a few hours a week on a regular schedule, to provide company but not care. The occasional company and conversation of someone who brings good cheer can be a wonderful diversion. These services are mostly volunteer-staffed and community-funded, so there is usually no charge for using them.

d. Housekeeping and Grocery Services

Many state and local government Departments of Social Services or volunteer programs offer grocery shoppers and part-time housekeepers to do occasional work for low-income physically disabled or impaired elders. When available, these housekeeping and grocery services are offered free or at a very low cost.

e. Telephone Safety Service

Particularly valuable for people who live alone and do not have family in the vicinity, telephone reassurance programs make a daily call, at the same time each day, to check in with an elder living at home. Besides being a safety check, these calls allow the elder to have a brief conversation with someone during the day.

A related service, called Lifeline, is available in many places. It provides a telephone emergency response service usually connected directly to a hospital or other emergency health facility. The line can be connected to your phone and maintained for a nominal cost. ■

Organized
Senior Residences

Many seniors are no longer able, or no longer willing, to live completely independently at home. For some, home care may offer help, but it may not deliver the sense of security and companionship that the elder needs. For seniors at the other extreme, the amount of home care they need may be prohibitively expensive, but they may neither want nor need the institutional care of a nursing facility.

Elder residences have evolved to fill this gap. They combine some of the comforts and independence of living at home with some of the care and security of a nursing facility. Elder residences come in various shapes and sizes, provide different services and levels of care and carry different price tags. But they share at least one thing: They provide shelter and services for the elderly without the institutional feel and high cost of nursing facilities.

These organized residences range from seniors-only apartment complexes and retirement communities for relatively independent elders, to assisted living facilities for people who need help with activities of daily living (ADLs). Some residential communities offer both independent living and assisted living in the same location. Still others provide continuing care, including a nursing facility, which guarantees that a resident can move from one level of care to another as needed.

While organized senior residences may provide excellent living situations, they are not for everyone. Some facilities deny entry to seniors who are over a certain age, while others mandate a certain level of physical capability. And most carry substantial pricetags or monthly payments that are beyond the means of many elders. The exception is federally subsidized housing for low-income seniors, which may charge rent and provide some services on a sliding scale based on income.

And financial assistance is hard to come by. Medicare, Medicaid and private insurance do not cover any of the cost of independent living residences. Nor do they pay for most assisted living facilities, although this is slowly changing. (See Section B.) Nonetheless, most of the residential alternatives discussed in this chapter are less expensive than nursing facilities and are worth considering if some care short of a nursing facility is needed.

HELP IN FINDING RESIDENTIAL FACILITIES

A growing number of sources offer help in finding suitable residential facilities:

- American Association of Homes and Services for the Aging can provide you with information about its member residential facilities in your area. Phone: 202-783-2242; Internet: www.aahsa.org.
- Assisted Living Federation of America provides a list of assisted living facilities that belong to the federation. Phone: 703-691-8100; Internet: www.alfa.org.
- Eldercare Locator, run by the National Association of Area Agencies on Aging, can provide referrals. Phone: 800-677-1116.
- Your local Area Agency on Aging provides information about subsidized housing and residential facilities. (See the Appendix for contact information.)
- The Senior Referral and Information service listed in the white pages of the telephone directory can refer you to local facilities.
- A geriatric care manager may be able to direct you to residential facilities (especially assisted living facilities), might know the reputation of particular local residences and can help you evaluate whether a particular place is likely to meet your needs. (See Chapter 1, Section G.)
- Religious, ethnic or fraternal organizations are often good sources of information about senior housing.

A. Independent Living

Independent living complexes are housing built or renovated for older people who are, for the most part, able to care for themselves. The main purpose of these residences is to provide senior-friendly housing and social services.

IF MORE CARE IS NEEDED

Independent living residences do not provide personal care or monitor a resident's physical condition. But some include separate floors or wings with assisted living units where such care is provided. (See Section B.) In these facilities, a resident may move to a higher level of care when needed, but only if such a housing unit is vacant. (See Section C1.)

Other independent living residences are combined with both assisted living units and a nursing facility. In these continuing care communities, residents are guaranteed whatever level of care they need. (See Section C2.) A resident whose health or physical condition changes may move to a different level of care without having to wait for available space. This guarantee makes continuing care communities more expensive than multilevel facilities that permit seniors to move only when there is a vacancy.

---

1. The Basics

Independent living residences come in many forms. For people with a good deal of money and independence, there are luxury, gated housing developments, often with a golf course or other extensive indoor and outdoor recreation amenities. In these developments, people purchase their own homes or townhouses.

There are also more moderately priced rental apartment or condominium complexes with a selection of differently sized units, common dining and socializing areas and services for residents, but without the extensive private grounds and recreation facilities of gated communities.

Independent living residences may also be simple urban apartment buildings with small rental units, limited common areas and few services. Some of these senior apartment buildings are subsidized by the federal government, which means that rent is considerably cheaper than market rates for units of the same size.

Many independent living residences refer to themselves as communities. This may seem like a big claim for what may be no more than a small apartment building, but a sense of community is just what these residences seek to create. The amount and type of services offered by an independent living facility vary, depending in large part on cost. But all independent living residences provide a specially tailored and protected living space—a community—by:

- limiting residence to seniors, which means the people who live there tend to have similar experiences, physical capabilities and limitations
- designing and outfitting common areas and individual living units specially for elders, with elevators, ramps, wide hallways, good lighting, handrails and extra safety and security devices
- having common dining areas and providing meals—some included in the general fees paid, others for an extra charge—specially prepared for older tastes, digestion and nutritional needs
- providing some laundry and housekeeping services, although there may be extra charges for these
- offering some commercial services on the premises, such as banking, a beauty salon, shops, a library or local transportation
- organizing social, educational and recreational events both on and off the premises, and

- having a nurse or paramedic on duty, or some other medical emergency system.

INDEPENDENT LIVING PLUS HOME CARE

You may be one of many people considering a move to an independent living community, but wonder whether you are independent enough. You may need more personal care than an independent living community offers, but not need all the services an assisted living facility provides. The difference may be something as simple as needing help to take a shower. If you need only a little personal care, you may not want the close monitoring and regulations of assisted living—or the higher cost of help that you don't need. But without a small amount of extra care, you cannot quite manage on your own.

One solution may be for you to arrange for outside home care in your independent living residence. (See Chapter 2.) You may be able to hire just as much home care as you need, without the unwanted and costly care provided by assisted living. Some independent living facilities even maintain a roster of reliable outside home care providers and will help arrange the care.

Other independent living communities, however, have rules about the type or frequency of outside care permitted. And some independent living facilities require that all residents maintain a certain level of physical capability—being ambulatory and able to get in and out of bed unassisted, for example. Such rules may make home care in those communities less useful than it could be. (See Section A3.)

---

2. Costs

Independent living residences range from federally subsidized studio apartments rented for a few hundred dollars a month to luxury homes sold for over a million dollars. And there are other important questions about cost to consider: Are there fees in addition to rent or purchase price? How much are rent and fees likely to be raised over time? What services are included in the price you pay, and what services cost extra?

a. Renting

Many independent living complexes offer studio, one-bedroom or two-bedroom rental apartments. Because of the services, facilities, staff and common areas that are also provided, rent for these units generally runs 50% to 100% higher than for a comparable apartment in the same locale. On the other hand, they are usually 50% to 100% less expensive than comparable assisted living units. And some are federally subsidized, which means that the rents there are lower for those who meet the eligibility requirements: a low fixed income and very few assets.

Although the initial rent for an independent living apartment may be affordable, you also need to consider rent increases. Because they provide more than just housing, independent living complexes are almost always exempt from city or county rent control laws. However, you may be able to control your own rent for a short time through a lease. Most independent living facilities will offer a one-year lease; some will offer two or three years. Longer leases are rarely offered, and are probably not a good idea for you, either. If it turns out that you do not like living in the apartment, or your needs change and you can no longer manage in independent living, a long lease might tie you down.

Before moving into a rental apartment, ask to see the facility's record of rent increases over the previous five years. If it has consistently raised rents by large amounts, the practice will probably continue. On the other hand, if it has kept rent increases low over the years, it might also do so for the foreseeable future.

b. Buying

Many independent living complexes are enclosed subdivisions with single family homes or townhouses for sale. Also, many senior apartments are sold as condominiums or cooperatives rather than rented. The prices of these houses and apartments vary widely, depending on size, quality, location and services. A senior housing unit tends to have less square footage than regular housing with the same number of rooms, but their special design, security and included services make the properties more expensive.

Unlike open market housing, many senior independent living complexes restrict an owner's rights to resell or mortgage the property. In all senior housing, a new buyer must qualify under the community's general rules, which generally require residents to be over a certain age and have a defined physical independence. (See Section A3.) But some complexes place additional restrictions on resale or refinance. For example, a housing complex may reserve the right to buy back the unit for some percentage more than the seller paid—or some percentage less than any offer the seller receives. Rules may also restrict an owner's right to refinance the house or to obtain cash by taking out a reverse mortgage. (See Chapter 2, Section H.) There may also be strict rules against renting out the property.

If at some point you need to move to a higher level of care than you can receive in independent living, or for any other reason you want to move out, these restrictions may make it difficult to sell your home. They will also reduce its market value. Your survivors would experience the same difficulties if you died while living in the property. So, before entering into any agreement to purchase an independent living house or apartment, thoroughly examine any rules relating to resale or refinance. If you are not certain how those rules might affect you, get a full explanation from an attorney, accountant or other financial advisor who is not connected to the facility.

c. Additional fees

At many senior residences, the price to buy or rent a house or apartment is only one of several costs. There is often an entrance fee that is partially or entirely nonrefundable. Many residential complexes also charge monthly maintenance fees. And some places include certain services (such as one daily meal and occasional cleaning services) in the basic rent or purchase price, but charge extra fees for other services, such as additional meals, laundry and access to recreational facilities.

Entrance fees. If you buy an independent living house or condominium, and in some cases if you rent, you may be required to pay a lump sum entrance fee, also called an endowment fee or a founders fee. These fees may range from $10,000 to $100,000—depending on how luxurious—or popular—the place is.

Sometimes, these entrance fees are fully refundable for a limited time; if you sell the unit within the first three to six months after you buy it, some housing complexes may refund the entire fee. At other places, you get back only a portion of the fee when you sell your unit—commonly, the entrance fee refund is reduced by 1% to 5% for each month you live in the residence.

Maintenance fees. Most independent living complexes in which residents own their house or condominium charge a monthly maintenance fee. For rental units, the maintenance fees are usually part of the rent. Most complexes charge a maintenance fee even if they also charge an entrance fee. Before you buy a residence, find out if there are any rules that control how much the maintenance fee may be raised per year. If there are no rules about fee increases, check the facility's records for the previous five years to see how often and how much the fees have been raised.

Fees for services. All independent living residences include some services in addition to a roof over your head. It is important to find out which services are included in the rent or purchase price and which cost extra.

Most independent living residences have a kitchen and common dining room in which at least one hot meal per day is served; some serve three meals, although breakfast and lunch may be informal buffets. But meals may not be included in your regular rent or maintenance fees; if you want meals, you may have to pay extra for them. Food is usually a senior's greatest expense after rent and health care. Shopping for, preparing and cleaning up after meals can be a significant burden for many elders. And good nutrition is a key to continued good health. For all these reasons, finding out how many meals are included in your basic rent or maintenance fee, and how much extra meals cost, should be an important part of your investigation of any independent living residence. Quality is important, too. If you plan to eat the residence's food, make sure to sample it; have at least two meals before you agree to move in.

INCLUSIVE CONTRACTS COVER EVERYTHING THAT IS OFFERED

Some independent living complexes offer what is called an inclusive contract or extensive agreement, which means that the rent or purchase price plus maintenance fees covers all the services the facility provides. If you can choose between an inclusive and a non-inclusive contract, you must determine if the extra cost of the inclusive contract is worth the extra services. If the extra services are not things you particularly care about, you may not want to pay for them.

Choosing between the two types of contracts will be less difficult if you are permitted to pay for individual services without having to buy the whole inclusive package. Then you may be able to pick and choose the few extra services you want—lunch and sessions with an exercise instructor, for example—without having to pay for all the other things in the inclusive contract that don't interest you.

Among the services commonly offered is recreation—exercise and dance, for example, and golf, tennis and swimming at the more expensive communities. You may be charged a separate fee for some of these services, or charged extra for unlimited or preferential access to them. Similarly, transportation, housekeeping, laundry and shopping services may be offered, but some or all of them only for extra fees.

Some independent living facilities also offer temporary personal assistance. If you need long-term help with dressing, bathing, eating or moving around, you will not be permitted to remain in independent living. (See Section A3.) But if your need for care is only short-term, some facilities provide it. Find out whether the facility offers this kind of personal care and whether it is included in your regular fees or requires paying extra.

3. Rules and Restrictions

Because they are organized facilities rather than merely a collection of residences, independent living communities tend to have numerous rules and regulations by which residents must abide. The rules range from simple things like the time meals are served or the decorations or modifications permitted in an individual living unit, to the extremely important matter of the physical condition a resident must maintain to live there.

a. Age and physical condition

Independent living facilities require residents to maintain a certain level of physical independence. There are usually two different standards: one to enter as a resident and another (somewhat less stringent) standard to remain.

Requirements to enter. To qualify to buy or rent a housing unit, you must have reached at least a minimum age—usually 55 or 60. But many residence complexes also have a maximum age; some have entry age limits of 75, 80 or 85.

In most residences, you must also be fully ambulatory—meaning that you are able to move around without a wheelchair or personal assistance. Most independent living complexes permit a new resident to use a walker, but some do not permit walkers or oxygen units in the common dining areas. Many independent living facilities also require that new residents be fully continent. Others insist that a resident must be able to eat without assistance, at least in the common dining area.

Requirements to remain. Residents in independent living units might not be permitted to remain if their physical conditions deteriorate, for more than a short time, past a certain point. Any of the following problems might disqualify a resident:

• inability to get in and out of bed without assistance

- full incontinence, or
- inability to eat without assistance.

Because of such rules, if you are already frail and are likely, within the foreseeable future, to fall below a residence's physical condition requirements, you should consider:

- an independent living residence with less stringent requirements, or with no requirements at all for continuing residents
- an assisted living residence instead of independent living (see Section B), or
- a facility with more than one level of care, so that if you must move, you will be able to remain in the same residential community. (See Section C.)

RULES FOR COUPLES

It often happens that one person in a couple—either a married couple, siblings or some other combination of people who live together—loses some physical capabilities before the other does. If one member of the couple falls below the facility's physical requirements while the other remains physically qualified, what happens next depends on the rules of the facility and the availability of another housing unit within the same complex.

In some residences, the couple must move—or one of them must move while the other remains. If the same facility offers assisted living units, this rule would not create quite as much of a hardship. Other facilities permit the couple to stay if the less able one can reach the minimum physical standards with the help of the healthier one, but without outside assistance.

Any couple considering an independent living residence must understand these rules, and make sure they are clearly spelled out in the written residence contract.

b. Number of residents, guests, assistants

Many independent living facilities limit the number of people who may live in any given unit. The maximum is usually two; only one resident might be permitted in a small unit. All residents must be over a certain age—generally 55 to 65. That means that children or grandchildren may not move in, even if they could provide needed personal care for the resident. Some communities also require that couples who share a residence be related. This restriction prevents residents from reaping the great cost savings of sharing with a housemate—and prohibits older couples who are not (or cannot get) married.

Most residences also have rules regarding overnight guests. Some prohibit guests in the units but offer guest rooms or apartments for short stays, usually with an extra charge to the resident. Some permit guests for short stays, but prohibit children under a certain age. Most places allow guests to stay for meals, for an extra charge to the resident; some even provide a separate, private dining room for groups or special occasions.

When you consider an independent living residence, find out whether and under what circumstances it permits home care for individual residents. Having a personal care aide come to your home on a regular basis to help you with activities of daily living—dressing, bathing, cooking and eating, getting in and out of bed or taking a walk—may mean the difference between remaining in independent living and having to move to assisted living or a nursing facility. But some residences limit the number of regular visits by outside personal care aides, or do not permit them at all except on a temporary basis while a resident recovers from an illness or injury. Such a restriction may not seem that meaningful to you if you are now hale and hardy, but it could become important if and when your physical condition takes a turn for the worse.

A CHANGE IN OWNERSHIP MAY NOT BE GOOD NEWS

Like many other businesses these days, seniors residences are frequently targets for takeovers by larger companies. National corporations that run senior residences around the country are gobbling up good, low-cost, locally owned facilities. And when the ownership changes, the quality and the cost often change, too.

New owners often change things to make their acquisition more profitable, which may mean less comfort and higher costs for the residents. If you are considering moving into an independent or assisted living residence complex, find out how long the current owners have operated it.

If it has been sold within the previous two years, talk with the staff and residents about recent changes. Cuts in services and staff may make residents less comfortable than they have been, and future cuts may make things worse. Also, you can no longer rely on what the previous owners did regarding rent or fee increases. Ask management for information on increases the new ownership has imposed not only at this residence but also at other facilities they operate, particularly ones they have recently purchased.

B. Assisted Living

Assisted living combines much of the homelike atmosphere of independent living with some of the personal care of a nursing facility. It provides extensive personal assistance and services, plus round-the-clock monitoring, that are not offered by independent living residences and would be extremely expensive if arranged through home care. On the other hand, assisted living permits residents to maintain some of the privacy and independence that are lost in more institutional, and more expensive, nursing facilities. Assisted living is the fastest growing type of senior residence—meeting the needs of millions of seniors who cannot make it entirely on their own, but who do not need nursing care.

The residences referred to in this section as assisted living are sometimes also called sheltered care or catered living. Although each facility or residence differs somewhat in the type of housing and level of services and staffing provided, all of them, regardless of name, have certain things in common. They provide:

- domestic services, including meals and housekeeping
- assistance with personal care and the activities of daily living (see Section 1b), but not nursing care, and
- close monitoring to help ensure residents' health and safety.

1. The Basics

Assisted living provides a room or small apartment—usually rented—to help maintain a homelike setting, plus a range of services to assist residents with those tasks of daily life made difficult for them by the loss of some physical or mental capabilities.

a. Types of living spaces

There are several kinds and sizes of assisted living housing: full-size one-bedroom apartments; studio apartments with small kitchenettes; studios without a kitchen, or with a partial kitchen that has no cooking facilities; single rooms; and shared rooms. An assisted living apartment or room may be furnished or unfurnished. Even if a space is furnished, some places permit residents to bring in some furnishings of their own, which can make a new place feel more like home.

Assisted living apartments and rooms tend to be smaller than living spaces intended for the general public. They are often fitted with safety devices such as handrails and special bathroom fixtures, and may include a hospital bed if needed. In addition to the small rooms and space-eating fixtures, people tend to bring more of their own furnishings than would otherwise fit easily into the space. As a result, many assisted living apartments feel crowded and even smaller than they are. It is often difficult for a new resident to adjust to the smaller, more cramped quarters.

SPECIAL CARE FOR ALZHEIMER'S OR DISORIENTATION

Many people suffer mild symptoms from the early stages of Alzheimer's or other age-related disorientation. Their need for monitoring and assistance make independent living too difficult or dangerous, but they do not need the high level of care provided by a nursing facility. For them, assisted living is often an excellent solution.

However, the kind of assistance these people need is different from that required by those who have only physical limitations. The same assisted living residence that provides good care for someone with only physical frailties does not necessarily work well for a person with mild dementia. If you are considering an assisted living facility for someone with early Alzheimer's or other mild dementia, be sure to read Chapter 5.

---

b. Services provided

The main difference between assisted living and independent living residences (see Section A) is that assisted living gives residents more help in meeting their daily needs. While assisted living does not offer the medical care or the level of attention of a nursing facility, it does provide personal care in a resident's living space and common areas, meals, household tasks and extensive monitoring of each resident's physical condition.

Personal assistance. Most people move to assisted living because they need help with one or more of what are known as the activities of daily living (ADLs). ADLs include eating, bathing, dressing, continence and using the toilet, walking and getting in and out of a bed or chair.

An assisted living facility will help a resident with any ADL—but not all the time, and not whenever a resident wants help. Instead, a schedule will be developed that takes into account the resident's needs and the staff's availability. For example, an aide might help a resident get in and out of bed in the morning, once or twice during the day, at bedtime and once again during the night. Or a resident might be given a full bath three or four times a week, but not every day.

When you consider a particular assisted living residence, ask precisely what help it offers for the specific ADLs with which you need assistance. If the facility offers you the kind and frequency of assistance you need, make certain that care is spelled out in the written residence agreement you and the management sign.

Health monitoring. In addition to help with daily activities, assisted living facilities monitor a resident's health. That does not mean nursing or other active treatment of a medical condition, however. Rather, it means keeping track of and helping the resident take the correct dose of medications, helping the resident with self-administered health aids such as prostheses and oxygen, providing emergency call systems and checking on a resident's well-being during the night.

Most assisted living residences have a nurse on duty to check on any resident who has health difficulty or whose physical condition seems to be changing, and to refer the resident for medical care if it seems necessary. Health monitoring may also include coordinating care with the resident's primary care physician and keeping track of a resident's medical appointments. And most facilities provide or arrange transportation to and from those appointments.

STRICT RULES AREN'T FOR EVERYONE

Assisted living offers close monitoring of residents' physical conditions. This includes keeping track of medications, checking on residents at night and making sure residents eat properly. Assisted living facilities accomplish this by setting up schedules that staff and residents must follow.

Sometimes, these schedules and rules are too restrictive for a competent, independent-minded person. (See Section B3, below.)

Depending on your needs, including your need to be left alone, independent living plus home care might fit your personality better than assisted living—even though you and your family will have to take charge of organizing your care.

Meals. For many people, one of the most attractive things about assisted living is that meals are provided. These facilities have a kitchen and a common dining room where at least two and usually three meals a day are served. The cost of meals is included in the resident's rent or fees. Residents are freed from shopping, cooking and cleaning up; they are assured of nutritious food; and they are brought together for the informal social exchange of a meal with other residents.

There are several things to check about an assisted living residence's food service. First, find out how many meals a day are included, and whether they are all full, hot meals. Then check on the quality of the food; it won't do you any good if you won't eat it. Try several meals in their dining room, and see if the residents seem interested in their food and in each other.

It is also important to find out what happens if a resident is not able to appear for a meal, or simply does not want a meal in the dining room. Are meals served at different times, or only at one set time? Under what circumstances are meals delivered to individual rooms or apartments? May a resident take food from the dining room back to a private room? If three meals a day are served, may a resident regularly choose to skip one or more of them? If so, does the resident need to prove to the staff that he or she is getting enough nutrition without the prepared meal?

Housekeeping. Assisted living facilities provide laundry service and also clean individual rooms or apartments. What that housekeeping includes, however, can vary considerably. Find out how often a resident's bedding and bath linen are laundered. Does the facility do a resident's personal laundry as well? Is there an extra charge for personal laundry? How often (and how well) is an individual room or apartment cleaned?

Social activities and exercise. It is one thing to assist residents with the basics of daily life such as dressing and bathing; that help is guaranteed in a contract with an assisted living residence. It is another thing entirely to help residents lead mentally, physically and socially active lives. This is not a matter of contract, but of the quality and style of service at a good residence. Most facilities plan group activities such as guest lectures and exercise classes, as well as regular gatherings for the residents to visit among themselves. The best facilities also help individual residents participate in these activities to the extent possible and provide alternatives—an assisted walk around the hallways, for example, or a one-on-one chat in a resident's private room—when it's not feasible to participate in a group.

There are several ways to get a sense of the quality of group and individual activities at a particular facility. You can always take a look at what is scheduled for any given week, but it is also important to visit during one of these planned activities to see if residents participate and seem to enjoy doing so. As for more individual attention, find out whether there are any rules against staff spending non-scheduled time with residents. And on all your visits, watch how staff members interact with residents: look for a friendly, relaxed manner on everyone's part. (See Chapter 4, Section B, for information on how to choose a nursing facility, much of which also applies to assisted living.)

2. Costs

Most assisted living spaces are rented, not purchased. The major exception is assisted living as part of a continuing care community. (See Section C2.)

a. Basic rent

Obviously, rent depends on the size of living space. A small room with no cooking facilities will cost much less than a spacious one-bedroom apartment with full kitchen. The rent also varies with the amount of services and staff provided, the location and the overall condition of the facility. And some facilities offer more than one type of rental agreement: A limited contract may include fewer meals and personal assistance than an inclusive or extensive agreement that includes all the services the facility has to offer. Given all these variables, rent for an assisted living unit generally runs 50% to 100% higher than for a comparable independent living unit in the same facility. But it will still be one-third to one-half the cost of a nursing facility of the same quality, in the same area.

b. Rent increases

As with any other rental housing, you must consider how much your rent may go up over time. A lease can guarantee the rent for a year or two. After that, rent increases are completely within the discretion of the facility's ownership, unless a yearly limit is included in your rental agreement. If there is no limit, check the facility's record of rent increases over the previous five years. If they have raised rents in large chunks, you have to consider whether they will price you out of your apartment in years to come.

c. Additional fees

Some assisted living facilities charge fees in addition to rent. There may be a one-time nonrefundable entrance fee. And there may be a fee for certain services not included in the basic assisted living contract, such as extra or delivered meals, extra housekeeping service, local transportation fees or personal care beyond the standard level of care offered in the facility.

d. Medicaid coverage

Medicaid (called Medi-Cal in California) is a federal program, administered somewhat differently by each state, that pays medical expenses for people with very low incomes and few assets. (See Chapter 7.)

Until very recently, Medicaid paid for home care and for nursing facility care, but not for any type of long-term care residence in between. Slowly, however, Medicaid administrators have begun to recognize that many people who live in nursing facilities paid for by Medicaid could be living more comfortably in much less expensive assisted living facilities if only Medicaid would pay for it. So, a number of states are now exploring the advantages of paying for assisted living for some people who would otherwise qualify for nursing facility care.

These programs are relatively new, however, and there are no national standards that establish when and where Medicaid will pay for assisted living. Medicaid assisted living coverage is currently available in only a few states, sometimes only in certain counties, and usually on a temporary, experimental basis. Even where the program exists, most assisted living residences are not certified to accept Medicaid.

Nonetheless, if you believe you might qualify for Medicaid now, or might qualify in the foreseeable future after spending most of your assets, it would be wise to take these steps:

- read Chapter 7 of this book regarding Medicaid eligibility
- contact the Medicaid office in the county where you plan to live to find out if the local program covers assisted living and if so, what the rules are, and
- if Medicaid does cover some assisted living, get a list from the Medicaid office of all the assisted living facilities in the area that are certified to receive Medicaid payments.

It may be better to find out whether a particular facility is covered by asking the Medicaid office directly rather than asking facility administrators. If the facility does not accept Medicaid, your question may scare off the facility operators even if you are currently able to pay your own way. They might worry that you are asking about Medicaid because you anticipate running out of money at some point, which could make them reluctant to take you on as a resident.

e. Long-term care insurance coverage

Virtually none of the private long-term care insurance policies issued during the 1970s and 1980s covers assisted living—they are all essentially nursing home policies, some of which also cover home care. By the mid-1990s, however, some policies began to offer coverage for assisted living. This was due in part to increased competition among insurance companies, and in part to the insurance companies' realization that if they have to pay on a policy, they would rather pay for assisted living than for a more expensive nursing facility.

If you have long-term care insurance and believe assisted living might be a better choice for you than either home care or a nursing facility, check the extent of coverage in your policy. If assisted living is covered, carefully examine the requirements to qualify under your particular policy.

Such policies usually require you to have physical or mental limitations to trigger the coverage—many policies will pay for assisted living only if you need assistance with at least two or three Activities of Daily Living, or ADLs. (See Section B1.) Some policies make this requirement a bit easier to meet by also looking at what are called instrumental ADL, such as the abilities to keep house, manage money and bills and manage medications.

There is also the question of who decides whether your condition meets these standards. The policy may require that your primary care physician certify that you meet the conditions, but the policy may also permit the insurance company to have its own doctor examine you before agreeing that the coverage trigger has been met. (Chapter 11 covers long-term care insurance in detail.)

3. Rules and Restrictions

Assisted living facilities take on the difficult task of providing different types and amounts of care and services to people who, like everyone else, have individual quirks and personality traits. One way these facilities manage is by setting standards regarding who is an appropriate resident, and creating fairly strict rules by which all residents must abide.

a. Becoming and remaining a resident

Just as assisted living fits between independent living and nursing care, its residents' physical and mental capabilities are supposed to fit between complete independence and total dependence. To ensure this fit, assisted living facilities establish standards residents must meet to enter and to remain.

The entrance requirements for potential residents may begin with a minimum age—55 or 60—and sometimes a maximum—80 or 85. Then there is the matter of the care needed by a potential resident. Facilities will usually accommodate someone who doesn't need much assistance but wants the personal attention offered by an assisted living facility (and is willing to pay for it). Some facilities (especially those with few vacancies) might suggest that a relatively healthy potential resident try independent living instead. But assisted living facilities are usually careful not to accept a resident who needs more care than they can deliver. Most of them scrupulously assess each potential resident's physical and cognitive capabilities before agreeing to let the individual into the facility.

Rules for entering and staying in such facilities commonly mandate that residents:

- require regular staff assistance with no more than two to four of the Activities of Daily Living (ADLs)—eating, bathing, dressing, transferring in and out of a bed or chair, using the toilet and walking
- not be completely incontinent
- not require daily nursing care, and
- not present a danger to themselves, staff or other residents and not require extremely close monitoring or physical control—unless the facility has a special care unit for Alzheimer's or other dementia sufferers.

Unless it is part of a continuing care community which guarantees each resident the right to remain in whatever level of care is required (see Section C2), an assisted living facility may force a resident to move out—usually to a nursing facility—if he or she falls below the facility's standards.

However, assisted living facilities are often more flexible with existing residents than with potential ones. For example, a facility may permit a resident to remain if he or she hires outside assistance for the extra care the facility is unable to provide, depending on the facility's rules regarding how much outside assistance is permitted.

WHO DECIDES WHETHER YOU MUST MOVE?

A resident must meet physical standards to remain in an assisted living facility. But who decides exactly what a resident's condition is? The answer to this question is very important, because it could determine whether you are required to move to a nursing facility

Some changes in condition will obviously require a change. If a resident becomes completely bedridden, there will be no argument that he or she no longer meets the facility's standards. But often, the issue is murky. The degree of a resident's incontinence may be unclear, for example. Or a resident might suffer a fall that could be permanently disabling—or could permit a slow recovery.

An assisted living contract should clearly describe how this decision is made. Facilities always reserve the right to make the final decision. But it should take into account the resident's primary care physician's opinion and be reviewed by an independent physician or geriatric social worker.

---

b. Outside assistance

Some assisted living residences place strict limits on visits by outside nurses and personal care aides. Some permit them only on a temporary basis while a resident recovers from an illness or injury. Others permit regular visits by outside help, but limit the type or frequency. If the personal care assistance offered by an assisted living facility does not seem to match your needs, but you believe you can fill the gaps with outside help, find out whether the facility's rules would permit it. If so, make sure the rules are clearly spelled out in your written residence agreement.

c. Staff control over residents

One of the important services provided by assisted living staff is round-the-clock monitoring of the residents' well-being. This is often achieved through strict schedules by which staff and residents must abide. For example, some facilities serve meals at a precise hour and require residents to appear in the dining room for all of them. Or a staff aide might enter each resident's room one or more times every night to check on the resident's condition. Or the staff might control all of a resident's medications, even nonprescription ones, to ensure that the resident uses them properly and to protect against adverse drug interactions.

This constant caretaking is more than some residents need or want. It is therefore important to find out not only about the facility's rules and schedules but also about its flexibility. For example, if a resident does not want three meals a day in the dining room, do the rules allow checking in without having to appear? Can some meals be delivered to a resident's quarters, or must the resident provide his or her own food if a meal is skipped? Can nightly check-ups be eliminated if the resident finds them more disturbing than beneficial? May medications be left with the resident if the resident has sufficient awareness and orientation to monitor them without help?

d. Right to return after an absence

Many assisted living residents have serious medical crises that force them into the hospital or a nursing or rehabilitation center for extended stays. Often no one knows for months whether the resident will recover sufficiently to again live in assisted living, or instead will need to move to a long-term care nursing facility. During this time, the resident may not want or be able to pay for an unused assisted living room or apartment to which the resident might never return.

Most facilities have rules regarding a resident's right to return after an extended absence. Many facilities will hold a room or apartment for a short time, then offer a longer period—often six months or a year—during which the former resident has priority over new applicants for the next available equivalent room or apartment. Without such protection in an assisted living contract, one serious medical crisis—even one from which you eventually recover—could force you to search for a new home.

C. Combination Residential Facilities

The first two sections of this chapter discuss independent living communities and assisted living residences, while Chapter 4 covers nursing facilities. But many senior communities combine two or three of these care levels in one place. This section explains the different combinations available—and the benefits and risks of each.

1. Extended Care Residences

Many senior residence communities offer both independent living and assisted living in the same complex of buildings and grounds. Because many design features and services are common to both, it can be economical for the same ownership to build and operate the two levels together. This makes it possible for a senior to move into an independent living residence and conveniently transfer to assisted living, if necessary.

That both independent living and assisted living are offered within the same seniors community, however, does not necessarily mean that you may move from one to the other whenever you choose. In an extended care community, you may be given an opportunity to move from one level to another, but not a guarantee. This differentiates it from continuing care and life care communities in which, for considerably more money than a simple extended care facility, you lock in the right to move to a different level as needed. (See Section C2.)

In an extended care community, an independent living resident may move to assisted living only if there is a vacant unit that fits the resident's needs and budget. Some people move into assisted living first, then to independent living if they regain strength or mobility. But most move first into independent living and later to assisted living.

If there is no vacancy, the resident must wait. This is not always a major problem—often a resident's need for increased care develops slowly, as physical strength diminishes. And the wait may be shorter if the facility gives priority for vacancies to existing residents. That should be spelled out in the written residency agreement.

If you do eventually need assisted living, an extended care community offers advantages that may make it worth the potential delay:

- You can remain within a familiar physical setting and routine. In most places, many of the community's common areas are used by both independent living and assisted living residents. And although your private living space would change if you move from one level to another, it would still have a familiar look and feel—in design, bath and kitchen fixtures, for example.

- Many of the people on staff will be the same, so you don't need to get to know a whole new crew, and they don't need to become newly acquainted with you.
- The other residents whom you have come to know will still be your neighbors.
- You avoid the strenuous and always disorienting process of packing up, moving to a new location, settling in and getting to know a new area, a new living space, new rules and regulations and new people.

2. Continuing Care Retirement Communities (CCRCs)

A Continuing Care Retirement Community (CCRC) provides any level of care and services you need—independent living, assisted living or custodial nursing care—for as long as you are a resident. (See Chapter 4 for information on custodial-level nursing care.) The basic agreement of a CCRC is that the resident pays a hefty entry fee and monthly charges to live in the community, and the facility guarantees that the resident may move from one level of care to another as the resident's physical and mental condition require. The phrase often used to describe this guarantee is "aging in place"—that is, to live in the same place through all the stages of growing old. And while some CCRCs truly offer an "age in place" guarantee, others fudge a bit on the "place." (See Section 2a.)

Some CCRCs offer a year-to-year arrangement to residents, after an initial entrance fee. These facilities may also have monthly maintenance fees; these fees are sometimes tiered—meaning that they are higher for assisted living than for independent living, and highest for nursing care. Other CCRCs offer an extended lease, which locks in maintenance fees and other charges for the period of the lease. And a special, more expensive kind of CCRC arrangement, called a Life Care contract, promises care for as long as the resident lives. (See Section 2d.)

a. Basic arrangements

All CCRCs provide continuing care, but not all of them do so in the same location. Almost all CCRCs offer independent living and assisted living in the same place. And some CCRCs also have an on-site nursing facility. But many CCRCs have no separate nursing wing; instead, a resident who needs nursing care must receive it in an assisted living apartment. When that is not practical, the resident must move into a separate off-site nursing facility with which the CCRC has a contractual arrangement.

ON-SITE OR OFF-SITE NURSING FACILITIES

A CCRC with its own nursing facility is not necessarily better than one that has contracted with an outside facility. In fact, some on-site nursing facilities are no more than rooms in a separate section of assisted living where nursing care is delivered. Of course, there are advantages to remaining in the same location with some of the same staff and your neighbors nearby. But if an on-site nursing wing does not get much of the community's attention, expertise and money, it may be better to move to an off-site nursing facility that provides only one level of care and does it well.

Find out whether a CCRC's on-site nursing facility is certified by the state. If not, find out whether it contracts with a separate local nursing facility to take residents for whom they can no longer care. If it does, visit that facility and assess it as thoroughly as possible. (See Chapter 4.)

Beware that some CCRCs only admit residents who are initially able to qualify for independent living. It costs less for the CCRC to provide care and services for an independent living resident, and facility administrators want to make sure that they get several years of providing this less expensive level of service before they have to provide more costly assisted living or nursing care. Some CCRCs also have a maximum entry age of around 80.

CONSIDER THE FUTURE

People who consider moving into a CCRC do so because they want to provide not only for their immediate needs, but also for the care they may later require. Unfortunately, when investigating specific communities, too many people focus on the independent living quarters and services where they would first live, and only casually look into the assisted living and nursing facility care. This nearsightedness is often encouraged by the community's sales staff, who know that independent living is always a more cheerful and inviting part of the community to show a prospective resident.

Investigate the assisted living and nursing facility living quarters, services and costs as closely as you do independent living. You may never need those levels of care, but if you do, you will want them to measure up. You will have already paid a lot of money for them. And if someday you need the care they offer, you will have to depend on them. This advice is important for all CCRCs, but doubly so if you are considering a Life Care contract. (See Section 2d.)

---

b. Costs

Because of its guarantee of care and services at any level needed at any time, a house or apartment in a CCRC is usually substantially more expensive than a comparable living space in a multiunit facility that offers no nursing care and provides no transfer guarantee.

Rentals. If an independent living house or apartment in a CCRC is offered as a rental, you can expect to pay anywhere from 25% to 100% more than a comparable rental in a non-CCRC independent living community. The amount of rent may depend on how steep the entry and maintenance fees are; sometimes high fees mean lower rent. The rent may also depend on the level of care and services you receive. That is, while you have guaranteed access to assisted living or nursing care if you need it, there may be higher rent for those services than for independent living.

You should also look into the possibility of rent increases. Some facilities agree in the rental contract to a percentage limit on rent increases. Others have no such limit, however. If there is no contractual limit on rent increases, it is important to investigate the facility's recent record on that score. (See Section A2.)

Purchases. Some CCRCs offer equity purchases rather than rentals. This usually means that you are buying an interest in a specific condominium. But in other CCRCs, you buy an interest in the whole community—a membership, so to speak—which does not give you ownership or the right to sell any particular living unit.

How resale works—what you have to sell and under what terms—is a crucial aspect of a CCRC agreement. If you buy into a CCRC, you must fully understand the limits placed on your ability to resell your interest if you choose to move out someday, as well as the equity that may remain for your survivors if you die while still living in the community. (See Section A2.)

Entrance and maintenance fees. There is usually a large entrance fee that is only partially refundable, and only for a short time, should you decide to move out of the CCRC. Fees range from $50,000 to $300,000 and up. The entrance fee may vary with the overall quality of care and demand for space in the particular CCRC, the size of the independent living unit and the type of nursing care contract.

There may also be monthly maintenance fees. Those fees may increase if you move from one level to another. And the amounts will go up over time. In the best residence contracts, the percentage that maintenance fees may be raised per year is strictly limited. If it is not limited at all, fee increases over the years could eat up your savings and, if you can't afford them, force you to move out.

Nursing care fees. Although all CCRCs guarantee nursing care should it become necessary, the terms of that care vary greatly from one community to another. We've already covered the issue of where care is provided—on-site or in a separate facility. (See Section C2.) But there is also the question of extra charges for nursing care, depending on where and for how long you receive it. Different types of residence contracts cover these variables in nursing care fees. Some communities offer only one type of contract; others offer a choice, at different prices.

- An extensive or all-inclusive CCRC contract provides unlimited nursing facility care of all levels, either on-site or in a separate facility, without any extra charge. (See Chapter 4.) Because there is no limit to how much expensive nursing care you might receive under such terms, the entrance and monthly fees for these contracts are the highest. A Life Care contract includes unlimited nursing care. (See Section 2d.)

- A modified CCRC contract guarantees a certain number of days (usually 30–90) per year of free nursing care. The number of days may vary depending on whether the care is delivered on-site or requires moving to a separate nursing facility. After you have used your free days, you are charged additional fees, ranging from $25 to $200 per day, depending on the level of care provided. These contracts are less expensive than all-inclusive arrangements.

- A fee-for-service CCRC contract guarantees you nursing care as needed, provided in your living unit, in the community's own nursing wing or in a specific separate facility, but charges you a daily fee for the care. The amount of the fee often varies, depending on the level of nursing care you receive and where you receive it. Because these charges partially offset the community's cost of providing nursing care, the entrance and monthly fees for such a contract are the lowest.

c. Decisions about levels of care

It is one thing to know that many levels of services and care are available to you in a CCRC. It is another thing to know who decides which level of care you need. No CCRC permits a resident to have the sole authority to decide what level of care is appropriate. On the other hand, you should not enter any CCRC that reserves for itself the exclusive right to decide when to move you in or out of independent living, assisted living or nursing care.

A CCRC should have specific written standards in its residence contract that spell out what physical or mental conditions require or permit residence in one community level or another. Whether you need nursing care should be determined by your primary care physician. The CCRC, however, may reserve the right to decide whether you are to receive that nursing care in your residence, in a nursing care wing of the community or in a separate, off-site nursing facility. That decision should be made only after the community's management obtains an assessment of your condition and needs from a physician, nursing supervisor or geriatric social worker, in consultation with your primary care physician.

d. Life Care contracts

One form of arrangement with a CCRC provides care for the life of the resident. A Life Care contract makes a very large promise: If you enter a residence in your 70s, as many people do, the facility might have to provide you with 20 or 30 years of care. In exchange, the entrance fee is extremely high—$100,00 to $500,000 or more. And that may not include the cost of your individual residence and other fees. In other words, that may be merely the cost of your lifetime membership in the community.

Because your investment is so large, you must judge a Life Care contract and the community that offers it with extraordinary care. What you buy with a Life Care contract is no different from what you get in any other CCRC; it is just guaranteed to last longer. And the length of the contract is the source of its two major potential problems. The first is uncertainty concerning the quality of care the community will provide in the future. The other is the amount of monthly maintenance charges the facility will levy years down the road.

A resident is not handcuffed to the community. If the quality of care and services becomes poor, or the maintenance fees too high, you are free to leave. But you will have lost the lifetime benefit your huge entrance fee was intended to cover. And losing that money may make a move somewhere else unaffordable. Also, if you have purchased an equity interest in specific living quarters, the contract terms may prevent you from recouping much of your equity when you sell.

Diminished quality. There are many scenarios in which a dazzlingly luxurious and well-staffed Life Care community might become unable to provide high-quality services after 10, 20 or more years. The operators of the community may not have calculated fees and costs properly, or may be poor administrators who squander the funds needed to maintain high-quality premises, services and care over the long haul. Or the buildings and equipment may not be constructed to last, and may require unaffordable refurbishing. And there is the problem of profit-taking: Owners may take too much money out of the business for themselves, leaving too little to maintain high-quality operations. Similarly, the business may be sold to new operators who have a stronger commitment to their profits than to the quality of care.

Increased fees. To make up for poor planning and management (or simply to increase profits), the owners might begin to raise monthly maintenance and nursing care surcharges at a steeper rate as both you and the facility age. Unless your contract limits how much the fees and surcharges may be raised, they may get to levels that are difficult for you to pay, or that eat up the money you had intended to pass on to your survivors or use for other purposes.

UNDERSTAND A LIFE CARE CONTRACT

Because of the enormity of your investment and the many ways in which that investment may be at risk for the long term, you should thoroughly understand the terms of any Life Care contract and the financial condition of the facility and its owners. Before you enter into a Life Care contract, have a financial advisor, lawyer or accountant review all documents, investigate the financial status and reputation of the facility and its ownership and carefully explain to you the implications of that information.

Among the things an advisor should discuss with you are:

- **Terms of resale.** Do you own an equity interest in a specific piece of property or only a membership in the community? What are the terms under which your ownership interest may be sold, if at all, or left to your survivors?

- **Refund of entrance fee.** What amount of your entrance fee may be refunded to you if you decide to move out of the community?

- **Fee increases.** What are the limits on increases of monthly maintenance fees for each level of care, and on surcharges for nursing care?

- **Level of care.** Who decides the level of care and services you need, and how is that decision made?

- **Status of nursing facility.** Does the community maintain its own nursing facility on-site, and if so, is it certified by the state? If the community contracts with a separate offsite nursing facility, what are the terms of their agreement?

- **Financial stability.** Do the financial records of the facility indicate that it is on sound footing? What is the financial record and reputation of the parent company that owns the community? Are there any bankruptcies in the company's history? Is there a substantial reserve fund to cover unexpected decreases in revenues or increases in operating costs?

Long-Term Care Facilities

Despite significant recent increases in home care and alternative seniors residences, nearly one out of every two women and one of four men over age 65 will enter a long-term care facility at some time in their lives. Many nursing facility stays are short ones to allow a senior to recuperate from an illness, injury or surgery. But many other stays are extended: More than a third of all nursing facility stays last more than a year and many last three years or more.

PLANNING AND FINANCES

If at all possible, searching for a long-term care facility should not be a hurried, emergency procedure. As soon as you begin to see that your current living arrangements may become insufficient and neither home care nor assisted living will provide the care or monitoring you need, begin planning.

Finding out what long-term care facility might be the best in a particular area can take time. Many good ones operate at full capacity, so they may not be able to accept a new resident on short notice.

You must also consider how you will pay the facility. You'll have to calculate family assets and income along with reverse mortgages (see Chapter 2) and the amounts that might be contributed by Medicare and veterans' benefits (see Chapter 6) and any long-term care insurance (see Chapter 11). Medicaid coverage may be available for people with low incomes and few assets other than a home. (See Chapter 7.) It helps to understand Medicaid rules, both perhaps to save some assets by advance planning and to make sure that Medicaid will cover care in a particular facility if and when the resident qualifies.

There is a great range in the levels of care available in long-term care facilities. Skilled nursing facilities provide short-term, intensive medical care and monitoring for people recovering from acute illness or injury. Other facilities—called nursing homes, board and care homes, sheltered care homes or something similar—provide custodial care: long-term room and board, 24-hour assistance with personal care and health care monitoring, but not intensive medical treatment or daily nursing.

Many people would prefer to remain outside a care facility. However, some seniors, because of their condition, circumstances or the unavailability of in-home services or affordable assisted living residences, can only receive adequate care in a residential care facility. Unfortunately, as we've all heard on the news, some facilities provide substandard living conditions and even a dangerous lack of care. Still others give basic care that meets technical health standards but offer little else, and have an atmosphere that is debilitating or demoralizing to the residents.

However, there are also excellent long-term care facilities that provide high-quality care while assisting residents to maintain active lives with a full measure of dignity. But because there are many levels and types of nursing and personal care, your task is to find a good, affordable facility that is right for you.

HOW TO FIND OUT ABOUT LOCAL LONG-TERM CARE FACILITIES

The federal government and the states have teamed up to create an online service that lists and compares the qualities of every certified nursing facility in the country. This service is called "Nursing Home Compare" and can be found at Medicare's official website, www.medicare.gov.

This service provides contact information about every nursing facility in any geographic area you choose. And for any particular facility, the service lists information from the facility's official record regarding staffing, resident care and inspections.

However, while this website is a good starting point and reference, you should not depend primarily on its information when choosing a facility. The site statistics—which are often well over a year old—may provide you with an important warning about a facility with a bad record. But "good" statistics cannot tell you much about the quality of life for residents in a facility. Only several in-person visits, looking at and talking about the various factors discussed in this chapter, can give you a good sense of the facility.

You should also speak with people who have personal experience of nursing facilities in your area. Your doctor may have a good or bad impression of certain local facilities. And your relatives, friends and neighbors may have had experience with a nursing facility or know someone who has.

A. Levels of Care

Care in long-term residential facilities ranges from intensive 24-hour care for the seriously ill, which is called skilled nursing care, to long-term personal assistance and health monitoring with very little active nursing, often called custodial care. Some facilities provide only one level of care, while others provide several levels at the same location.

Most people who are in long-term care facilities cannot function without 24-hour monitoring and extensive personal assistance and nursing care because of illness or physical or mental limitations. Some residents are in relatively good physical and mental health, but too frail to live alone at home. If they had more family or resources, many of these people might be able to make do with extensive home care (see Chapter 2) or residence in an assisted living facility (see Chapter 3). For lack of an alternative, they become long-term care facility residents.

Your task is to find a good and affordable long-term care facility that provides not just care, but the right type of care. For someone with severe physical or mental limitations, it is crucial to find a facility that provides the kind of attention and care that meets the individual's specific needs. For people who need little or no actual nursing care, the task is to find a facility that provides physical, mental and social stimulation rather than just bed and board.

Your toughest challenge may be footing the bill. Long-term care facilities of all levels are very expensive, but depending on the type of care needed and the type of insurance you have, you may get some help covering the cost. Skilled nursing facilities run between $300 and $500 per day, although stays there are relatively short and Medicare or private health insurance often picks up much of the tab. (See Chapter 6.) Long-term custodial care—the kind that may last for years—costs between $3,000 and $10,000 per month. Neither Medicare nor medi-gap private insurance supplements pay any of the cost of custodial care. Long-term care insurance, for those who have it, may cover some of the cost of custodial care. (See Chapter 11.) And Medicaid pays the full cost of custodial nursing facility care for people with very low incomes and few assets. (See Chapters 7 and 8.) Some veterans may also find coverage for custodial care through the Veterans Administration. (See Chapter 6.)

If a facility is certified by the federal government, it may also be more affordable. The Health Care Financing Administration has certified about 85% of all nursing facilities; HCFA certification means that the facility is eligible to receive Medicare and Medicaid payments. Some facilities do not meet HCFA standards. Other facilities charge high prices and simply do not want to accept residents who depend on Medicaid payments. Unless you have an unlimited supply of money to pay for long-term care, make sure that any facility you consider is certified. Certification means that the facility meets certain minimum health, safety and care standards. And certification also means that if someday you should need and qualify for Medicaid coverage for your stay, you will be able to receive it without having to move to a different facility.

1. Hospital-Based Skilled Nursing Facilities

Hospital-based skilled nursing facilities, also known as extended care facilities, are departments within hospitals. They provide the highest levels of medical and nursing care, including 24-hour monitoring and intensive rehabilitative therapies. They are intended to follow acute hospital care due to serious illness, injury or surgery.

Unlike other nursing facilities, hospital-based facilities are not for permanent residence, but for a short-term stay until a patient can be sent home or maintained elsewhere. Hospital-based facilities are very expensive ($300 to $500 per day), but the average stay is generally short (usually a matter of days or weeks) and, for those who qualify, is usually covered by Medicare or private insurance. (See Chapters 6 and 11.)

2. Skilled Nursing Facilities

Nonhospital-based skilled nursing facilities (SNFs) provide a relatively high level of nursing and other medical care, as well as personal care and assistance, for people whose illnesses or impairments require close monitoring.

Around-the-clock nursing is available from licensed vocational or practical nurses, with at least one supervising registered nurse on duty at all times. In addition to nursing, most other prescribed medical services can be provided, including various rehabilitative therapies. A SNF is almost always for short-term recovery from a serious illness, injury or surgery that required hospitalization. A few people may spend months in a SNF, but most stays last only days or weeks.

The cost of SNF care ranges from $200 to $500 per day. Medicare, Medicaid and private insurance usually pay for SNF care, but only up to specific coverage limits.

3. Intermediate Care Facilities

Intermediate care facilities (ICFs) provide less nursing and other medical care than SNFs. ICFs are for long-term residents with chronic illnesses or impairments whose conditions are not as acute as those of SNF residents. Residents in an ICF are usually ambulatory, for example.

Staff is geared as much toward personal care and assistance as to medical care, although there is always a licensed vocational or practical nurse on duty. ICFs generally care for people who need a long recovery period from serious illness, injury or surgery, but who no longer need the level of nursing care and high-tech monitoring that a SNF provides.

Costs range from $150 to $400 per day. Medicare does not cover ICFs and private insurance coverage is rare, usually requiring prior approval. Medicaid, however, may cover much of the cost of ICF care. (See Chapter 7.)

Very few facilities are set up solely as ICFs; most are part of an SNF or a custodial care facility. (See Section 4.)

MEDICAID CERTIFICATION

One of the first things you should check about any facility is whether it is certified by Medicaid (called Medi-Cal in California). If it is certified, Medicaid will pay for the resident's care in the facility if the resident qualifies for Medicaid benefits. If you plan to pay for the facility out of your own pocket and are not currently eligible for Medicaid (see Chapter 7), this may not seem important. But if you stay in the facility for an extended period, you may spend enough of your assets to qualify for Medicaid coverage. If this happens, you will want Medicaid to pay for your care in the facility where you have been living—and this can happen only if the facility is Medicaid-certified.

---

4. Custodial Care Facilities

Custodial care facilities come in a variety of shapes and sizes—and offer a variety of services. They also go by a number of different names: nursing facility, board and care home, rest home, congregate living facility, sheltered care facility, group home and RCFE (residential care facility for the elderly), among others. Some are small facilities, with five to ten beds in a converted private home. Others are 100-bed facilities with large common areas and extensive social, physical and educational activities—and that unmistakable institutional feel. Costs range from $30,000 to $150,000 per year.

Despite these differences, all facilities that provide custodial care share these basic elements:

- They provide room, board, assistance with the activities of daily life (ADLs), health monitoring and social, recreational and exercise activities.
- They do not provide nursing, physical therapy or other skilled medical care.
- They are intended for people who need help throughout the day and night with personal care and mobility but do not need constant medical attention or intervention.
- Residents are there for the long term—for months or years—and not merely while recovering from an acute physical condition.
- Because residents live in rooms—often shared—rather than a private apartment, and because no expensive medical care is provided, they cost much less than skilled or intermediate care nursing facilities.
- Because residents receive all meals and round-the-clock monitoring and assistance, they are more expensive than assisted living facilities.

The remainder of this chapter will help you choose a facility that meets your needs—and your budget.

WHAT'S IN A NAME?

In most cases, the name a facility goes by won't tell you much about the quality of life it provides residents. Instead, you have to judge a facility by whether if will offer the services you need at a price you can afford. However, the title a long-term care facility uses—for example, nursing facility, board and care home or residential care facility for the elderly (RCFE)—may tell you something about the state rules and regulations that the facility has to abide by.

   Different types of facilities are subject to different sets of rules, and are certified and inspected by different state agencies. In some states, a nursing facility may have to follow stricter rules (about number and training of staff members, for example) than a board and care home does, even though the facilities are very similar in most respects. In some states, non-nursing facilities have very few rules to follow—and are subject to almost no inspection or other oversight by state agencies. If you are seriously considering a particular facility, ask what state agency oversees it. Then contact that agency to find out whether it has information for consumers on the rules and regulations the facility has to follow. And be sure to review the facility's recent inspection reports. (See Section B3.)

B. Choosing the Right Facility

Once you have determined which facilities in your area are affordable and provide the appropriate general level of care, you must decide which one best suits your needs and preferences.

The experts to turn to for guidance are the residents themselves. Most nursing facility residents, studies have shown, care very little about high-tech medical gear, or even about medical care. Rather, their most important concerns involve their ability to maintain some independence, to participate in decisions about daily life and to retain contact with the outside world.

Because these and other concerns discussed below cannot be guaranteed in writing or demonstrated in a quick tour, it is important to spend as much time as possible at a facility before making a decision to receive care there. Make separate visits during the day, evening and night, and during one or more meals. And to the extent possible, talk with current residents and their families.

SPECIAL CONSIDERATIONS FOR THOSE SUFFERING FROM ALZHEIMER'S DISEASE

All of the factors discussed in this section apply to people with Alzheimer's Disease or other forms of age-related dementia. However, choosing the right long-term care facility for these elders will require you to consider other issues as well. These matters are treated separately in Chapter 5. Before you move on to that chapter, read through the information in this section. Then use it—along with the material in Chapter 5—to choose a facility that will fit the bill.

---

1. Ownership and Management

The quality of daily life in a long-term care facility is determined primarily by on-site management and hands-on care personnel. And the owners of a facility determine how well management can do its job through the funding provided for equipment, food and staffing.

However, the form of ownership (for example, whether a facility is a nonprofit or is run by a particular religious group) may not tell you much about the quality of care any particular facility provides.

a. For-Profit Facilities

About three-fourths of all long-term care facilities are operated for profit, often by big corporations. There is a popular but not necessarily accurate belief that in profit-making facilities, the dominating desire to make money means skimping on patient care. Research has shown that this is not always the case. Profit-making facilities may be better managed than nonprofits, and therefore deliver better care for the dollar. Similarly, studies have found that patient satisfaction is important to for-profit facilities because their economic health depends on keeping their beds filled. As a result, a for-profit facility may be just as likely as a nonprofit facility to provide good quality care for the price.

b. Nonprofit Facilities

The flip side of negative beliefs about profit-making facilities is the notion that those run by nonprofit philanthropic, charitable or religious organizations will provide quality care because their only interest is to "do good" for residents. But nonprofit organizations often give no more than their name and tax advantages to a long-term care facility, while everyday management is contracted out to others. Even when the nonprofit organization takes an active role in running the facility (usually several facilities), there is no guarantee it will be any better at the job than profit-making managers. The test of care quality comes on the floor of the facility itself, not in the boardrooms of its owners.

c. Group Affiliation

Some long-term care facilities are operated by or affiliated with religious, ethnic or fraternal organizations. Depending on your interest and on how the affiliation affects daily life in the facility, this can be either good or bad. A particular affiliation may mean that you and the other residents will have similar backgrounds and interests, which can make for a real feeling of community. Also, there may be specially targeted activities at the facility in which you will enjoy participating.

On the other hand, if a group or organization to which you do not belong dominates the social activity of a facility, it may make you feel like an outsider and may limit the availability of other, nonsectarian activities.

2. Cost

Although it may generally be true that higher costs lead to better quality, that is not necessarily the case with nursing facilities.

With nursing facilities, high price often means sophisticated and expensive medical equipment and staff. And although most residents will never need them, every resident ends up paying for them. Similarly, some facilities are expensive because they have to foot the bill for a shiny new building.

Many smaller, less expensive facilities with less high-tech equipment can provide a more comfortable setting with more individual attention and participation for residents. Of course, you must make certain that lower cost does not reflect a lack of essential services or of qualified personnel. But these are things you will have to investigate—the cost of the care alone won't tell you much about the quality of the facility.

> ### MORE IS NOT LESS
>
> While one might guess that larger facilities cost less because they operate on an economy of scale, in general it is just the opposite. On the average, larger facilities cost more to operate than smaller ones, due in part to their higher-level medical services and larger administrative staffs.

3. The Facility

a. Location

For a number of reasons, the location of a facility can be extremely significant. Continuing contact with people and life outside the facility is one of the residents' greatest concerns, and location can affect that contact in a number of ways.

Visiting. Can friends and relatives get there easily? Is it near public transportation? The ease with which people can visit has a direct bearing on how often they do.

Outings. Are there places nearby—a park, library or senior center—where elders can be taken for outings, either by visitors or by staff?

Immediate surroundings. Is the surrounding area noisy, peaceful, ugly, safe? What can be seen and heard through the windows during the day and night? Are short walks or a bit of lounging outside possible?

b. Number of Beds and Residents

As with most questions about long-term care facilities, there is no simple guideline about whether a large or small one is best. It is mostly a matter of your own needs and tastes, and of the quality of care delivered. When assessing large facilities (those with over 100 beds), consider whether their size means they're too institutional or too cold. Do they still provide personal attention and permit residents to participate in their own care?

A small facility, on the other hand, may not have all the services and skilled personnel (such as dieticians, rehabilitative therapists, and social workers) that a larger one has. But smaller facilities tend to be more personal and homey and allow residents greater control over their own daily lives.

c. The Facility's "Feel"

What is your first impression when you walk through the door? It is probably the same general impression, conscious or unconscious, that a resident has all the time.

Homeyness. A facility should be as unlike a hospital as is consistent with good health care. It should be colorful, with personal, individual touches on walls and tables. Some facilities encourage residents to decorate their rooms and common areas; others have regulations against it. There should also be plenty of light, both from windows and lighting.

Healthfulness. The facility should be clean and free from strong odors. Infections and viruses pass easily in group living situations, and they can be very serious for elders. The space should not feel cramped; crowding is both physically and psychologically unhealthy. And the air should not be too hot, too cold or too stuffy.

Odors may mean that food, linen, residents' clothing or personal hygiene are not receiving proper attention.

CHECK THE INSPECTION REPORT

Every licensed nursing facility and most other licensed long-term care facilities are inspected regularly by state health care officials, usually about once a year. The inspectors check for violations of state and federal health, safety and care standards. The state agency then describes those violations, along with residents' complaints, in a written report called a State Inspection Report or Compliance Survey. All facilities are supposed to make these reports readily available to the public. Most good facilities will post the most recent report on a bulletin board and have other copies available.

Read a facility's latest report carefully. Even the best among them will have some minor violations or complaints from residents. But a report that mentions many serious health violations, or repeated neglect of residents, should raise a red flag. The administrators at a facility should be willing to discuss the report with you and to explain what they are doing to address violations and complaints.

While a bad report means the facility has some explaining to do, a good report does not necessarily mean everything is hunky dory. Most facilities know roughly when an inspection is due— and some load up with extra staff to bring the facility up to par for the inspection, then sink back to fewer staff and poorer conditions as soon as the inspectors leave. When evaluating a facility, depend first and foremost on your own inspection.

d. Public Areas

Prospective residents often pay much less attention to common rooms than to residents' private rooms. But the comfort and attraction of the public areas affect the amount of time a resident spends out of his or her room or out of bed—and so may have a bearing on how active the resident remains. Consider each of the following areas:

A quiet room. Although one advantage of a long-term care facility is that residents do not spend too much time alone, this can also be a problem. Most residents share rooms, and privacy can sometimes be difficult to find. It's important that some room or area is available where residents can enjoy some solitude or at least quiet—where there is no radio, television or group activities and where it is understood that people are to be left to themselves.

Eating areas. Food and rules about eating are discussed more fully below, but you should spend time where the food is served and eaten—dining room, private rooms or other areas of the facility—while residents are actually eating. If possible, you should also eat a few meals there with the residents.

Social, TV and activity rooms. While television can be good company for facility residents, it can also become a real annoyance. If televisions are always on in all common areas, that can interfere with other activities such as having a simple conversation. It may also signal that the staff is using television as a distraction rather than interacting with the residents. Whether or not there is a "quiet" room, it should be possible to socialize somewhere without a TV blaring.

The social and activity rooms should be clean and comfortable and should have some personal touches. A simple way to tell whether the residents find these common rooms inviting is to see how many people are using them.

Outside areas. Is there a garden, courtyard or other outside area where residents can spend time? Both the fresh air and change of scene can be very inviting to residents.

Visiting areas. Is there a place other than the resident's room for private visits? Must visiting take place in a room used for other purposes as well? Does the facility encourage visiting or make it seem like a bother?

e. Residents' Private Rooms

Many people who enter a long-term care facility have not shared a room with anyone else for a long time, yet most long-term care facilities provide only double or triple rooms. Adjusting to the loss of privacy and need for compromise that go with sharing a bedroom can be difficult. The set-up and rules of the facility can make this transition easier or harder. Here are some things to look for:

Size. Are there single rooms, double or triple? Are there adjoining bathrooms? Are the bathrooms set up to ensure privacy?

Light. Is there a window that lets in natural light? Are there individual reading lights near each bed? Can the lights be used without disturbing a roommate's sleep?

Structure. Does the set-up of the room, furniture and perhaps a curtain between beds allow some privacy for each roommate? Is there someplace to sit other than on the bed? Are there places for visitors to sit and visit privately? Can furnishings be moved around?

Security. Theft is a common problem in nursing facilities. Is there a place where personal possessions can be kept safely and easily retrieved? Is there a call button within reach of each bed that connects to the central aide station and can only be turned off at the bed?

Comfort. Is private furniture allowed in the room? Can residents in the room control its temperature? Are telephones, radios or televisions permitted in the rooms? If so, what rules protect roommates from too much noise?

GETTING HELP FROM AN OMBUDSMAN

Every licensed nursing facility has one or two people called ombudsmen, who act as advocates for residents and their families when conflicts arise about facility rules or with facility staff. These ombudsmen are usually volunteers or employees of the state or county, not hired or paid by the facility. As independent observers, ombudsmen should be able to provide you with good, unbiased opinions about the quality of a particular nursing facility you are considering. And because an ombudsman usually works at more than one facility, he or she will probably be able to compare one facility with others in the area.

The operators of the nursing facility can give you the name and phone number of the local ombudsman for that facility, or let you know when he or she is slated to visit. The local ombudsman can then give you a picture in private of the facility and its staff, compare it with other area facilities and discuss whether the facility is particularly good or bad with residents who have similar physical or mental capabilities.

There is also a state ombudsman who oversees the local programs and tracks formal complaints and health and safety violations against nursing facilities. If you call the state office, you may be able to get an overall assessment of several facilities you are considering. (See the Appendix for contact information.)

4. Services and Activities

Long-term care facilities do not all offer the same services and activities beyond basic personal and medical care. Some facilities focus on exercise and therapy for physical impairments, others on social or educational programs, still others on developing residents' independence and memory. It is important to match services and activities with your needs. For example, if a resident does not have the physical or mental capacity to be very active, recreational and social programs may be much less important than how much attention personal staff pays to cleanliness, comfort and conversation. For more active residents, though, activities that encourage independent thought and movement may be crucial to maintaining the highest possible levels of health.

You cannot match services and activities with needs entirely in advance, because you may have trouble anticipating what needs will be most important. Also, needs change over time. Try to choose a facility that encourages resident input into services and activities, and is attentive to a resident's individual needs. Discuss the flexibility of services and activities with the staff and listen for indications that residents' dignity, independence and individual differences are valued.

a. Rehabilitation Therapy

Is the particular physical, respiratory, speech or other therapy you need regularly available in the facility, or must you make special arrangements? Will you have to go outside the facility to receive the therapy? Will it cost extra?

WHAT YOU CAN LEARN FROM CONSULTING CARE PLANS

By law, a licensed nursing facility must develop a written care plan for each resident. This plan includes an assessment of the resident's physical and cognitive abilities, needs, personality and social skills. Based on that assessment, the facility develops a plan for care, which should include nursing, therapy and physical and memory exercise requirements; prescribed medications (and medicine combinations to be avoided); social activities the resident favors and is able to join; and nutrition needs, including dietary restrictions and required eating assistance.

When considering a facility, ask to see some of the resident care plans that have recently been developed. Privacy need not be an issue; names can easily be blackened out in a copy. The plans should be tailored to meet each resident's individual limitations and needs; they should not all look the same. Also, ask about the facility's procedures for regularly updating the plans. And ask to see samples of plans that have been changed to meet a resident's changing condition and needs.

b. Social Activities and Other Services

The greatest concern of many long-term care facility residents is to maintain contact with the outside world—by seeing family and other visitors, physically leaving the facility and receiving news, phone calls and mail.

Outings. Does the facility regularly organize outings to places and activities such as the library, park, local senior center or shopping areas? Is transportation provided? Are escorts available for a simple walk?

Incoming activity. Are visiting speakers and activities scheduled regularly? Is there a program of outside volunteers who participate with residents in some program or activity?

Organized events. Look at the facility's weekly or monthly calendar of events. Is there stimulation for mind and body—education, information and exercise—as well as entertainment? Do organized activities take place in the evening as well as the day? Do people from outside the facility participate?

Personal care. Are there services for personal grooming and cleanliness, such as a visiting barber or hairdresser and a way to have clothes washed and cleaned? Does a dentist or dental hygienist visit the facility?

Social service assistance. Is there a counselor or social worker who can assist with family problems, paperwork, financial organization and referrals for outside services?

c. Facility-Wide Rules

Every facility has rules by which all residents and visitors must abide. Ask to see the written rules and try to find out about important rules of daily life which are not listed. Do they seem reasonable? Do the administrators seem willing to be flexible with those rules to meet individual needs?

Visiting. When and where is visiting allowed? Are there any particular rules about children? What about phone calls in and out? Can visitors eat facility meals with residents?

Meals. Are mealtimes flexible? If you miss a meal, is there other food available to eat? Must meals be eaten in the dining area? Can you bring in food from outside the facility?

Hours. Is there a set time when all residents are awakened? Is there a rule about having to get dressed? About going to bed? Watching television? Lights out? Is there a curfew for residents who have gone on an outing?

Bathing. If a resident needs assistance bathing, does he or she retain a reasonable choice about when and how often?

Privacy. Can a resident keep the private room door closed at will, or only during night hours? Must staff knock before entering? Is there privacy in the bathroom?

Privately hired aides. Some facilities allow residents to supplement the personal care staff with privately hired aides. This flexibility may be a good thing, but be wary if the practice is common. It may mean the staff relies on the outside aides and gives less care and personal attention to residents.

d. Medication Control

Overmedication is a serious problem for many older people. Some elders have trouble keeping track of when and how often they are supposed to take their various medications, or of dosage amounts. And sometimes a doctor may prescribe medicine without carefully considering how it might interact with other drugs the patient is taking. Long-term care facilities can add to these problem by encouraging residents too strongly to take "as needed" medications—such as sedatives, relaxants and sleeping medications—instead of dealing with the resident's specific problem or need.

For all these reasons, it is important to find out how carefully a facility monitors residents' medication. The facility should:

- keep a written record for the personal physician and family to review
- have a policy of periodic review of all medications a resident is taking
- have a policy that any new medication shall be cleared in writing with a responsible family member, and
- have a clearly stated rule about the residents' right to refuse unwanted medication, including "as needed" medication.

SPECIAL WARNING ON DRUG USE AND RESTRAINTS

A few nursing facilities prescribe and administer psychotropic drugs, also known as "chemical straightjackets." These drugs make residents easy for the facility to care for because, in essence, they turn active residents into zombies. Not only do these drugs rob residents of their humanity while they're directly under the influence, but they can do lasting physical and emotional damage as well.

Any good nursing facility should be willing to show you its written policy on psychotropic drugs. The policy should specify that no such drugs can be administered to a resident without the written consent of either the resident or certain designated family members, that any such written consent will be valid only for a limited period of time and that the designated family members and the resident's physician will be notified of the administration of any such drugs.

There are legal limits on the use of physical restraints to hold a resident in a bed or chair. Both health care experts and nursing facility advocates seriously frown on the practice. Although in some limited circumstances restraints may be necessary (for people who are in danger of falling if left unattended, for example), some facilities use restraints like psychoactive drugs merely to "manage" residents who require more attention than the facility wants to give. Make sure to find out what the facility's policy is on the use of restraints. It should permit restraints only when the resident presents an immediate danger of physical injury to himself or herself or to others, and should require a designated family member to be notified when restraints will be used.

e. Medical Records

Although technically required to keep records only of certain medical and nursing procedures provided, a thorough facility will also keep a written record of a resident's medical condition and outside treatment by doctors, clinics and hospitals. It can also be very helpful to a resident and to his or her physician if the facility keeps a written record of health problems that have not warranted medical treatment but have affected the resident's comfort and well-being—such as problems with elimination, digestion, sleeping, depression, too much time in bed, bedsores, eating problems or weight changes.

5. Other Residents

When considering a long-term care facility, try to make several visits there and speak to some of the residents as you consider the matters discussed below.

a. Similar Levels of Care

Small facilities should admit only residents with relatively similar care needs; large facilities should provide only one level of care in each separate area or wing. There are several reasons for this. First, when care is kept to one level, personnel can be specialized—they may be better at what they do if they have fewer things to do. Costs may also be lower because residents aren't paying for services they don't need.

There are also less tangible reasons for wanting to be with people whose needs are similar to your own. Residents can share their concerns and their ways of coping with common problems. Also, they need not be confronted daily with problems much different or more severe than their own. This is particularly important where mental orientation or capacity is concerned. Good facilities may separate the rooms of severe Alzheimer's or other dementia sufferers from the rooms of other residents. And when all the residents are together, the staff should pay special attention to residents who are disoriented.

b. Room Assignment

Some small long-term care facilities offer residents private rooms. Larger facilities that offer private rooms usually charge considerably more for them. However, most facilities have two beds per room; some large nursing facilities have three beds in each room.

In facilities where people share a room, resident surveys show that roommate selection is very important to the residents' happiness and well-being, ranking only behind contact with family and friends. Some people prefer to have a roommate in similar physical condition so that they can better understand each other's needs and concerns. Other people do not mind having a roommate with greater needs; it allows them to be of help. Still others would prefer a roommate in better physical condition so that they can receive extra help. Whatever your preference, find out whether the facility will take it into account in assigning a roommate.

There is also the matter of finding someone with common interests, religious or ethnic background, language and habits—smoking or late nights, for example. Will the facility consider these things when assigning a roommate? If so, make sure to let them know the things that are most important to you.

c. Residents' Condition and Activity

You can tell a lot about a long-term care facility simply by walking around and looking carefully at the residents. Are most extremely ill or disabled? Do people appear comfortable? Are they reasonably neat and clean? Do you see smiles, hear friendly conversation among residents and between residents and staff? Are residents moving about the facility and being active in some way, or are they mostly in their rooms? Are people sitting alone and unattended in chairs or in wheelchairs in the hallway?

By checking the common areas, you can tell whether the residents are doing things together or only on their own. It may take several visits, at different times of the day, to get a feel for this. Are there any ongoing communal activities, such as a newsletter, a garden, regular outings or some volunteer project? Be sure to ask.

6. Staff

Getting a sense of the staff also requires spending some time at the facility during a normal day's activities.

a. Personal Care Aides

In virtually every nursing facility, 90% of direct resident care is provided by personal care aides—also called assistants, attendants or orderlies. These are the foot soldiers of long-term facility care, and their competence and attitude are most important to the health and well-being of residents. There are several things to find out about them.

Numbers. Although there are no hard and fast rules about how many attendants there should be for each resident, there must be enough so that the residents receive attention most of the time when they want it, and any time they need it. Generally, a good facility will have one aide on duty in a given wing or section of a facility for every five or six residents there. At night, the figure may drop to one aide for every 15 or so residents. On the other hand, during meals, when resident needs are high, aides should be supplemented by volunteers or other assistants so that there is one person to help every three or four people. In addition to these numbers, use your eyes to judge whether there are enough aides: Are there residents who seem to want or need attention from an aide but are not getting it?

Turnover. How long have people worked at the facility? Long-term employment generally means that both aides and residents are satisfied with the aides' work. A rapid turnover of aides may be a bad sign, although even the best facilities sometimes have a hard time keeping staff (particularly in the aide jobs, which are usually high in stress and low in pay).

Language. If English is not the first language of the resident, how many people on the staff speak the resident's first language? The reverse may also be important. What percentage of the staff speaks understandable English?

Intangibles. The courtesy, friendliness and efficiency of the personal care aides to both residents and visitors are very important considerations. But the only way to judge this is to see the aides and residents in their daily interchanges. Is there easy conversation? Do the aides seem to pay attention to what the residents want? Do the aides have a neat and professional appearance?

Remember, as with any group of people, not every aide and every resident are going to get along. The crucial thing is not that every interaction is smiling and efficient, but that most contacts are cordial and responsive to a resident's needs.

b. Available Professional Staff

It doesn't really matter how many people with impressive certificates and licenses are listed on a facility's letterhead. What counts is how much time any of them actually spends with residents. How often does the facility's physician check on medical care standards? How often do licensed nurses make rounds? How easy is it to schedule a rehabilitation therapist? How much hands-on care do professional personnel provide, and how much do they just supervise? To what extent can a resident request direct care from one of the professional staff?

Except in emergencies, direct physician care will come from your own physicians, not from the facility's doctors. Find out whether the facility restricts visits from outside physicians and whether it provides transportation to outside medical appointments. Also, many physicians will not make visits to a nursing facility. Ask whether your primary care physician will make such visits, and if so, whether he or she will come to the particular facility you have in mind.

c. Outside Help

Find out whether the facility permits or arranges for extra outside help.

Volunteers. Many facilities make good use of volunteers from public service agencies and programs. Some simply provide extra personal attention or companionship, while others bring special educational skills or social programs. These volunteers are a good link to the outside world and give residents a change of pace and face from the regular staff.

Private aid. Does the facility allow part-time private assistance of any sort from outside the facility, such as a private duty care assistant, chiropractor, massage therapist or private duty nurse?

7. Food

In a long-term care facility, the importance of meals goes beyond merely getting the right nutrients. Meals are central activities in a resident's day—a social event and a source of pleasure when many other events and pleasures may be limited. In inquiring about a facility's food service, don't restrict yourself to looking at a menu or seeing that a dietician is an official member of the staff. Instead, visit the facility's dining areas during one or more meals and eat the food with residents. There are several things to ask, look and taste for:

Tastiness. Don't overlook the simple fact that the nutritional value of food doesn't matter if you don't eat it. If food tastes lousy, people eat less of it. Freshness and variety also help keep people interested. Check menus from a week or two and see how often fresh foods are served and how often dishes are repeated.

Preferences and restrictions. No group living facility can cater to the different food whims and desires of all its residents. But residents should be offered some choice in meals, and the facility should respond to strong likes and dislikes. Dietary restrictions, whether for health, digestive or religious reasons, must be strictly followed. The facility should keep a written record of any such restriction for each resident, and the kitchen staff should consult it when planning and preparing meals.

Extra food. Not everyone's appetite runs by the standard meal clock. Some people prefer, or need, to eat a little bit several times a day. Other people who are up at "odd" hours get hungry. And many people get pleasure from special foods made by friends or relatives or a favorite neighborhood bakery. A facility that is too rigid about food is not taking care of important needs.

Does the facility serve snacks, tea or coffee between meals, or at least make such things available to residents? Do the snacks include fresh fruit and other healthful foods? May residents eat the snacks where and when they want—particularly in their own rooms—or only at designated times and places? May residents be given food from outside the facility? And if so, is there an easily accessible place where it can be kept?

Dining area. The first thing to pay attention to when you visit the dining area during a meal is whether the residents are eating the food. That will tell you a lot. Observe whether the staff is helpful with residents who need assistance eating. Are residents comfortable? Is the area clean? Ask if dining times are flexible. Do residents have enough time with their meal, or is food rushed in and out?

8. Family Involvement

One benefit of a long-term care facility is its ready-made community of companions and helpers. However, active family involvement in the resident's life also provides important benefits. Residents rate personal contact—by visits, phone, mail and outings—at the top of their list of concerns. And no matter how good a facility's own outreach programs are, a resident's ability to stay in touch with the larger community requires help from friends and relatives.

Whether family and friends are actively involved in a resident's life depends to no small degree on whether the facility encourages their participation. Families should be regularly invited to participate in activities with residents. Visiting should be encouraged rather than merely tolerated. There should be adequate space, comfort and privacy in visiting areas and wide and flexible visiting hours. Visiting should be permitted during meals, and there should be wide latitude in taking residents for outings.

Together, the staff and resident's family should regularly review the resident's condition and care. Find out what the procedures are for family consultation about problems or changes in the resident's care plan or room or roommate assignment. Ask whether there is an organized family support group or network for residents' families to keep in touch.

9. Decision-Making

Residents' long-term health and comfort depend directly on a facility's procedures for making decisions about their care. A good facility should have standardized procedures for making daily care decisions. Review them before deciding on a particular facility. If a licensed facility refuses to respond to a resident's complaints, there are state and local government agencies which can step in. (See the discussion of the Nursing Facility Ombudsman, below.)

a. Residents' Problems and Complaints

It is a sad but widely recognized truth that patients are abused and neglected in some nursing facilities. There are also many smaller problems that, if unattended, can make a resident's life miserable. Therefore a facility must have specific procedures for residents and family members to lodge a complaint or discuss a problem about a particular staff person, a method or type of care or a facility rule or condition.

The danger of not having an explicit complaint procedure is that a resident will not know with whom to speak, or will get a run-around from staff members who claim they have no authority to do anything to right the wrong. Find out how complaints are handled and make certain that the process guarantees a response from an identifiable person in authority.

Similarly, there should be a regular procedure for registering complaints or discussing problems about a roommate or other resident. Find out what these procedures are and what a resident must do to request a room change.

b. Facility-Imposed Changes

For financial and other reasons, a facility may want to move residents around when there are vacancies in double rooms. Or, because of a change in a resident's condition that requires a different level of care, the facility may believe a room change is necessary. However, the resident may not want to move. It is therefore important that a resident have a right to be notified in advance of a room change, and that the facility have rules that limit the circumstances under which such changes can be made.

As with a room change, the facility may decide that the particular nonmedical care a resident has been receiving is no longer necessary, or that new types of costlier or more restrictive care are required.

Find out how these decisions are made and what rights the resident has regarding them. Also make sure there is a provision for consultation with, and notification of, the family.

For all decisions about medical care or changes in condition, specific written rules should be set out, including:

- what decisions can be made by aides and what must be decided by the nurse on duty
- when the facility's attending physician must be consulted about a change in medical care or condition
- when the resident's personal physician must be consulted about a change in condition or a possible change in care, and
- when the resident's family must be notified of a change in care or condition.

c. Nursing Facility Ombudsman

The federal government funds a program, administered by each state's Agency on Aging, which makes available to nursing facility residents an ombudsman—a kind of troubleshooter to mediate unresolved problems between residents or their families and a nursing facility. The ombudsman has regular visiting hours and days at the facility and should also be available by phone. There is no charge for using the services of the ombudsman.

C. Entering a Formal Residence Contract

All facilities have a formal written document that both you and a facility representative sign. It does not matter whether this document is called a "contract" or an "agreement" or something similar. What does matter is that all important terms and conditions of residence and care are included, so that both you and the facility are clear about them. If you are unsure of any terms and conditions, consider having an attorney or someone else familiar with nursing facility care review it with you before signing. Even if you do not consult with anyone else, take the agreement home and review it carefully before signing.

If something important to you is not included in the facility's preprinted agreement, discuss it with the proper facility official. When you've reached an agreement, write it on a separate piece of paper, signed and dated by both of you, and attach it to the rest of the agreement.

1. What to Look for in a Written Agreement

The agreement should spell out the specific health care, personal care, equipment and supplies you will get for your regular daily, weekly or monthly fee. This should include frequency of nursing care, physical or other therapies, number of meals and special dietary needs.

Room. The agreement should specify the number of beds in the resident's room, as well as any other features that distinguish the type of room from others in the facility and are important to you—such as the room size, bathroom facilities, windows or location in the building.

Extra charges and adjustments. The agreement should specify what services, equipment and supplies are charged as extra (above the regular rate). The agreement should also specify whether you will get any discounts for such things as meals eaten outside of the facility and time spent off the premises, such as vacations or time in the hospital.

Some contracts require residents to purchase their medications at the facility's own pharmacy. Since the rates there may be considerably higher than at outside pharmacies, this is in effect a forced extra charge. Find out in advance whether this is the policy at any facility you are considering.

Rate changes. The agreement should spell out whether, and how much, the regular rate will go up or down if the level of care is changed, whether the regular rate is guaranteed to remain the same for any length of time and how much notice must be given before rates are raised.

Change in funding. As discussed in Chapter 6, Medicare and private insurance coverage for nursing facility care is very limited. And Medicaid coverage, while extensive, is not available to everyone at all times. (See Chapter 7.) Also, some facilities provide certain rooms for Medicaid residents and other, better rooms for private paying patients, so that even if Medicaid begins to cover you at some point, you may be forced to move to a different, less desirable room to receive it.

Be sure to find out not only what your coverage is when entering the facility, but also what your personal financial responsibility would be, and how the facility would respond in changing circumstances such as:

- using up your allotted Medicare skilled nursing facility coverage
- moving from skilled to intermediate or personal care, neither of which is covered by Medicare or private insurance
- becoming eligible for Medicaid
- declaring personal bankruptcy; many facilities require proof of your ability to pay for two years as a condition of admission.

Discharge policy. There are situations in which either you might want to move out of the facility or the facility might want to discharge you even though you want to stay. Find out the facility's policies and procedures, including how much written notice must be given, in these and other discharge situations:

- if the resident's need for care changes and the resident wants to leave the facility to receive different care
- if the resident's need for care changes and the facility wants the resident to move out and receive care elsewhere, or
- if the resident's source of funds changes.

CHECK THE POLICY ON TEMPORARY HOSPITALIZATION

It is not uncommon for a long-term care facility resident to need hospitalization for some period of time. Find out what the policy is on holding a resident's bed during hospitalization. If you may be going back and forth to the hospital and you can easily lose your place in the facility while hospitalized, you may want to choose a different facility.

■

Care for Elders With Alzheimer's Disease

Y ou can find extensive general information about home care, assisted living and long-term care facilities in Chapters 2, 3 and 4 of this book. But long-term care for those with Alzheimer's Disease presents special additional problems, both for the elder and for the caregivers. This chapter explains the special needs of Alzheimer's patients—and the ways those needs can be met at home, in assisted living residences and in long-term care facilities.

As discussed in Section A, below, Alzheimer's Disease is a progressive condition. It begins with mild symptoms and slowly, but inevitably, becomes worse. What type of care is appropriate depends in large measure on how far an elder's disease has progressed. An elder with mild Alzheimer's symptoms can often manage very well at home, or in a family member's home, with a combination of home care and strong family support. Or the elder could receive home care in an organized senior residence. When the elder's symptoms become more severe, however, providing care at home can become extremely difficult. For many people in the middle stages of the disease, some sort of assisted living or long-term care residential facility works best. And as the disease progresses to its most severe stages, patients almost always require the round-the-clock care provided in a custodial care nursing facility.

OTHER TYPES OF COGNITIVE IMPAIRMENT

This chapter focuses on the particulars of Alzheimer's Disease. But older people may suffer diminished mental capabilities—called "cognitive impairment" or "dementia"—from other causes, such as a stroke, Parkinson's Disease or the loss of brain cell function that has traditionally been called "senility". Whatever its cause— and no matter what name it goes by—diminished mental capacity often presents the same symptoms as Alzheimer's, such as disorientation, memory loss, anxiety, sleeplessness, loss of balance and coordination and eventual difficulty with body functions. This chapter provides information about dealing with these and related symptoms, whether they result from Alzheimer's Disease or from another type of cognitive impairment.

A. The Symptoms and Stages of Alzheimer's

If you are organizing care for yourself or a loved one with Alzheimer's, you should learn the symptoms of the disease in its various stages *before* those symptoms fully appear. Alzheimer's is a progressive disease in which a person's condition slowly deteriorates. The course of the disease—from mild early symptoms to severe late stages—may last from five to twenty years. But within that slow decline, symptoms may appear abruptly, without warning. Knowing what to expect can help you cope with these changes as they develop.

This section looks at the three stages of Alzheimer's Disease as the medical and care communities now understand and describe it. But the symptoms of Alzheimer's and other forms of dementia vary widely from person to person. Some people will show only some of the symptoms on the "standard" list or suffer a milder version of some symptoms and a more severe version of others. Other people will develop the classic symptoms but not in the order or severity of the disease's normal progression. And no clear dividing line separates one stage of the disease from another. Although learning about the disease's usual progression can help you prepare for the future, no brief summary can cover the many ways in which this complex disease appears. And long-term care is for a person, not a disease. It is that person's individual needs that must dictate care, not those of a theoretical person with supposedly "average" Alzheimer's symptoms.

1. Early Stage Alzheimer's

In its earliest stages, Alzheimer's symptoms may be subtle and hard to recognize. How do you distinguish between the "normal" signs of aging—lower energy, slower movements and thinking that isn't quite as sharp—and the more serious loss of cognitive functions that may indicate the onset of Alzheimer's? Even physicians find it very difficult to make the distinction. And these same symptoms can result from an undetected physical problem, such as a small stroke, Parkinson's Disease, overmedication or a potent interaction of several medicines. If you begin to notice some of the symptoms listed here, see a physician who is experienced with Alzheimer's. If your personal physician does not have that experience, ask to be referred to a doctor who does. This doesn't mean you cannot continue to be treated by your regular physician, even if you do have Alzheimer's. But an accurate early diagnosis of Alzheimer's, if that is what you have, will help you, your family and your physician plan for what is to come.

As the early stage of Alzheimer's progresses, even its relatively minor symptoms can make life difficult and dangerous for the person who has the disease and for those with whom that person lives. Once several of these symptoms are occurring regularly, you will need to arrange for close monitoring and care. (See Section B, below.)

These are the most common early symptoms of Alzheimer's Disease:

- **Confusion about time and place.** One of the tell-tale signs of early Alzheimer's is increasingly frequent mistakes about the day, time or location. Some loss of date and time awareness is common in older people, especially if they have no fixed daily schedule. But elders who are confused on a regular basis, or seem not to know where they are, should be checked for Alzheimer's.

- **Short-term memory loss.** Some memory loss is a normal aspect of the aging process. Over time, most elders will suffer from fading long-term memories—an inability to reconstruct events long in the past. But elders with Alzheimer's begin to lose short-term memory. In the afternoon, a person may not be able to remember what happened that morning. Or a person might repeat a task he just completed, because he has no memory of having done it already.

- **Difficulty with routine tasks.** A person with early stage Alzheimer's may be unable to figure out how to write a check, count out the right amount of bills to pay at the grocery store or change channels on the radio or television.

- **Making senseless decisions.** An Alzheimer's sufferer may make choices or decisions that are illogical, like putting on a heavy coat to go out on a hot summer day, putting the cordless phone away in the fridge, getting undressed for bed right after breakfast or putting ten loaves of bread in the grocery basket.

- **Mood swings.** Those who have Alzheimer's sometimes "lose" their normal personality. A person with early stages of the disease may become moody, restless and irritable for no apparent reason, may be unable to concentrate on anything or indifferent to surroundings. These mood swings tend to occur most often and acutely at dusk, as the light is changing—which is why doctors refer to this phenomenon as "sundowning."

INFORMATION AND REFERRALS ABOUT ALZHEIMER'S

There are two excellent national nonprofit organizations that can provide a wealth of information to people coping with Alzheimer's Disease. These organizations offer materials that can help you understand the disease, its symptoms and its treatments. They also provide descriptions of and referrals to local health care organizations and facilities that specialize in Alzheimer's care. They connect families caring for someone with Alzheimer's to support groups of other families in the same situation. And they provide a continuing stream of valuable information via newsletters, brochures and websites. Anyone dealing with Alzheimer's should make use of the resources of one or both of these organizations:

Alzheimer's Association
919 North Michigan Ave., Suite 1100
Chicago, IL 60611-1676
800-272-3900
www.alz.org
email: info@alz.org

Alzheimer's Disease Education and Referral Center
P.O. Box 8250
Silver Spring, MD 20907-8250
800-438-4380
www.alzheimers.org
email: adear@alzheimers.org

2. Middle Stage Alzheimer's

An elder in the middle stages of Alzheimer's Disease may suffer a more severe version of the early stage symptoms—and will begin to exhibit new symptoms. Some medications—antidepressants, sleep aids and anti-anxiety drugs—can help alleviate some of these symptoms, at least for a while. But the disease's progression can only be slowed, not stopped. It becomes increasingly difficult for elders with Alzheimer's to communicate and to care for themselves. This makes it much harder for family members to be the sole caregivers. You can get outside help from a home health agency or independent personal attendants, either in a family home or in an organized senior residence. (See Section B.) As the symptoms worsen, however, the patient will require extensive monitoring, supervision and assistance. At this point, many families will have to make the difficult choice to move the elder to an assisted living or long-term care facility. (See Section C.)

These are the symptoms most commonly associated with middle stage Alzheimer's:

- **Confusion as to time, place and persons.** An elder's confusion about times, dates and places worsens. This is compounded by one of the most heart-breaking aspects of Alzheimer's: the elder's inability to recognize other people. An Alzheimer's patient will mix up names and identities; as the disease progresses, the patient will no longer recognize even the most familiar faces.
- **Memory loss and transposure.** The short-term memory loss that begins in the early stages of the disease becomes acute. People with middle-stage Alzheimer's may remember very little that they have recently done. Long-term memory is also affected. Those suffering from Alzheimer's often transpose events and people, creating a hodgepodge of recent recollections and childhood memories that they can no longer sort out.

- **Wandering.** People with middle stage Alzheimer's have a tendency to wander away from home—or from a companion on an outing—and become lost. This can cause great anxiety and difficulty for both patient and caregiver—and a variety of dangers (from exposure, traffic or crime, for example) if the person winds up in unfamiliar territory.

- **Loss of simple logic.** Patients are no longer able to go from one simple thought to the next, or to figure out the basic steps they will have to follow to complete a task. For example, an Alzheimer's patient might not realize that a door must be unlocked before it can be opened.

- **Language problems.** As Alzheimer's progresses, people lose their facility with language. Someone with middle stage Alzheimer's may have trouble finding even simple words, may use words incorrectly and will likely have difficulty reading.

- **Motor function difficulties.** The early symptoms of Alzheimer's are mostly cognitive—that is, they affect the patient's ability to think and understand. In the middle stages the patient's body begins to suffer, too. Elders may lose hand-eye coordination, making simple tasks difficult. They may have trouble with balance, meaning that dangerous falls may occur. And they may become incontinent.

- **Extreme mood swings.** People with middle stage Alzheimer's often ride an unpredictable roller coaster of emotions, from deep depression to high good humor, from intense anger to weepy sentimentality.

- **Impulsive behavior.** People with Alzheimer's are known to "act out" in impulsive and unexpected ways, such as loud talking or shouting, arguing, disrobing, making inappropriate personal commentary or touching others and engaging in other antisocial or embarrassing behaviors.

- **Paranoia and hallucinations.** As the disease progresses, a person may begin to exhibit paranoid behavior, showing fear or mistrust of strangers, caregivers and even close family. Someone with Alzheimer's in the middle stages may also begin to have visual or auditory hallucinations—that is, they might start to see or hear things that aren't there—which can be very disturbing to patients and caregivers alike.

3. Late Stage Alzheimer's

Because Alzheimer's Disease may take up to twenty years to run its full course, many people die of some other disease or condition before their Alzheimer's progresses to its final stages. Those who do reach the late stages of the disease almost always require care in a nursing facility. At that point, the disease weakens the body as much as the mind.

In its late stages, Alzheimer's can cause:

- **Complete loss of cognitive functions**. People with late stage Alzheimer's are unable to recognize anyone, to communicate or to help with their own care.
- **Physical deterioration.** Someone with late stage Alzheimer's has difficulty chewing and swallowing, suffers severe weight loss, is completely incontinent and often develops trouble breathing.

B. Home Care for Alzheimer's

In its very earliest stages, the symptoms of Alzheimer's may be no more than a nuisance. With the help of a spouse or other family members, someone with Alzheimer's may be able to manage without any outside care. As the early stage symptoms become persistent, however, elders will require some assistance from outside personal care aides. Caregivers can come to the elder's home, a family member's home or an organized senior residence. However, once patients reach middle stage Alzheimer's, with its deepening confusions and disorientation, they will require round-the-clock monitoring, often in a residential care facility. (See Section C.)

Before considering the issues peculiar to home care for someone with Alzheimer's, read Chapter 2 to familiarize yourself with more general matters of home care.

FAMILY PARTICIPATION IS CRUCIAL

To care for someone with Alzheimer's at home, you will need substantial family participation. Patients in the early stages won't need much assistance. But as their condition worsens, they will need monitoring and assistance round the clock. Most people cannot afford 24-hour outside help—which means that they will have to rely on their spouse, grown children and grandchildren. Unless family members are ready and willing to make this commitment, home care won't be a workable solution over the long term.

---

1. Care in a Family Home

Staying in the comfortable surroundings of home can be very important to someone with Alzheimer's—even more so than to an elder with frailty or other physical problems. As elders lose their memories and grow increasingly confused, the familiar faces and layout of a family home can provide a sense of stability and well-being.

With the help of a healthy and physically capable spouse, someone with Alzheimer's may be able to get along well at home for quite awhile. The spouse can serve as the main caregiver and organize other sources of care. This will be easier, and less expensive, if adult children or grandchildren live nearby and can help out. If no adult children or grandchildren can provide substantial help, a spouse may have to consider moving with the patient to an organized senior residence (see Section B2, below) or moving the ill spouse to an assisted living or residential long-term care facility (see Section C).

Patients who don't have a healthy and physically capable spouse to help with care might consider moving into the home of an adult child, grandchild or sibling. If there are a number of people living in the home, they can share the caregiving responsibilities. A person with Alzheimer's will probably find a family home is more comforting than a residential facility. And it will be less expensive, at least initially.

The larger the number of family members helping to provide care—either in the elder's own home or in a family home—the less outside care will be needed. As the elder's need for care increases, however, it will become more difficult for family members to handle alone. And the more outside assistance is required, the more expensive home care becomes, until at some point the elder will probably have to move to an assisted living or residential long-term care facility.

In addition to the factors listed in Chapter 2, here are some additional things to consider when setting up home care for an elder with Alzheimer's.

a. Caregiver Experience

As explained in Chapter 2D, you can get home care assistance from a home care agency or independent home care aides. Someone in the early stages of Alzheimer's will require safety monitoring, minor assistance with daily tasks and companionship—but not necessarily medical or therapeutic care. Therefore, you probably won't need the more medically skilled personnel offered by a home care agency, at least at the beginning. Instead, you should look for an individual caregiver who has the right skills and temperament for Alzheimer's care.

Caring for an elder with Alzheimer's requires a special kind of patience, a soothing personality and an ability to sort through the workings of a confused mind. Someone who has these personality traits but doesn't have experience working with Alzheimer's patients may turn out to be a wonderful caregiver. Generally, however, you should try to find outside caregivers with Alzheimer's experience. A home care agency that can guarantee that it will send Alzheimer's-experienced aides will save your family the time and effort of finding experienced help. If the agency cannot guarantee experienced aides, however, you should consider spending the time to find aides on your own. Your efforts will pay off in higher quality care—and in lower expenses, as independent aides generally charge less than a home care agency.

b. Continuity of Caregivers

Someone with Alzheimer's should see the same aides, at the same time of day, to the extent possible. The aides will get to know the patient's individual needs and preferences—and will learn what works (and what doesn't) in responding to those needs. The person receiving care will see a familiar face, which can be very important for someone whose world may otherwise be quite confusing. And because people with Alzheimer's become disoriented as to time, it is best to have the same aides work at the same time each day. A patchwork schedule can contribute to a patient's disorientation.

ALZHEIMER'S SUPPORT GROUPS AND DAYCARE

Coping with the early stages of Alzheimer's can be emotionally trying for the person with the disease. People with early stage Alzheimer's still have most of their mental faculties. They are often painfully aware of the onset of the disease, the problems they are having and, worst of all, what the future might hold. Losing their cognitive abilities is distressing, embarrassing and frightening.

The early and middle stages of Alzheimer's are also physically and emotionally exhausting for family members, who not only have to manage not only their own fears, anxiety and sadness over their loved one's condition, but also must arrange and provide care.

Fortunately, there is an extensive network of support groups for people with Alzheimer's and for their families. People with Alzheimer's can share their fears, frustrations, angers and coping devices with others who are in a similar stage of the disease. Family members can share experiences and ideas with others who face the same daunting caregiving tasks.

Some support groups are only for people with Alzheimer's. Others are for family members only. And still others are for both. Some support groups also offer adult daycare (see Chapter 2J), which provides companionship and perhaps some therapeutic classes for the person with Alzheimer's—and a welcome break for family members.

To find out about Alzheimer's support groups near you, contact the Alzheimer's Association or the Alzheimer's Disease Education and Referral Center. (See Section A, above.)

c. Sundowning

Many people with Alzheimer's become particularly disoriented, anxious and agitated as day turns to night and natural light is replaced by the dark and/or electric lights. No one knows exactly why this phenomenon, known as "sundowning," occurs. But if you must cope with sundowning, you can do two things to minimize its effects. First, ask the family member or outside caregiver with whom the patient is most comfortable to be "on duty" during those hours. This can help diminish the patient's disorientation. Second, alter household lighting to avoid abrupt changes in light as night falls. For example, you can install and use dimmers on overhead lights and lamps, turn on lights before it gets dark and avoid high-intensity bulbs. Because shadows are also known to disorient those with Alzheimer's, you might also try to eliminate patterns of bright light and dark.

d. Wandering

One of the most common and frightening symptoms of early and middle stage Alzheimer's is the phenomenon of wandering. Even a patient who is usually competent and clear-headed can have a lapse in concentration, wander out of the house or away from a companion on an outing and quickly become lost and disoriented.

You can do several things to manage with this problem. Make sure the person with Alzheimer's engages in lots of physical activities, including regular walks and other outings, to reduce restlessness and the inclination to wander. You can also remind any caregiver or family member who takes the patient on an outing to stay alert. Some also find it helpful to talk regularly to the person with Alzheimer's about where he or she is—this helps patients orient themselves and reassures them that they are where they should be (that is, at home or in another safe place).

Because you may not be able to curtail entirely a patient's inclination to wander, make sure to keep all doors leading to the outside locked. You can also install door alarms and other security devices (see Section e, below). You might also let your neighbors know that the elder could wander off, so they will know to alert you if they see the elder heading out alone. Finally, the Alzheimer's Association (see Section A, above) has a program called "Safe Return" which helps identify and return Alzheimer's wanderers. Some local police agencies have similar identification programs.

DON'T IGNORE OTHER AILMENTS

Sometimes, family members caring for someone with Alzheimer's dismiss the elder's complaints about physical ailments as just another of the disease's delusions. But caregivers have to bear in mind that people with Alzheimer's are no less susceptible to physical ailments than other people of the same age. So, when someone with Alzheimer's complains about a physical symptom—even if the complaint's isn't entirely clear—make sure to have a physician look into the matter. Remember, Alzheimer's patients depend on their caregivers to communicate their problems to physicians. If you ignore physical complaints, you might allow what could have been a minor, treatable problem to become more serious—or even terminal. What's worse, your delay might force the elder to suffer through physical pain that could have been alleviated.

---

e. Safety

Making a home safe for an elder who is frail or has mobility problems is generally a simple matter of eliminating loose electrical cords, installing hand rails and rearranging furniture and other obstacles. But for someone with Alzheimer's, the task is much more difficult. An elder with Alzheimer's has to be protected not only from obvious hazards, but also from his or her own thoughtless acts. For example, someone with Alzheimer's might momentarily forget that an iron or stove might be hot or that a knife is sharp.

An Alzheimer's patient's tendency to wander and frequent wakefulness at night when caregivers are sleeping can magnify these safety concerns. An elder who is disoriented, lacks judgment and coordination and wanders around the house in the dark can easily come to harm.

The best way to protect against injuries is to be extremely vigilant. But no caregiver can watch every move an Alzheimer's patient makes, particularly at night. This makes preventive measures very important. Because an elder with Alzheimer's has reduced balance and coordination, your home should be cleared of tripping hazards—such as cords and loose rugs—and sharp, protruding corners that could cause serious injury in a fall.

Some other things that can make your home safer for someone with Alzheimer's include:

- deadbolt or inaccessible locks or gates, not only to the outside but also to stairways and to areas of the house that should be off-limits without supervision
- protected access—child-proof locks, for example—to sharp or otherwise potentially harmful appliances, objects and substances, particularly in the kitchen, bathroom and garage
- lowering hot water settings, to avoid scalding
- night-lights in the person's bedroom and other rooms accessible at night, to permit safe movement
- extra lighting and contrasting floor colors at doorways, stairways and landings, to make it easier to see the difference in surface, and

- motion sensors and door alarms, to alert caregivers when the elder moves around at night.

2. Home Care in an Organized Senior Residence

Those in the early stages of Alzheimer's can also receive home care in an independent living senior residence, sometimes called a "retirement home" (see Chapter 3A and C). This option works well for single people with Alzheimer's, as well as for couples in which only one spouse or partner has the disease.

Some single people in the early stages of Alzheimer's can get by safely on their own but cannot fully manage the daily running of a household. If these elders do not have an adult relative with whom they can or want to live, an organized senior residence can provide a number of advantages. Similarly, a spouse who provides care for an Alzheimer's spouse may find it difficult to manage both caregiving and housekeeping responsibilities. If your home is large, open or isolated, you may find it especially hard to care for a spouse. Moving together into an independent living residence for seniors may considerably improve the situation.

Because independent living units are usually small apartments or rooms, they are physically easier to manage than larger apartments or houses. Also, these living units are designed to make life easier for older people, with built-in safety features and easy-to-use appliances. Senior residences often offer meals in a common dining room, which can eliminates the hassle and dangers of cooking and cleaning up.

Independent living residences do not offer personal assistance with the activities of daily life, nor do they provide round-the-clock supervision. But they do have some staff on hand all the time. The staff and other residents provide not only a social community, but also a kind of neighborhood watch—they can provide physical and emotional support while keeping an eye out for trouble. A single person may feel more secure in such a community. And a caregiver spouse won't have to provide constant care and companionship, because there will always be familiar faces nearby.

Although an independent living senior residence offers many advantages, an elder with Alzheimer's may also need outside home care as time goes on. As the disease moves into its more difficult stages, a person with Alzheimer's may need more help than the community alone, or a caregiver spouse, can provide. Most independent living residences are used to having outside home care aides regularly work with residents. In fact, most residences have a formal or informal referral service for home care aides—and work with those aides to make life easier for residents. However, some independent living communities restrict access by outside care aides, or do not permit residents to remain if they are not able to function independently. (See Chapter 3A). If you are considering an independent living community for yourself or someone else with early stage Alzheimer's, make sure its rules permit continued residence and unlimited outside home care as the disease progresses.

C. Residential Care Facilities for Alzheimer's

As discussed in Chapters 3 and 4, there are many types of residential facilities for older people who are no longer able to live independently and who cannot or do not want to rely on home care. For example, assisted living residences provide a small amount of daily assistance plus round-the-clock monitoring. (See Chapter 3B.) Long-term care facilities—also called board and care homes, residential care facilities, custodial care facilities, sheltered care residences or the like—provide 24-hour personal assistance but not much nursing or other medical care. (See Chapter 4A.) And nursing facilities provide round-the-clock personal assistance plus nursing and other medical care. (See Chapter 4A.) These facilities can eliminate or limit an elder's need for outside assistance, reduce the physical space and daily tasks the person with Alzheimer's and caregivers have to navigate and provide a community of people offering round-the-clock companionship.

As someone's Alzheimer's symptoms become more severe, caring for that person at home can become extremely difficult. If you use a lot of paid outside assistance, care may quickly become prohibitively expensive. For these reasons, most people with middle to late stage Alzheimer's eventually move to an assisted living, residential care or nursing facility. And many of those people later have to move to a higher level of care, either within the same facility or in a different setting.

No specific type of facility is best or "right" for someone with any particular stage of Alzheimer's. Much depends on the facility's location. In most cases, the only practical choices will be facilities that are near the home of the family member—usually a spouse or adult child—who will supervise care. Cost may also limit your choices. Some otherwise suitable facilities may simply be too expensive.

Once you've found affordable facilities in the right area, you should select the facility that can best meet the needs of an elder with Alzheimer's. Someone with Alzheimer's requires a different type of care from someone who has only physical limitations. The same assisted living or long-term care facility that provides excellent care for people with physical frailties will not necessarily work well for a person with dementia.

Below are some of the special factors you should consider when choosing a residential care facility for someone with Alzheimer's. Use the information here to supplement the more general discussion of residential facilities in Chapters 3 and 4.

HELP FROM A GERIATRIC CARE MANAGER

Geriatric care managers are professional advisers who help seniors and their families arrange long-term care. They know most of the agencies and facilities in a given geographic area and can help arrange complicated combinations of home health and personal assistance care. They are particularly useful to people who are trying to arrange care for someone from long distance. They can also help people find a residential facility for someone with Alzheimer's. Particularly in urban areas where there may be many residential facilities, a geriatric care manager who has experience placing people with Alzheimer's may know which facilities do well with Alzheimer's residents (and which ones do not.) To find out more about geriatric care managers, see Chapter 1G.

---

1. Physical Space

You should always look for a facility that is roomy and comfortable. But for someone with Alzheimer's, a facility's physical design and layout can be equally important. If the person is physically active, as many people with middle stage Alzheimer's are, the facility must provide space to move about freely, without a sense of confinement. But because Alzheimer's patients often wander and become disoriented, the space must also be safe and constraining. Some facilities combine space and constraint by using a circular design for hallways, which permits Alzheimer's patients to walk about in any direction, for as long they want, without being stopped or confused by dead-ends or doors. When combined with a protected inner courtyard or patio for fresh air and a bit of greenery, these circular designs allow someone with Alzheimer's to feel a sense of movement and visual variety without risk. Avoid facilities with intersecting corridors, locked doors and dead-ends, where someone with Alzheimer's can quickly grow frustrated and disoriented.

2. Other Residents

Some long-term care facilities advertise a separate "special care unit" or "Alzheimer's care unit" exclusively for people with dementia. If a separate unit truly is designed and operated for dementia sufferers, its special features and staff may provide distinct advantages for those with Alzheimer's.

But a separate unit does not guarantee high-quality care. Unfortunately, some special units or wings offer nothing more than a higher price. And in some facilities, Alzheimer's residents are segregated into a separate unit merely because it is easier for the staff to control them there—and to prevent them from mixing with other residents.

Facilities that admit only Alzheimer's residents can provide some advantages. The staff can organize meals, activities and care including the monitoring of nighttime wandering—solely with Alzheimer's residents in mind. And because the staff only cares for people with Alzheimer's, they are likely to develop good skills in handling the particular difficulties Alzheimer's presents. Also, some Alzheimer's-only facilities have programs of Alzheimer's education, family counseling and support groups that might not be available at other facilities.

But facilities that mix Alzheimer's residents with those who are only physically limited also offer some benefits. People in early and middle stage Alzheimer's often benefit from contact with non-Alzheimer's residents. The conversation and activities of these other residents can help people with Alzheimer's remain oriented, alert and calm. However, if there is a mix of residents in an open facility (one that permits its non-Alzheimer's residents to go in and out freely), make sure that the facility pays close attention to the safety and security of Alzheimer's residents. Some open facilities rely solely on the watchful eyes of staff to monitor the movements of Alzheimer's residents. Others add closed-circuit monitors, door alarms or sensors—used with a wristband or other device—to alert staff when an unattended Alzheimer's resident wanders at night or attempts to leave the facility.

3. Staff Skills

Perhaps the single most important quality to look for in a residential care facility is the staff's skills in dealing with Alzheimer's. Unfortunately, it can be difficult to gauge staff skills during brief visits to a facility. Therefore, you should try to visit a facility several times before you make your choice.

Be sure to visit at different times of day, including meal times. Meals are the highlight of the day for most residents—how well the staff helps residents in the dining room will make a big difference in how happy residents are. Try to make a night visit also—night is a particularly difficult time for people with Alzheimer's, and the facility may have different people staffing the night shift.

Your initial visit to a long-term care residence will almost certainly be conducted by the facility director, administrator, general manager or other top level official. This person may have a very impressive professional resume. He or she may also be charming and helpful both to you and to the residents you encounter on your tour. Except in a very small facility, however, this administrator is likely to spend much more time dealing with paperwork and staff than directly caring for residents. Of course, if the administrator is obviously awkward or callous in direct contacts with residents, this is a bad sign; such an attitude can easily rub off on the rest of the staff.

Your main focus should be on how the line staff—the personal care aides—interact with the residents. They are the facility employees who will spend the most time with residents. Are they calm and soothing with residents, or cold and abrupt? Do they treat the residents like children, or respectfully as adults? Do they acknowledge resident comments and requests and offer solutions—or do they simply try to quiet or distract residents? Do they have good language skills, either in English or a resident's other first language?

Make sure you see how the staff does with Alzheimer's residents, not just residents who are physically limited. And try to observe them with the most seriously ill Alzheimer's residents—this will be your best measure of staff attitudes and capabilities. Do the Alzheimer's residents seem comfortable with the staff? If a resident is distressed or disruptive, as people with middle stage Alzheimer's often are, how well do staff members respond?

4. Family Participation

In either an assisted living facility or a residential care facility, regular visits from family members can greatly improve an Alzheimer's resident's comfort and sense of well-being. Some facilities make family visiting easy and encourage participation in a resident's care. They maintain avenues of communication for family members, readily accepting family comments and requests and willingly acting on them. Other facilities, however, set limits on visits and treat family members as aliens who must be tolerated but should not be encouraged.

You may have trouble getting a sense of a facility's attitude toward family members during your first visits. Try to see how family members of current residents interact with the staff. Do family members move about the facility easily, or do they seem like uncomfortable guests? Do they know staff members by name, and vice versa? See if the facility will give you the names and phone numbers of some immediate family members of current residents with Alzheimer's. If so, give them a call and find out how their relatives have been doing at that facility.

5. Special Programs for Alzheimer's Residents

Alzheimer's residents can benefit from programs designed to address symptoms particular to the early and middle stages of the disease. Special arts and crafts work, reading, word games and outings can help residents stay mentally alert. Memory enhancement programs can slow memory loss. Resident participation in room and hallway decoration can help keep the resident oriented within the facility. The facility can offer physical exercises tailored to people with relatively healthy bodies but poor balance or coordination. And staff can pay special attention to residents during the hours around sunset, to minimize the effects of sundowning (see Section B, above).

6. Incontinence

Almost everyone with middle stage Alzheimer's Disease becomes incontinent to some degree. At first, they will have only occasional loss of bladder control. Later, they are likely to develop nearly total incontinence. This presents several problems. It is embarrassing to the person with Alzheimer's. It is unpleasant for other residents and staff. It can be physically uncomfortable. And, if it is not properly attended to, it can present health problems.

For all these reasons, you should try to get a sense of how a facility handles residents' incontinence. A facility cannot be expected to keep a resident completely clean every moment. But some things can be done to help minimize incontinence, particularly in its early stages. Does the staff try to help residents control the problem, if possible? And when incontinence is beyond control, does the staff regularly monitor and clean residents—day and night—so that they are reasonably comfortable?

7. Medication and Other Medical Care

Find out whether the facility is licensed—usually this means it has a registered nurse on duty—to administer drugs by injection and to deliver other types of nonself-administered medical care. People with Alzheimer's are not immune to other ailments and may need regular medical attention. Assisted living residences and small long-term care facilities might not have staff who can administer such medical care. If you are looking for a facility for someone who has a physical condition that may soon require regular medical intervention, make sure the facility can deliver it.

Also look into the facility's policy on using medications to control Alzheimer's symptoms themselves. There are drugs that can help control the anxieties, aggressiveness, agitation and sleeplessness of people with Alzheimer's. The proper use of these drugs can make life more comfortable for the resident. And facility staff may legitimately need to use accepted Alzheimer's medication to help control the extreme behavior of some residents in the later stages of the disease. But who decides what drugs, what doses and what frequency? Ask the director about the facility's policy (it should be in writing) on the use of behavior-controlling medication. To what extent is a resident's personal physician consulted regarding medications? What about family? And does the facility keep a written record of each administration of these medications, including dosage and frequency?

6

Medicare and
Veterans' Benefits

Brace yourself for some serious numbers. The cost of nursing facility care averages $3,500 to $5,000 per month—and some facilities cost as much as $10,000 per month. Even the least expensive custodial-only care facilities average almost $3,000 per month. And these amounts are increasing much faster than the general cost of living. Many people exhaust their personal savings within months of entering a residential care facility. Yet many long-term care residents stay in facilities for two years or more, with total costs often reaching $100,000 to $200,000. Home health care, too, can cost many thousands of dollars a year if you need skilled or frequent services.

Who pays for all this? For the most part, the answer is you—at least until all your money is gone, when Medicaid may begin to pay. (See Chapter 7.) Many believe—incorrectly—that the Medicare system "covers" nursing facility care. The truth is that Medicare pays only about 10% of all nursing facility costs nationwide. On average, Medicare pays for less than 30 days of nursing facility care—and that applies only to skilled nursing care. Medicare covers no long-term nursing facility or other residential care, and its coverage of home health care is equally limited.

Private long-term care insurance may pay some of the cost of nursing facility care. But even if you have such insurance, you may wind up having to pay so much out of pocket that you will deplete your savings. (See Chapter 11.)

Medicaid provides the only comprehensive coverage of long-term care. This federal government program for low-income people, administered by the states, pays for almost half the nation's total nursing facility costs and for much home care as well. But, as discussed later in Chapter 7, a person is not eligible for Medicaid coverage until he or she has used up almost all personal assets. In other words, if you have money saved when you begin long-term care, you must pay the bills yourself until your money is nearly gone; only then will Medicaid begin to pay.

If you choose to receive home care, government programs or private insurance won't pick up much of the cost. Even so, your out-of-pocket expenses may be lower than for residential care. If you do enter a residential facility, you will probably wind up personally paying for the bulk of your care until your assets are nearly gone.

There is no easy way out of this staggering financial crunch. Your task is to make your money last as long as possible. You want to be able to use your assets for things other than long-term care. And you want to maintain sufficient assets to pay for long-term care services not covered by any government program or insurance.

Once you actually need long-term care, the best way to protect your assets is to get only the services or level of care you really need from the most cost-efficient provider. (See Chapters 1 through 4.) Also, be aware of how much and under what rules Medicare, the Veterans' Administration and Medicaid may pay for long-term care, so that you can get the most from these programs. And even long in advance of your need for long-term care, you may be able to take some steps to protect some of your assets. Long-term care insurance is one avenue to consider. (See Chapter 11.) Transferring some of your assets to others may also allow you to save some money.

A. Medicare Coverage for Long-Term Care

Most Americans age 65 and older are eligible for Medicare coverage, but few understand how it works. Medicare is a federal government program created to assist older Americans with medical costs. The program is divided into two parts. Part A is "hospital insurance," which covers some of the bills for a stay in a hospital or a skilled nursing facility. Part B is "medical insurance," which pays some of the costs of doctors and outpatient medical care. If you are 65 or older and eligible for Social Security retirement, survivor's or dependent's benefits, you are automatically eligible for Part A coverage. For a monthly premium, anyone 65 or older can enroll in Part B coverage, whether or not they are eligible for Part A.

FOR ADDITIONAL INFORMATION

Even people who are not eligible for Social Security benefits may be eligible for Part A Medicare when they reach age 65. For a complete discussion of Medicare eligibility, see *Social Security, Medicare & Government Pensions: Get the Most Out of Your Retirement and Medical Benefits*, by Joseph Matthews with Dorothy Matthews Berman (Nolo).

One of the worst misconceptions about Medicare is that it covers nursing facility care. In fact, Medicare nursing facility coverage is severely limited, which leaves most people to pay for virtually all long-term care out of their own pockets.

Because home health care can be considerably cheaper than nursing facility care, it would seem sensible for the government to encourage home care by covering a sizable portion of the cost. Unfortunately, it does not. Medicare pays much less for home care than such logic might lead you to expect. And it pays nothing at all for custodial care in nursing facilities or other residential long-term care facilities.

It's important to know what long-term care Medicare pays for so you can get the most out of available coverage. But it's just as important to find out what Medicare does not pay for, so you can be prepared either to gather the funds elsewhere or to obtain most of your care and coverage from other sources.

1. Skilled Nursing Facility Care

Part A of Medicare covers a small amount of skilled nursing facility care, as follows:

- up to 100 days per benefit period—that is, per continuous period of treatment—in a skilled nursing facility
- a semiprivate room (two to four beds); if you want a private room, you must pay the difference in cost yourself, unless the private room is medically necessary as prescribed by a doctor and approved by the facility and the Medicare intermediary—an insurance company that administers Medicare funds in your state
- daily, regular, skilled and special nursing as medically necessary, but *not* a private duty nurse
- skilled rehabilitation services—such as physical, occupational or speech therapy—if medically necessary, as long as you are showing improvement, and
- medications, medical supplies and equipment, and dietary requirements as supplied by the facility.

WARNING—MEDICARE DOES NOT COVER

- custodial care (nonmedical assistance with normal daily activities such as eating and bathing), unless it is part of skilled nursing care in a skilled nursing facility
- nursing care or therapy provided in a facility that is not certified by Medicare as a *skilled* nursing facility, or
- doctor's care while you are in a nursing facility. However, Medicare Part B "medical insurance" covers doctor's care in a nursing facility under the same terms as any other medical care.

a. Conditions Limiting Medicare Coverage

Unfortunately, Medicare's conditions for coverage of nursing facility costs eliminate far more types of care than they cover. When you also consider that Medicare partially pays for only 100 days of care in total, it is easy to understand why Medicare covers only about 10% of all nursing facility costs.

Here are some Medicare coverage restrictions:

- **Immediate prior hospital stay.** Medicare pays for your stay in a skilled nursing facility only if you have first spent at least three consecutive days (not counting the discharge day) in a hospital. And you must be admitted to the nursing facility within 30 days of your discharge from the hospital.

- **Daily skilled nursing care or therapy.** Medicare pays only for the skilled nursing care or rehabilitative therapy you need and receive every day. If you receive such care intermittently, you do not qualify for Medicare coverage.

- **Prescribed by a physician.** Your daily skilled nursing care or therapy must be "medically necessary"—that is, it has to be specifically prescribed by a doctor.

- **Medicare-approved skilled nursing facility.** You must receive care in a *skilled* nursing facility certified by Medicare. Medicare checks on the quality of care in each nursing facility and certifies only those that meet its standards. Ask to see the current Medicare certification documents of any nursing facility you are considering. Medicare also won't cover care that is, or could be, received in a lower level facility.

- **Only while condition "improving."** Even though Medicare covers up to 100 days in a skilled nursing facility, and even though you may need daily skilled care for each of those days, Medicare will cover you only as long as your condition is "improving." Once Medicare determines, after a review, that your condition has stabilized, it will no longer pay for skilled nursing facility care—no matter how serious your condition remains or how much skilled nursing care you continue to need.

MORE COVERAGE FOR ALZHEIMER'S PATIENTS

Prior to the year 2002, elders who sought Medicare coverage for therapies and treatments related to Alzheimer's were routinely denied. The reason? The government's official stance was that those who suffer from Alzheimer's were not capable of medical improvement, and therefore did not qualify for such services.

Recently, Medicare has announced a policy change. These claims may no longer be routinely denied, but must be considered just like any other claim for benefits. Advocates for Alzheimer's patients say the change is long overdue—and will result in cost-savings in the long run, as Alzheimer's patients who receive therapeutic care will be able to live longer on their own.

- **Approval on review.** Even if your doctor prescribes "medically necessary" skilled nursing care for you in a skilled nursing facility and continues to certify that your condition is improving, this does not guarantee that Medicare will provide nursing facility coverage. The doctor's opinion must be approved by both the nursing facility's Utilization Review Committee—facility doctors who review patient conditions—and by the Medicare "intermediary."

b. How Much Medicare Pays of Nursing Facility Costs

During the first 100 days of coverage, Medicare pays these amounts:

- **Days 1 to 20.** You are responsible for paying up to your yearly Medicare Part A deductible, if you have not already reached it. Once you have paid the yearly deductible, Medicare pays all your covered nursing facility charges.
- **Days 21 to 100.** After the first 20 days of coverage, Medicare pays all covered charges except what is called a "coinsurance" amount, for which you are personally responsible. In 2003, that coinsurance amount was $105 per day; the figure goes up slightly each year.
- **Days 101 on.** After 100 days in a skilled nursing facility, you are on your own. Medicare pays nothing toward your stay there.

2. Medicare Home Care Coverage

Although Medicare coverage for home care is extremely limited, it does provide substantial payment for the most expensive part of home care—skilled nursing or therapy—during the time immediately after an illness or injury, when you are most likely to need it.

a. Home Health Services Covered by Medicare

The home health care services Medicare covers are listed below, limited by the conditions discussed in the following section:

- skilled nursing
- physical and speech therapy as needed during recovery, while your condition is improving, and
- supplemental care. If (and only if) you receive skilled nursing or physical or speech therapy, Medicare may also pay for limited visits by a home health care aide to help you with personal care— usually only if there is no one else at home to help. Medicare may also cover required medical social services, some medical supplies

or equipment provided by the home care agency and the services of an occupational therapist to help you relearn daily household tasks.

WHAT'S NOT COVERED

Medicare home health care does not cover custodial personal care, drugs, meals or homemaking services.

---

b. Restrictions on Home Health Care Coverage

As with nursing facility care, a number of restrictions limit home health care coverage. Medicare covers care only during periods of recovery from acute illness or injury, or following a change in condition while you are learning how to administer drugs or otherwise care for yourself.

Intermittent skilled care. It must be "medically necessary" for you to receive skilled nursing care or rehabilitative therapy on a part-time only basis. Full-time nursing care at home is not covered. Note that this is the opposite of the requirement for covered care in a skilled nursing facility.

Doctor-prescribed. A physician must have ordered the skilled care.

Only during recovery. Care is covered only while you are recovering—that is, while your condition is improving. As soon as your condition has stabilized, as determined by a Medicare review, coverage ends.

Injury, illness or medical condition. Your need for care must be the result of a specific injury, illness or medical condition. If you need home care because of general frailty, Medicare will not pay for it.

Confined to home. Care is covered only while you are confined to home (except for brief, infrequent occasions out, usually related to receiving medical care). Medicare consider you to be "confined to home" if you are unable to leave home without difficulty and without the assistance of another person or a medical device such as a wheelchair. Confined to home does not necessarily mean bedridden, however.

Approved agency. Care must be provided by a Medicare-certified home care agency or other provider. This sometimes eliminates independent nurses and therapists. Always ask the home care agency or other provider to show you its Medicare certification documentation before beginning care.

c. How Much Medicare Home Health Coverage Pays

In general, Medicare pays 100% of the "approved costs" of covered services provided by a certified home care agency or other provider. "Approved costs" are the standardized charges Medicare decides are appropriate for specific services, based on a national cost average. You are personally responsible for the cost of any services that aren't covered, such as homemaking or unapproved personal care from a home care aide.

No matter what the home care provider might normally charge for the covered services, it must accept as payment in full whatever Medicare decides is the approved cost. The home care agency will submit all bills for covered services directly to Medicare. You don't have to be involved in the paperwork.

In some situations, it may not be clear whether Medicare will cover a particular service. In that case, the home care agency or other provider must notify you of the problem, in writing, before it provides the service. If it does notify you and you accept the service anyway, you are personally responsible for the bill if Medicare denies coverage. If it does not notify you in advance, the provider cannot bill you.

LONG-TERM CARE COVERAGE BY HMOS AND MEDI-GAP INSURANCE

Many people have private health insurance that supplements their Medicare coverage, commonly called medi-gap. Many others get supplemental coverage through membership in an HMO or other managed care plan. Most medi-gap and managed care plans cover no more of nursing facility or home health care costs than Medicare. If Medicare does not cover it, a medi-gap policy or managed care plan usually does not cover it either. And medi-gap or managed care payments plus Medicare's payments may still leave some part of the bills unpaid—even for covered care.

A few managed care plans do offer extra home care and nursing care coverage beyond what Medicare covers. This coverage is not for long-term care, but it may pay for a few extra weeks. Given the cost of nursing facility and home care, even a few weeks of coverage is worth collecting.

B. Veterans' Benefits for Long-Term Care

The Veterans' Administration (VA) operates more than 150 hospitals and a number of outpatient clinics throughout the United States that provide free or very low cost health care for veterans and their dependents. The care at these facilities is often very good, but in-patient care is limited. Although there are many hospitals and over 100,000 beds, there are millions of veterans and their dependents, so the VA reserves in-patient care for the treatment of acute conditions, with priority to veterans with service-connected illnesses and injuries and veterans who cannot afford care elsewhere. The space available for in-patient long-term care for the elderly is severely limited.

1. Eligibility for Veterans' Benefits

Many elders may be eligible for Veterans' Administration medical benefits based on their military service or their spouse's service, even if their current need for long-term care has nothing to do with any service-connected disability. Disability compensation for "service-connected disability" and pension benefits for financially needy veterans are not covered here, but they may provide you with extra sources of income. Check with your local Veterans' Administration for more information.

In general, any veteran who cannot afford care elsewhere is eligible for medical care from a VA facility. Dependents and survivors of veterans with service-connected disabilities, veterans who receive veterans' pensions or veterans who are eligible for Medicaid are also eligible to receive medical care from VA facilities if they are unable to afford care elsewhere.

2. Home Health Care Covered by Veterans' Benefits

The number of home health care units connected to Veterans' Administration hospitals and clinics is growing. And the care is free of charge. But unless there is such a home care unit in your area, the VA will rarely pay for care provided by an outside agency.

If a VA facility near you has a home health care unit, it can provide complete medical and personal care as often as necessary. Usually you will only be eligible for care while you recover from acute illness, injury or surgery. If you need specific medical care, it may be available on a long-term basis.

3. Nursing Facility Care Covered by Veterans' Benefits

A number of VA facilities provide long-term skilled nursing and intermediate residential care for veterans. In general, simple custodial care for those who don't need regular nursing or other health care is not available, but where the VA draws the line in a given case may depend on the availability of beds in a particular facility.

The VA may cover skilled or intermediate care in a private facility if similar care is not available in a VA facility. Eligibility depends on financial need and the connection (if any) between the disability or impairment and military service. Because the quality of free VA health care tends to be very good, you should investigate both your eligibility and the availability of long-term residential care in a VA facility. Begin your search for information by contacting your local VA office and any VA medical facility in your area. ∎

Medicaid Coverage
for Long-Term Care

Medicaid (called Medi-Cal in California) is a federally funded program, administered by the individual states, that helps pay for medical care for financially needy people. For low-income older people who qualify, Medicaid supplements Medicare to cover many of the costs of long-term care—including home care and almost all types of long-term residential facility care for an unlimited time. The Medicaid program pays for about half of the country's total nursing facility costs.

To qualify for Medicaid, an elder must have a low income and very few assets. Unfortunately, this means that many people are not eligible until they have spent almost all their savings paying for residential facility or home care themselves. Medicaid allows you to keep more assets if one spouse remains at home while the other lives in a long-term care facility.

Because Medicaid pays a lower rate than that charged to privately paying residents, some facilities either do not accept Medicaid residents or put them only in less desirable rooms. So, if you are dependent on Medicaid when you look for a long-term care facility, your choices may be limited. And if your funds diminish to the point that you become eligible for Medicaid after you are a resident, the facility is legally prohibited from discharging you, but it might move you to a different room. Before choosing any long-term care facility, find out the details of its Medicaid policy.

A NOTE ON FINANCIAL PLANNING

As discussed below, Medicaid is a program intended to help people who have low income and few assets. Its rules severely restrict how much of your savings you can keep and still be eligible for coverage. These rules also prevent people from getting around the eligibility requirements by simply moving their money around.

However, a few options are available to people who are likely to need Medicaid coverage for long-term care but have slightly too many assets to qualify for Medicaid—or who want to try to keep at least some of their assets to pass on to their survivors. These options may require advance planning. And some require the older person to give up control over some assets, which some are reluctant to do. Even with these drawbacks, however, you should consider whether one or more of these options might work for you—and what you need to do now to plan for the future. These issues are covered in Chapter 8.

A. Eligibility for Medicaid

Each state has its own Medicaid eligibility standards—check with your county's social services agency to get the rules for your state. Federal government standards require your assets and income to be below certain levels (with special rules for nursing facility residents), which differ greatly for married couples and unmarried individuals. Medicaid defines the term unmarried to include divorced people and widows or widowers.

1. Home Care: Income and Asset Limits

You are eligible for Medicaid assistance for care you receive in your home only if your income and assets (such as savings, investments and property) fall within guidelines established by the federal government. Some states have stricter rules—and some are more liberal. To find out about your state's income and asset limits, contact your local county's Department of Social Services or Welfare Department (see Section C, below.)

a. Income limits

Medicaid figures out your income by adding up the money you receive from Social Security and other government benefit programs, wages or self-employment income, interest and dividends from savings or investments, rents, royalties, pensions, annuities and gifts. If one spouse in a couple is still working and earning income, about half of that money does not count against the other spouse—that is, Medicaid will not consider about half of the working spouse's income when figuring out the income of the other spouse.

Once your income is tallied, states use the total in one of two ways to decide whether you are eligible for home care coverage. Some states offer Medicaid only to those who qualify as "Categorically Needy." A person whose monthly income is about $400 to $600 often qualifies for home care coverage under this type of system. For married couples, the income limit is higher—roughly $600 to $800 per month. Because state rules vary—and because they can be quite complicated—you should apply for coverage even if your income exceeds these figures substantially. (See Section C, "Finding Out About Medicaid In Your State.")

Other states provide Medicaid home care coverage to those who qualify as "Medically Needy." This category includes people whose income is over the state's general eligibility limit, but whose medical expenses would reduce their income below that limit (subtracting medical expenses from income in this way is referred to as "spending down.") This type of system is more generous to people who have high medical expenses.

The following states offer home care coverage to those who qualify as medically needy, based on their current or anticipated medical expenses. Keep in mind, however, that not every state on this list will subtract the entire cost of your anticipated home care from your income to determine your eligibility— each state has its own rules about whether and to what extent home care services constitute medical expenses for purposes of spending down.

Arizona	Louisiana	North Carolina
Arkansas	Maine	North Dakota
California	Maryland	Oklahoma
Connecticut	Massachusetts	Pennsylvania
District of Columbia	Michigan	Texas
Florida	Minnesota	Utah
Georgia	Montana	Vermont
Illinois	Nebraska	Virginia
Iowa	New Hampshire	Washington
Kansas	New Jersey	West Virginia
Kentucky	New York	Wisconsin

b. Asset limits

People who don't live in a nursing facility may have nonexempt assets worth no more than $2,000 ($3,000 for a couple). Fortunately, a number of assets are exempted from these figures—that is, their value doesn't count towards these limits. The most significant exempt asset is your home, if either you or your spouse live in it. Also exempt are your car up to a value of $4,500 and most of your household goods and personal effects. These are approximate figures—you must check with your local county social services office to find out the specific rules in your state.

Some states permit people to qualify for Medicaid home care services if paying their medical expenses would force them to spend their assets down to a level below the Medicaid eligibility limit. The states that recognize this "medically necessary" category of eligibility are listed in Section a, above.

c. Whose Money Counts?

Medicaid has a number of rules for deciding which assets and income to consider in determining eligibility:

- The assets and income of children, grandchildren or other relatives do not count toward Medicaid limits, even if they live in the same household as the elder applying for Medicaid—unless they provide regular financial support to the elder. Regular financial support is not limited to money but can include food and clothing or other personal items.
- If a married couple live together, both of their incomes and assets are counted toward the Medicaid limits (except as explained in Section 1a, above).
- If a couple is divorced or legally separated and living apart, only the income and assets of the spouse applying for Medicaid are counted, including any actual support received from the other spouse.
- If a couple live together but are not married, only the income and assets of the person applying for Medicaid are counted, including any direct financial support received from the other partner.

> ### MEDICAID MAY PAY FOR ASSISTED LIVING
>
> Some states are beginning to experiment with Medicaid coverage for some assisted living as well as nursing facilities. Where coverage is available, it is provided only to people in assisted living who require nursing care. The same rules determine Medicaid eligibility for assisted living residents as are used for people in nursing facilities.
>
> For a complete discussion of assisted living as an alternative to nursing facility care, see Chapter 3B. To find out whether Medicaid covers assisted living in some parts of your state, see Section C of this chapter.

2. Special Long-Term Care Facility Medicaid Rules

Once a resident of a Medicaid-certified long-term care facility has qualified, Medicaid pays virtually all facility costs for as long as a person remains there. But as with home care, a long-term care facility resident is only eligible when his or her assets are below a certain level. Until then, the resident must pay. Once Medicaid begins paying, almost all of an individual's and much of a couple's income will go to the facility to reduce the amounts Medicaid pays.

Because Medicaid rules for long-term facility residents are quite different for unmarried individuals and for married couples, this section is divided in two parts. The first section explains the income and assets that a single person who enters a long-term care facility can retain. The second section explains the income and assets that each member of a married couple can retain when one spouse enters a long-term care facility.

a. Unmarried Individuals

Remember that for Medicaid purposes, "unmarried" includes a person who is divorced or whose spouse has died. If your marital status changes after you qualify for Medicaid, the Medicaid limits on your income and assets will also change.

Income Eligibility Limits

About 30 states have no limits at all on the income an unmarried long-term care facility resident can have and still be eligible for Medicaid coverage. However, as discussed below, the resident will have to pay virtually all of that income to the nursing facility, with Medicaid paying the balance of the cost.

The rest of the states do have eligibility income limits, which vary from about $500 to $1,600 per month. An unmarried long-term care facility resident in one of these states whose income is over the limit does not qualify for Medicaid coverage at all.

To find out about your state's eligibility rules, contact your local Social Services or Welfare office (see Section C, below).

Income Retained by the Resident

If an unmarried long-term care facility resident qualifies for Medicaid, all of that person's monthly income will go to the facility (and Medicaid will pay the balance of the bill), except:

- small monthly amount for personal needs—books and magazines, grooming and toilet articles—ranging from $30 to $70, depending on the state.
- income the resident spends directly on Medicare premiums, deductibles and co-payments, on medical insurance and on out-of-pocket medical expenses not covered by Medicare or Medicaid.
- in about 30 states, $150 to $600 a month for upkeep and repairs on the resident's private home. This home maintenance allowance continues for up to six months if the resident's doctor gives a

written prognosis that the resident is expected to be able to return home within six months after entering the facility.

Asset Eligibility Limits

Medicaid will cover an unmarried person's stay in a long-term care facility only if that person's savings and other assets are below certain limits. If your assets exceed these limits, you will qualify for Medicaid coverage only after you have paid enough for facility coverage out of your own pocket—referred to by Medicaid as "spending down"—to reach these limits. Medicaid asset limits are:

- no more than $2,000 in savings or other liquid assets such as stocks or certificates of deposit (this limit varies slightly from state to state)
- household and personal items, usually limited to several thousand dollars in value
- one automobile up to a value of $4,500
- one wedding and one engagement ring of any value
- a burial plot and up to $1,500 in a separately maintained fund for burial costs
- a life insurance policy with a face value of no more than $1,500
- a home, under limited circumstances. Some states won't count your home in determining Medicaid eligibility for long-term care facility coverage—but only if your doctor certifies in writing that you are likely to recover sufficiently to leave the nursing facility and return home. Some states also add a six-month to twelve-month time limit, no matter what your doctor says. In other states, your home remains exempt if you merely indicate on your nursing facility admission form that you intend to return home; even if the chances of returning are remote, you must indicate your intent to do so to qualify for this exemption.

Even if your state's Medicaid program allows you to keep certain assets while you live in a long-term care facility, that won't protect your assets after you die. Medicaid may seek reimbursement from any of your remaining assets for payments it made on your behalf (see "Medicaid Will Seek Reimbursement," at the end of this section).

Note that Medicaid rules do not permit you to simply give away assets to relatives or friends and then qualify for coverage. The few permissible methods to protect some assets are discussed in detail in Chapter 8.

HOW DOES MEDICAID KNOW WHAT ASSETS YOU OWN?

A natural question arises when people read that Medicaid coverage is available only to people whose assets are below certain levels: How does Medicaid know what my assets are?

The answer is that Medicaid workers ask you—and examine your financial records. When you apply for Medicaid, you must fill out extensive application forms that ask you to list all your assets. You must also show the Medicaid eligibility workers copies of all ownership documents, bank books and the like. If there are any large or regular withdrawals from your assets in the 36 months prior to your application, you will have to show where that money went and why. Remember, too, that Medicaid will have your Social Security number, so it can cross-check many financial transactions. Medicaid eligibility workers can also pay home visits.

If you fail to report income or assets and are caught by Medicaid, you run the risk of being denied coverage, being forced to repay any money already paid on your behalf and even getting hit with additional penalties and fines.

---

b. Married Couples With One Spouse in a Long-Term Care Facility

While many states do not set income limits for unmarried people entering a long-term care facility, different rules applies to couples.

Whose Income Counts for Eligibility?

Most states use a "name-on-the-check" rule to determine whether income received by a married couple is counted against the Medicaid eligibility of the spouse in the long-term care facility. This rule basically says that if the income is received solely in the name of the at-home spouse, it is not counted toward the state's maximum income limit for the facility spouse's Medicaid eligibility.

Two states—California and Washington—have "community property" rules that can help a facility resident spouse qualify for Medicaid coverage even though the name-on-the-check rule would deny eligibility. If the facility resident spouse in a community property state receives income in his or her name that is over the state's Medicaid limit, Medicaid will look at the at-home spouse's income as well. If one-half the total community property income (the combined income of both spouses) is not over the limit, then the facility resident spouse will qualify for Medicaid.

Three other states—Indiana, Nebraska and West Virginia—also count the at-home spouse's income over certain limits as part of the facility resident spouse's income when calculating eligibility.

Income Retained by Each Spouse

Of income received in his or her own name, the facility resident spouse may keep between $30 to $70 per month for personal use, plus amounts to pay for Medicare, other medical insurance and medical expenses not covered by Medicare or Medicaid. The rest of the facility resident spouse's income goes to the facility, except for any amount necessary to give the at-home spouse a minimum allowance.

The at-home spouse is allowed to keep all income in his or her own name. If more than half the couple's joint income is in the facility resident spouse's name, the at-home spouse is allowed to keep some of that income up to a basic living allowance of between $1,493 and $2,267, when combined with the at-home spouse's own income. The specific amount varies from state to state. Check with your local social services agency to find out your state's limits.

Assets Retained by Both Spouses

The name-on-the-check rule does not apply to assets—savings, property and investments, for example. Formerly, if a couple transferred all their assets to the sole name of the at-home spouse, the facility resident spouse might qualify for Medicaid. No longer. Medicaid now looks at the combined assets of both spouses, regardless of whose name is on the asset. The combined assets a couple may retain and still qualify for Medicaid coverage of the facility resident spouse are:

- the home in which the at-home spouse lives, regardless of its value

- a Community Spouse Resource Amount equal to one-half the value of the couple's nonexempt liquid assets (such as cash, bank accounts and bonds) for the at-home spouse to use, in an amount between $18,132 and $89,280—the maximum amount varies from state to state and both amounts increase yearly with the cost of living

- one automobile, regardless of its value

- furniture and household goods, regardless of value

- one wedding and engagement ring each, regardless of value

- life insurance with cash value of $1,500 for each spouse, and

- two burial plots and a separate savings account of up to $1,500 per person for burial costs.

You should establish the total value of your assets through bank records or other documentation when the facility resident spouse enters a facility, so that you can claim and retain everything to which you are entitled.

MEDICAID WILL SEEK REIMBURSEMENT

A Medicaid recipient and his or her spouse may retain a certain amount of assets—including a home of any value if at least one of them lives in it—while Medicaid pays for long-term care. However, Medicaid has a right to seek reimbursement from the property of the Medicaid recipient for everything Medicaid spends on long-term care after the recipient turns age 55.

Medicaid cannot force the sale of a home while either a spouse, or a minor or disabled child, lives in it. But it can seek reimbursement from the estate of the Medicaid recipient once the recipient and his or her spouse have both died. Those who take title to the property after the second spouse's death must either pay off the Medicaid amount or sell the property and have Medicaid collect its reimbursement out of the proceeds of the sale.

However, with some advance planning, it may be possible to protect the value of the property from some of Medicaid's reimbursement right. (See Chapter 8.)

B. What Medicaid Pays For

What Medicaid covers and how much it pays varies by state. In general, though, Medicaid pays for extensive home care and the full cost of long-term facility care as long as either is necessary.

1. Medicaid-Certified Providers Only

Medicaid pays only for covered services performed by a Medicaid-certified provider. Some home care agencies and long-term care facilities do not meet Medicaid quality standards and therefore are not certified to participate in the program. Also, because Medicaid pays less than what agencies or facilities charge private consumers, some providers choose not to participate in the Medicaid program. However, once a facility has accepted a resident who pays privately, it must allow that resident to remain if the resident switches to Medicaid coverage. Finally, many individual home care providers choose not to seek Medicaid certification because they want to be paid in cash.

It is important to find out whether a facility, agency or individual care provider participates in Medicaid before you obtain service. This is particularly true for long-term care facilities. Even if you are not initially dependent on Medicaid, you should find out the facility's policy on Medicaid patients. Some facilities maintain different, less desirable rooms for Medicaid patients. Switching to Medicaid later may affect the quality of care you receive.

FACILITY MUST KEEP YOU IF YOU BEGIN MEDICAID COVERAGE

Many people enter a long-term care facility as privately paying residents, but later run out of money and become eligible for Medicaid. Because Medicaid pays less than the facility could charge a privately paying resident, a facility might prefer to move out those who becomes eligible for Medicaid and move in waiting residents who can pay their own way. But federal law forbids that.

Facilities that participate in the Medicaid program may not discharge a resident who becomes eligible for Medicaid. A facility may not avoid this law even by withdrawing from the Medicaid program altogether. No one who resided in a facility while the facility participated in the Medicaid program may be discharged if he or she later becomes eligible for Medicaid, even if the facility drops out of the Medicaid program.

The only people left out of these legal protections are residents of facilities that have never participated in Medicaid, or those who move into a facility only after it has entirely dropped out of the Medicaid program.

---

2. Medicaid Home Care Coverage

Unlike Medicare, Medicaid does not usually have stringent rules about either the kind or duration of home care services it covers. In most states, Medicaid pays most of a certified home care agency's reasonable costs, even if care is primarily custodial, and covers many services by nonagency providers (as long as they are Medicaid-certified). In some states, Medicaid also pays for extra-duty nursing, rehabilitation therapies provided outside the home, prescribed medications and medical supplies. To find out whether Medicaid covers a particular service in your state, check with both the provider of the service and your local social service office.

If Medicaid covers a service and the provider accepts payment from Medicaid, the provider cannot then charge you for any amounts over that payment. But, of course, the provider can and will charge you for services not covered by Medicaid.

In some states, Medicaid charges additional fees such as:

- **Enrollment fee.** Some states charge a small, one-time-only fee of a few dollars when you first enroll in Medicaid.

- **Monthly premium.** States are allowed to charge a small fee to "medically needy" Medicaid participants—those who would not normally qualify because of their income or assets, but who become eligible because paying their medical bills would drop their income or assets below the eligibility levels. The amounts of these premiums vary but are usually only a few dollars a month.

- **Co-payments.** States may charge a co-payment—as Medicare does for the first few days of nursing facility care—which is a fixed amount for each covered service you receive. States can only charge those who qualify for Medicaid as "medically needy" (see above) or receive "optional" services (those the state program decides to cover, even though federal law doesn't require it).

3. Medicaid Long-Term Care Facility Coverage

Unlike Medicare, Medicaid can be a lifesaver when it comes to long-term care facility bills. In general, Medicaid pays for all levels of care in certified facilities for an indefinite period of time.

a. Levels of Care Covered

In all states, Medicaid covers residence in certified skilled nursing facilities. But unlike Medicare, this coverage does not require a prior hospital stay.

The greatest advantage Medicaid has over Medicare is that state Medicaid programs also cover residence in certified intermediate care and custodial care facilities, as well as some assisted living residences in a few states. This means that Medicaid will cover the situation that most commonly exhausts a family's savings: a long-term stay in a personal care facility where the resident receives primarily non-medical custodial care.

Unlike Medicare, Medicaid coverage is not limited to a certain number of days. Medicaid covers residence in a certified long-term care facility indefinitely. However, if you are in a skilled or intermediate care facility, Medicaid may review the level of care you are receiving. If Medicaid determines that the higher level of care is no longer medically necessary, it can require you to move to a custodial care facility, if you want Medicaid to keep paying for your care.

b. How Much Medicaid Pays

Some state Medicaid programs pay only a certain percentage of the cost of care. Check in advance with both the facility and your local Medicaid social worker to determine what Medicaid will cover and how much it will pay.

In general, Medicaid pays a nursing or other qualifying residential facility a daily rate that covers medical and personal or custodial care, rehabilitation therapies provided by the facility and room and board. For anything Medicaid covers, the facility must accept Medicaid's payment as payment in full. The facility cannot bill you for any additional amounts for covered services. Among the personal care items for which the facility may not charge extra to a Medicaid resident are nonprescription drugs, incontinence supplies, razors, soaps, tooth care items and services such as laundry and basic hair and nail grooming. In some states, more items and services are covered. You can get a full list of what is covered from the facility, the facility's ombudsman or the social services office that administers Medicaid in the county where the facility is located.

C. Finding Out About Medicaid in Your State

PROTECT YOUR ASSETS

Before you apply for Medicaid, read Chapter 8 and consider taking the steps explained there to help protect some of your assets from nursing facility and other costs.

To qualify for Medicaid, you must file a written application to the agency that handles Medicaid on the local level, usually the county Department of Social Services, Health Department or Welfare Department. If you or a family member is already hospitalized or in a long-term care facility, ask the institution's medical social worker to assist you in obtaining and filling out the applications.

You should bring some financial documents with you when you apply. Even if you do not have all of the following documents, go ahead and begin the application process. The Medicaid eligibility workers can help you get whatever papers and documents are necessary, including:.

- recent interest and dividend statements, your previous year's income tax return and recent pension and Social Security benefit papers or deposit slips indicating your current income

- papers showing all your financial assets, such as bank books, insurance policies, stock certificates and car registration (if you used the assets worksheet in Chapter 1, bring documents relating to all the assets you listed there)
- rent receipts, lease agreement or canceled rent checks if you are a renter, or your mortgage payment book and latest tax assessment on the property if you're a home owner
- your Social Security card or number
- if you live with your spouse, information about his or her income and separate assets, and
- medical bills from the previous three months. If you are planning on home care or residence in a care facility in the near future, bring medical records or reports that confirm your condition will require that type of care. If you don't have records or reports, bring the names and addresses of doctors who are treating you.

A Medicaid eligibility worker will interview and assist you in filling out your application. Write down his or her name and telephone extension in case you have specific questions during the application process.

You may have to make several visits and wait through some delays in processing your application while the proper documents are located and reviewed. Normally you will receive a decision within a few weeks; the law says the agency must make a decision within 45 days after your application is complete. If you don't hear from Medicaid within 30 days after completing your application, call the Medicaid social worker who interviewed you and ask what's going on. Social service and Medicaid agencies are very overworked; sometimes a person's application gets delayed in the shuffle. Stay on top of things so your application isn't delayed any more than necessary.

> **THE RETROACTIVE COVERAGE RULE**
>
> If you become eligible for Medicaid, you may be covered for
> home care or long-term care facility costs incurred since the
> beginning of the third month before you filed your application.
> You must present proof that you incurred covered costs during
> that time. Make sure to tell your Medicaid eligibility worker
> when you apply that you want retroactive coverage.

D. What to Do If You Are Denied Medicaid Coverage

If you are notified that you do not qualify for Medicaid, or that
coverage is denied for a particular service, facility or time period, you
have a right to what is called a "fair hearing" to determine if the
decision is correct. If you receive notice of a decision that you think is
wrong, inquire immediately, at the office where you applied, about
the procedure in your state for getting a fair hearing.

The rules for a fair hearing vary. In general, you are permitted to
have a friend, relative, social worker, lawyer or other representative
appear with you and testify about your financial situation, medical
condition or expenses if such evidence would be helpful. The hearing
itself is informal—you will be able to explain your position in your
own words, without having to worry about legal technicalities or
jargon. If your medical condition or need for treatment is in question,
a detailed letter from your doctor would be of great help. The hearing
officer who makes the decision is a Medicaid eligibility specialist
rather than a judge.

HELP FROM HICAP

The Health Insurance Counseling and Advocacy Program (HICAP) can be a tremendous help to seniors trying to qualify for Medicaid. HICAP is funded through a combination of government grants and private donations. It provides free counseling to seniors about Medicaid and related medical coverage matters. HICAP's trained staff can counsel you about your state's Medicaid eligibility standards—and the documents you will need to prove that you meet those standards. To find the HICAP office nearest you, call the toll-free number for your state's central HICAP office. You can find this number in the Resource Directory in the Appendix.

Although the odds of getting a Medicaid denial reversed at a fair hearing are not in your favor, such reversals do happen. And the amount of money at stake is large enough to make it worth the effort. Even if the fair hearing officer decides against you, there may be procedures in your state for further appeal. You will probably receive information about that appeal along with the fair hearing decision. If not, check with your local social service office.

FREE ASSISTANCE GETTING NURSING FACILITY COVERAGE

If you are entering a nursing or personal care facility and are having trouble either being accepted for Medicaid or getting Medicaid to cover that facility, contact your state's Nursing Home Ombudsman. The ombudsman program is financed by the federal government. Its purpose is to assist people with problems relating to nursing facilities. There is no charge for using its services. You can find your local office of the Nursing Home Ombudsman under that name in the white pages of your telephone directory, or through Senior Information and Referral. Your area, state or local Agency on Aging, or the central ombudsman office for your state can also refer you to the ombudsman. (See the Resource Directory in the Appendix at the back of this book.)

■

8

Medicaid and Asset Protection

A. Medicaid Rules on Transfer of Assets

As discussed in Chapter 7, a person is only eligible for Medicaid when his or her assets are reduced to minimum levels, which vary depending on your state's rules, your marital status and the type of care you need. A person (and spouse) must personally pay all long-term care costs—for home care or a long-term care facility—until assets have been spent down to Medicaid levels.

To avoid spending all their savings on long-term care before Medicaid begins coverage, many people used to give away assets—or at least transfer legal title—to children or other relatives, then apply for Medicaid. But Medicaid rules now severely restrict such transfers. Today, there is no simple way to keep your assets and also qualify for Medicaid. Long-range planning may permit someone to qualify for Medicaid while his or her assets remain with family members, but only if the Medicaid applicant has relinquished personal control over the assets.

Before learning about the few ways to protect family assets through long-term planning, you have to understand the basic rules Medicaid uses to judge whether a transfer of one type of asset or another is proper.

1. Penalized Transfers

There is one basic Medicaid rule limiting your ability to transfer assets: Anything transferred out of your name during the 36 months before you apply for Medicaid or enter a long-term care facility (if you are already receiving Medicaid), is considered an invalid transfer. If you have placed the asset in an irrevocable trust rather than transferring it to another person, the look-back period is 60 months, not 36. The effect of this rule is that your eligibility for Medicaid will be delayed for a period of time beginning on the date of the transfer. Medicaid calculates this delay by dividing the value of the asset transferred by the average monthly nursing facility cost in your state. In essence, this rule wipes out any potential benefit from the transfer by requiring you to come up with an equivalent amount of money to pay for your care.

Example. *You transfer a certificate of deposit worth $10,000 to your daughter a month before applying for Medicaid long-term care facility coverage. The average monthly long-term care facility cost in your state is $3,333. The penalty for your transfer within the 36-month period is figured by dividing the amount transferred ($10,000) by the average monthly facility cost ($3,333), which equals 3. So, for three months from the date of the transfer, you would be ineligible for Medicaid and would have to pay your own costs.*

A QUESTION OF ETHICS

This section of the book discusses ways in which Medicaid rules permit people to transfer assets to become eligible for Medicare coverage and to protect assets from Medicaid reimbursement. In other words, these rules permit people to keep their money, yet have their long-term care costs paid for by the government as if they were broke.

These rules—and the way some have chosen to apply them—have rankled many. Medicaid was enacted as a safety net for the poor. Many elderly people truly become impoverished because of their high medical costs. Medicaid saves their dignity, and prolongs their lives, by guaranteeing a decent level of care. But this care comes at a cost to taxpayers—a cost that our society has declared a willingness to pay. However, the public hasn't yet voiced support for assisting the elderly who have assets. A truly compassionate society might provide free long-term care for all its citizens, but ours has not shown a willingness to pay—through taxation—for it.

Despite recent changes tightening up the rules, some people with sizable assets are still able to skirt around the edges of the law and get Medicaid to pick up the tab for their long-term care. Following the rules carefully makes this legal. Whether it is entirely ethical—that is, whether it is a violation of the spirit of the Medicaid law and of the position of those who have refused to support long-term care for all—is a different question. And one which each person who considers these rules must answer privately.

2. Permissible Transfers

Medicaid permits some exceptions to this 36-month rule. These exceptions differ considerably depending on marital status. And they vary greatly depending on whether an asset is exempt or non-exempt. (To review which assets are exempt, see Chapter 7A.)

a. Unmarried Individuals

An unmarried person can transfer the assets listed below without any eligibility penalty.

Home. A home can be transferred:

- to the Medicaid applicant's minor child (through a custodianship or trust arrangement) or to the applicant's blind or disabled child of any age
- to the applicant's child of any age, if the child has lived in the home for two years prior to the parent's entry into a nursing facility and cared for the parent, allowing the parent to remain at home rather than enter a nursing facility during that time, or
- to a brother or sister who already has some ownership interest in the property and has lived in the home for at least the previous year.

Other exempt assets. You may transfer to anyone, at any time, your car worth up to $4,500, personal or household belongings, your engagement or wedding rings or other exempt assets. (See the list of exempt assets in Chapter 7.)

Nonexempt assets. You may transfer any asset, at any time, to your minor, blind or disabled child. You may also transfer any asset at any time to any person if you can prove to Medicaid that you made the transfer for some reason *other* than to qualify for Medicaid eligibility, such as to help a relative in need.

b. Married People Entering a Long-Term Care Facility

As discussed in Chapter 7A, Medicaid rules give married couples an advantage over unmarried people by permitting an at-home spouse to retain some liquid assets and income. The rules also provide an additional benefit by allowing the couple to change the title on their home when one spouse enters a long-term care facility.

Home. A married person can transfer title to a home to his or her spouse before or after entering a long-term care facility. Although the home is exempt as long as the spouse is living in it, it may be best to transfer title to the at-home spouse, who can then transfer the home to children or others in case the at-home spouse should die first. A married person can also transfer title to the home to any of the people an unmarried person can transfer to, as described above.

Other exempt assets. A married person can transfer exempt assets to anyone at any time. (Refer to Chapter 7 for the list of a married couple's exempt assets.)

Other assets. You can transfer any assets, at any time, to your minor, blind or disabled child. Any asset can also be transferred to anyone at any time if the person making the transfer can prove that the transfer was for some purpose other than to qualify for Medicaid eligibility. To qualify for this exception, you will need convincing proof that you made the transfer for a valid reason—for example, to help a brother or sister keep a failing business or to pay a child's medical costs that aren't covered by insurance.

Before applying for Medicaid, a spouse may transfer any nonexempt asset to his or her at-home spouse, but only if the at-home spouse does not transfer it to anyone else within 36 months for less than its true value. For example, nonexempt assets cannot be transferred to the sole name of the at-home spouse and then given immediately to the children.

B. Strategies to Protect Your Assets

This section discusses two separate but related questions.

Transfers for eligibility. If you have too many assets to qualify for Medicaid, are there lawful ways to transfer some of those assets so that you become eligible for Medicaid?

Transfers for asset protection. If you can qualify for Medicaid, are there lawful ways to transfer some assets so that they are out of reach when Medicaid seeks reimbursement after your death?

Each of the options discussed in this section has some drawbacks, and not all of them will be available to everyone. Carefully read through the rules to decide whether any of these options might be right for you.

> ## MEDICAID MAY RECOVER COST OF CARE
>
> Medicaid has the right to collect the entire amount it has spent on long-term care—whether home care or care in a long-term care facility—for anyone age 55 or over. It recoups this money out of any assets in the Medicaid recipient's estate at death. If assets have been lawfully transferred out of the Medicaid recipient's name before death, without violating Medicaid's transfer rules (see Section A2), those assets cannot be taken for Medicaid reimbursement.
>
> Usually, the largest asset from which Medicaid can seek reimbursement is the recipient's home. Medicaid can place a lien on the property and collect on the lien whenever the property is sold, if the recipient:
>
> - is in a long-term care facility
> - is not expected to return home as certified by a physician, and
> - has no spouse, minor or disabled child or sibling who has an equity interest in the property and lives in the home.
>
> However, if the recipient, spouse or minor or disabled child or sibling with an equity interest in the property is living in the home, or the recipient intends to return to the home, the rule is different. In these situations, Medicaid cannot place a lien on the home but must wait to collect its reimbursement out of the recipient's estate.
>
> The amount to which Medicaid is entitled as a reimbursement may be decreased if the Medicaid recipient had secured a state partnership long-term care insurance policy. (See Section B7.)

1. Transfers 36 Months Before Medicaid Application

Although many people need long-term care as the result of an accidental injury or the sudden onset of illness—a stroke or heart attack, for example—many others need care because of a slowly deteriorating physical or mental condition. If you are gradually heading toward the need for long-term care, one of the ways you may financially plan for it is to divest yourself of assets that might make you ineligible for Medicaid. Any asset you transfer more than 36 months prior to applying for Medicaid will not be considered in determining your eligibility.

As long as you do it well ahead of time, you can transfer liquid assets to your children or to others whom you would eventually want to give them to anyway. For many, the main problem with this approach is that when you give away assets, you lose control over them. If you later need the funds or change your mind about giving them away, you must depend on the cooperation of those to whom you gave the assets. And you risk the possibility that they will have already spent, invested or otherwise used them.

TAX CONSEQUENCES OF PROPERTY TRANSFERS

Transferring your home or other valuable assets may have unforeseen gift tax and income tax consequences. See Chapter 10 for information on these consequences—and how to minimize them.

---

2. Investments in Your Home

Because Medicaid rules often exempt a home of any value from asset eligibility limits, concentrating your assets in your home is a good way to protect them. Investing in your home may help you qualify for Medicaid. And if you follow some of the other steps discussed here, you can also protect the value added to your home from Medicaid claims for reimbursement. Both unmarried individuals and couples can use this strategy, but the rules are different for each and must be carefully followed.

Assuming you don't have other immediate needs for your savings or investments, you could put those assets into your home by:

- paying off your outstanding mortgage
- making home improvements or large-scale repairs, or
- buying a new home or condominium for more money than your present home is worth (for the home to be protected, you or your spouse must live in it).

a. Home Investment by Unmarried Individuals

The rules governing an unmarried individual's ability to affect Medicaid eligibility and reimbursement by investing in a home depend on whether the person lives in the home or moves into a long-term care facility. In either case, you may require some assistance from a lawyer or tax accountant familiar with Medicaid procedures. A brief explanation of possible options follows.

Long-term home care. As long as an unmarried individual continues to live at home, Medicaid will pay for long-term home care regardless of the value of the house. So if you have too many nonexempt assets to qualify for Medicaid, investing the excess assets in your house would permit you to qualify.

States without a strict "return home" rule. Medicaid rules in some states permit unmarried long-term care facility residents to exempt their homes—meaning that the value of their homes does not disqualify them from Medicaid coverage. This is true even if the individuals are unlikely to return to live in those homes. The only requirement is that the individual entering a facility must state on the admission form that he or she intends to return home. If you live in a state with such a rule, you may be free to invest assets in your home, thereby making them exempt. Check with the local Department of Social Services, Health Department or Welfare Department to find out the current rule in your locale. (See Chapter 7C.)

Exempt child or sibling. If your adult child or sibling lives in your home and would qualify the home as an exempt asset, you may want to invest further in the home. (See Section A2, above.)

Transfer to nonexempt adult child. Even if it would not qualify the house as an exempt asset, you may still want to consider investing assets in the house and transferring title to a son or daughter. This requires you to give up control over the property, so you must trust your child to manage it according to your wishes. Also, you should do this only if you want the home to belong to that child after your death.

If you transfer your home to your child, you won't have to sell the home to pay your own nursing facility bills. If you transfer the home more than 36 months before you apply for Medicaid for long-term facility coverage, the value of the home will not affect your Medicaid eligibility at all. If you transfer it within 36 months before entering a long-term care facility, your eligibility will be delayed for a period equal to the value of the home divided by the average monthly long-term care facility cost in your state. (See the explanation of the Medicaid 36-month rule in Section A1 of this chapter.) For example, if the equity in your home is $100,000, you could be denied Medicaid coverage for 18 months to three years, depending on the cost of care in your state. One month of coverage will be denied for roughly every $3,500 to $4,000 of equity.

Creating a life estate. A "life estate" is a legal maneuver that transfers title to property without affecting who has the right to use the property.

Here's how it works. The elder signs a legal document creating a life estate in the home, which permits the elder to live there for the rest of his or her life. The life estate "remainder"—the value remaining after the death of the homeowner—goes to the homeowner's children, or any other person designated.

The Medicaid advantage of a life estate is that it reduces the assets of an unmarried person in a long-term care facility. Most states normally count the full value of the home in calculating assets. The homeowner must sell it and use the funds to pay for facility care before becoming eligible for Medicaid. With a life estate, the elder no longer has the value of the entire home as an asset, but only has the value of remaining there for life. If a person must enter a long-term care facility with the possibility of not returning home or of not living many years there, then the value of the life estate is far smaller than the value of the home. The elder would only be required to spend an amount equal to the value of the life estate, rather than the greater value of the home, before being eligible for Medicaid.

Creating a life estate for Medicaid purposes is a technical legal maneuver that requires sound advice and assistance from an attorney experienced in estate planning and Medicaid rules.

b. Home Investment by Couples

A home is a particularly good place for a married couple to invest savings or other assets. Even if one spouse enters a long-term care facility, as long as the other spouse lives at home, the home is completely exempt from Medicaid eligibility limits—no matter how much it is worth.

Investing in the home may only be the first step towards protecting those assets. You can also consider these additional steps.

Title transfer to spouse. If one spouse enters a long-term care facility, he or she could transfer sole title to the property to the spouse who remains at home. The spouse at home could then transfer the property to children or others (but not back to the spouse in the facility). The transfer can be made by immediate gift, or by a provision in a will or living trust under which the property will not actually transfer until the at-home spouse's death.

This transfer protects against the possibility of the at-home spouse dying first. In that case, if the spouse in the facility still held title to the property, the value of the home would be used to reimburse Medicaid for all the money it had spent on care for the facility spouse.

Also, once the home is in the sole name of the at-home spouse, he or she may be able to make good use of the equity by, for example, selling the home and using the money. There are also other equity conversion devices an at-home spouse can consider. Reverse annuity mortgages, for example, allow a homeowner to use the home's equity as collateral for a loan; the lender then makes monthly or lump sum payments to the homeowner.

To know what effect transfer of title, sale of your home, living trusts or equity conversion devices might have on your tax liability and Medicaid eligibility, you should seek the advice of a lawyer, accountant or business advisor who is familiar with both Medicaid rules and tax laws.

3. Investing in Other Exempt Assets

A home is not the only asset automatically exempt from Medicaid eligibility limits. Those listed below are also exempt. Up to each state's limits, you can invest in these assets without affecting your Medicaid eligibility:

- an automobile (up to a value of $4,500 for an individual, of any value for a couple)
- furniture and household goods (of any value in some states; only up to a certain dollar limit in others)
- one wedding and one engagement ring per person of any value (individual or couple)—they don't have to be the original engagement or wedding rings; so you can buy a new ring at any time, and
- a burial plot and separate burial fund up to a cash value of $1,500 for each spouse.

4. Transferring Nonexempt Assets to At-Home Spouse

Although transferring nonexempt assets from a spouse in a long-term care facility to an at-home spouse will not prevent Medicaid from counting those assets towards its eligibility limits (unless they are then transferred to others before Medicaid is applied for, see Section 1, above), such a transfer can save a lot of money if the at-home spouse dies before the spouse in the facility.

When one spouse is a resident in a long-term care facility, Medicaid counts the joint assets of the couple and allows the couple to keep one-half of those combined assets—in some states up to $90,660. But an unmarried facility resident can keep only about $2,000. If the at-home spouse dies, the spouse in the facility becomes an unmarried individual who can only keep $2,000, and the $90,660 the couple had been allowed to keep then automatically goes to pay long-term care facility bills.

A couple can avoid losing most of this benefit by taking two simple steps. First, the facility spouse transfers the $90,660 into the sole name of the at-home spouse. Then, the at-home spouse makes a will or creates a living trust that leaves the money to the children or to anyone other than the spouse in the facility. If the at-home spouse dies first, the money goes to the children or other named beneficiary and not to the long-term care facility. (See next section.)

5. Transferring Assets to Children or Others

We've already discussed some strategies to protect your assets by transferring them to your children (or to anyone else other than your spouse) without jeopardizing your Medicaid long-term care facility eligibility. Here are a few more points to consider when transferring assets. Remember that transferring assets to children or others means giving up control of those assets. If you need to use the assets, you must depend on the goodwill of your children or anyone else to whom you have transferred them.

a. Transfers of Exempt Assets

Exempt assets—such as your home, car or household goods—may be transferred to children or anyone else even within the 36-month Medicaid no-transfer period. But if assets are exempt, why bother to transfer them? Look back at the Medicaid rules for exempt assets (Chapter 7) and you will see that the exemptions for a married couple with one spouse in a long-term care facility are far more generous than for an unmarried individual. But if the at-home spouse dies, a couple's exempt property—home, car, household goods of any value and up to $90,660 in savings—instantly becomes an unmarried person's nonexempt property—and so, a source for paying facility bills. To protect against that, some people transfer title to exempt property as well.

b. Payments to Children for Services

Unmarried individuals are at a disadvantage in trying to pass assets to their children or others. Because there is no spouse through whom assets can be transferred, many Medicaid exemption rules do not apply.

One way around this problem is to not transfer assets at all, but instead to pay a child or other person for services performed for you. Such services might be personal care or assistance, transportation, housekeeping or paperwork—almost any reasonable service you would otherwise have to pay someone else to do. Because these are payments rather than transfers, they do not count as transferred assets. However, the Internal Revenue Service and state tax agencies consider these payments as income to the people receiving them, and may require them to pay income tax on the amounts received.

As you might guess, Medicaid looks very closely at such arrangements to make sure they aren't fraudulent. The services performed must be reasonable—and you must have some proof that they were actually performed. Also, the payments must be reasonable for the services rendered: A thousand dollars for one housecleaning won't pass muster. But payment to an adult child or grandchild for regular housecleaning or transportation, for example, might be acceptable if you pay them about what you would have to pay a private house-cleaning company or taxi service.

6. Medicaid and Divorce

It may seem strange to think of divorce in connection with long-term care. Unfortunately, however, the Medicaid income and assets limits have forced more than a few couples to divorce for solely economic reasons. If all other methods for transferring or otherwise protecting your assets are unavailable, or continuing income presents an eligibility problem, you may at least want to consider the unpleasant alternative of divorce. Remember, though, that changing your Medicaid status requires only the formal, legal divorce. A couple need not stop living together, but they must separate their bank accounts and joint income, change title to property and otherwise shift their financial interests to reflect separate lives. Any asset they continue to own or control jointly will be considered part of the Medicaid applicant's assets.

This situation often arises when a couple must choose either to enter a long-term care facility and be covered by Medicaid, or to remain home without coverage. About 30 states have no income eligibility levels for Medicaid coverage of residential facility care; the other states have income levels of $700 to $1,500 per month for eligibility, but allow the at-home spouse to keep all income in his or her name. And all states allow the at-home spouse of a facility resident to keep between $18,322 and $90,660 in savings or other assets.

For nonresidential facility care, on the other hand, all states place severe limits on the amount of income and assets a couple can have and still qualify for Medicaid coverage. A couple may thus be forced to choose either to get care at home and be disqualified from Medicare, or to get divorced. A divorce permits the working spouse to keep all of his or her income without disqualifying the other spouse, and protects at least half of the couple's assets without limit. The spouse (now ex-spouse) needing care can then remain at home and receive Medicaid-covered home care.

A couple may face the same difficult choice even when one spouse is already in a long-term care facility. If a couple has considerably more in savings and other nonexempt assets than the Medicaid rules of their state would permit them to keep, a divorce settlement that gives more assets to the at-home spouse than Medicaid would have allowed the couple to keep may protect some of those savings.

These are all matters that depend on both the specific Medicaid rules and the divorce laws of your state. If divorce seems like the best last resort for you, consult a lawyer who is familiar with both sets of laws.

7. Special Long-Term Care Insurance Available in Some States

Programs in California, Connecticut, Indiana and New York provide some asset protection for those who buy special long-term care insurance policies. These states have watched many people use asset transfers to spend down their assets and then qualify for Medicaid—costing their state programs huge amounts of money. To get more people with assets and income to pay for some of their own long-term care, the Medicaid programs in these states encourage people to buy special state-certified long-term care insurance policies to cover a portion of their care. In exchange, Medicaid promises to permit the insured person to keep more assets than normal Medicaid rules permit.

These programs come in two types, and they protect different amounts of assets in different ways.

a. California, Connecticut and Indiana

In the California, Connecticut and Indiana programs, each state protects assets above its normal asset limits in an amount equal to the benefits paid under the special long-term care insurance policy. In other words, when the insured person applies for Medicaid coverage, whatever the special insurance policy has paid out in benefits is added to the amount of assets the Medicaid applicant is entitled to keep. However, these applicants still have to meet the same income eligibility rules as all other Medicaid applicants. These state partnership policies must also offer some of the best terms available for home care benefits, automatic inflation protection and nonforfeiture benefits. (But see Section C, "Additional Benefits and Risks," below.)

Example. *Mr. X, an unmarried man, purchased a state partnership long-term care policy. The policy paid $100 per day in nursing facility costs for Mr. X for two years, for a total of $75,000. Mr. X qualified for Medicaid coverage for continuing long-term care after his insurance benefits ran out and as soon as his savings and other countable assets were down to $75,000. Without the policy, Mr. X would have had to spend his savings down to $2,000 before Medicaid started to pay for his long-term care costs.*

b. New York

The New York model goes even further in protecting assets. A New York Partnership Policy requires the policyholder to use almost all of his or her income to pay for long-term care, once policy benefits run out. But Medicaid will pay all remaining long-term care costs. And the insured person may retain *all* of his or her assets, no matter how valuable.

c. Additional Benefits and Risks

In addition to their asset-protecting terms, most policies offered under these state partnership programs also have other relatively good features. They must offer—at some additional cost—home and community care coverage in addition to institutional care. Most of these policies also offer good benefits, inflation protection and level premiums. (See Chapter 11 for an explanation of these terms and their importance in choosing a policy.)

But as with all long-term care insurance, if you are considering a state partnership policy, you must compare its terms to those offered in other policies. Although these Medicaid-partner policies generally offer good terms and some asset protection, for most consumers they also present the same basic risks as do other long-term care policies. The first and foremost of these risks, as explained in Chapter 11, is that any long-term care policy is a gamble. These partnership policies, like all others, are expensive. Over the years, you pay significant premiums to protect against the chance that you will someday need substantial long-term care.

The likelihood that you will need a two- or three-year period of care in a long-term residential facility, however, is only about 30% for women and 15% for men who reach age 65. Only about 10% to 15%

remain in a facility for more than three years. The numbers of people who need some sort of long-term home care is greater, but the average cost of such care is significantly less than the cost of institutional care. If it turns out that you do not need long-term care at all, or need it only for a relatively short time, all the money you spend on years of insurance premiums will have been wasted.

A second risk is the possibility that you will not be able to afford to continue paying premiums and therefore will lose your coverage. Even state partnership policies are expensive. If your income drops in your later years, the premiums may become too much for your budget. If so, you may decide you have to drop your coverage just as you reach the years when you are most likely to need it. And the years of premiums you have already paid would wind up being nearly a total loss, depending on the level of reduced benefits or the non-forfeiture provision in your policy. (See Chapter 11G.)

Another risk with an asset-protecting policy is that the cost of long-term care in some urban areas may eat up most of your assets before Medicaid ever kicks in to cover you. For example, if you have a policy that pays $100 per day in long-term care facility costs, but the facility you choose charges $175 per day—as many do in California, Connecticut and New York—the uncovered part of your costs ($75/day) would mount up to $82,000 in three years. If you have well over $100,000 in assets to protect in addition to your home, the policy might work to preserve a portion of those assets. However, if you have less than $100,000 in assets other than your home, the policy would allow you to save very little—even though you will spend a tremendous amount in premiums over the years.

For some people, a major drawback with these asset-protection policies is that they do not protect income. If you expect to have substantial income while you receive long-term care, that income will be unprotected and may disqualify you from Medicaid—even though your assets would otherwise be protected. A Medicaid recipient may keep only a small amount of income—$30 to $75 per month for a residential facility resident, and $500 to $600 per month for someone receiving home care—even with a state partnership policy.

These state partnership policies also present the risk that, if you wind up receiving care in another state, that other state's Medicaid program will not honor the agreement with the state where you bought the policy. The policy itself will remain enforceable—that is, the insurance company must pay benefits—but the asset-protection provision will have gone out the window because you will be bound by the new state's Medicaid rules. This presents a particular risk if you are in your 50s or 60s when you buy a policy, because you may not know whether you will remain in the same state for the next 20 to 30 years. It may also be risky if most or all of your supporting family—siblings, children and adult grandchildren—live in other states. If so, you might want to move to receive care near your family.

Finally, all the other pitfalls of long-term care insurance apply to Medicaid partner policies as well. These problems are discussed in Chapter 11. Before making a decision, read that chapter carefully and examine and compare all the terms of an asset-protecting policy just as you would any other long-term care policy. ■

Protecting Choices About Medical Care and Finances

One of the difficult truths about aging is that, when physical or mental capacities diminish, many elders must depend on others to take care of life's business for them. A number of legal and practical roadblocks often complicate this shifting of responsibilities, however. And if an elder becomes entirely incapable of making decisions, there can be enormous problems, not only in getting matters decided, but in making sure those decisions reflect the elder's wishes.

This chapter discusses how elders can ensure that their rights, dignity and wishes are protected if they become incapable of making or communicating decisions about medical treatment. It also discusses how elders can arrange to have someone else manage if they become incapable of doing so.

A. Health Care Decisions

The increasing use of life-sustaining medical technology over the last decades has made many of us fear that our lives may be artificially prolonged against our wishes. The right to die with dignity, and without the tremendous agony and expense for both patient and family that prolonging life artificially can cause, has now been addressed by the U.S. Supreme Court, the federal government and the laws of every state.

The right to control medical decisions also extends to situations where doctors might wish to provide a patient with less extensive care than he or she would like. For example, a doctor may be reluctant to administer long-term treatments to a patient who has slim chances of recovering.

In 1990, the United States Supreme Court held that every individual has the constitutional right to control his or her own medical treatment. The Court also declared that medical personnel must abide by a person's wishes, as long as they are demonstrated by "clear and convincing evidence." (*Cruzan v. Director, Missouri Dept. of Health,* 497 U.S. 261.)

1. Documents Protecting Medical Care Choices

Every state has laws authorizing individuals to create a health care directive—a simple document that provides the necessary "clear and convincing evidence" of that person's wishes concerning life-prolonging medical care. States have come up with several different names for this document, including Living Will, Declaration or Advance Directive.

Medical personnel must follow the directions expressed in the document if an individual is no longer capable of communicating his or her choices regarding life-prolonging and other medical care. These documents take effect only when a patient is diagnosed to have a terminal condition, to be in a permanent coma or, in a few states, to have some additional serious medical condition. Health care directives are not used when a person is able to communicate those wishes to doctors in any way or is only temporarily unconscious or incapacitated.

Your written medical care instructions can help alleviate your fears that unwanted medical treatment will be administered to you or that desired medical treatment will be withheld. It can also help relieve family members from having to make agonizing decisions about your medical treatment. This can be particularly important when family members have conflicting ideas about what care you should receive. Also, doctors and hospitals have their own rules and beliefs about what constitutes proper medical treatment. Even if your family knows your wishes and tries to have them followed, medical personnel are not necessarily bound to follow them unless you have completed and signed a valid document.

2. Differences Among Medical Care Documents

The two basic types of documents that direct medical care are the health care directive and the durable power of attorney for health care or health care proxy.

The basic difference between the two documents is simple. The directive is a statement you make directly to medical personnel that spells out the medical care you do or do not wish to receive if you become terminally ill and incapacitated. It acts as a contract with the treating doctor, who must either honor the wishes for medical care that you have expressed or transfer you to another doctor or facility that will honor them.

In a durable power of attorney or health care proxy, you can appoint someone else to make sure your doctors provide you with the kind of medical care you wish to receive. In some states, you can also give the person you appoint the broader authority to make all decisions about your medical care on your behalf. In some states, you may spell out your medical care wishes and name a person to act on your behalf in a single document.

WHEN YOUR STATE FORM IS NOT ENOUGH

When it comes to health care directives, there are many state differences in the terminology, forms and formats used. Some state laws require you to use a specific form for your directive to be valid. However, regardless of your state's requirements, your goal is to make sure that your directions to doctors and other medical personnel are clear. If you feel strongly about a particular kind of care—even if your state law or form does not mention it—you should include your specific requests in your directive. If you are using a specific state form that does not adequately address your concerns, write them in on the form— and ask that they be respected and followed.

---

3. What to Include in a Health Care Directive

When completing their state forms directing health care, many people are unsure how to fill in the blanks—and are unsure what much of the terminology means. Although medical technology and treatments evolve over time, filling out the forms is not as difficult as it may seem at first. In most health care documents, you can direct:

- that all life-prolonging procedures be provided
- that all life-prolonging procedures be withheld, or
- that some procedures be provided—particularly comfort care, as discussed below—while others are withheld.

The following medical procedures and treatments are usually considered to be in the category of "life-prolonging." You can include specific directions about any or all of them.

- *Artificial breathing apparatus, such as a respirator or ventilator.* Some people specify that they want artificial breathing while they are conscious, but not if they lapse into unconsciousness.

- *Artificial administration of food and water, also called nutrition and hydration.* As with artificial breathing, some people want food and water administered artificially as long as they are conscious, but not if they become unconscious. A few states, however, do not permit a doctor or hospital to withhold food and water even if you request that it be withheld. Again, if you feel strongly that you don't want artificial administration of food and water, but you live in a state that restricts your right to direct that, add your request to the health care directive you fill out—and ask that your wishes be respected and followed, as is your constitutional right.
- *Comfort care—including relief from pain and discomfort, usually through medication.* Many people specify that they want pain medication, but do not want any other life-prolonging measures.

To make an informed decision about which procedures you do and do not want, you should discuss your health care directive with your physician. He or she can explain the medical procedures more fully and discuss the options with you. You will also find out whether your doctor has any medical or moral objections to following your wishes. If your doctor does object and will not agree to follow your wishes, you may want to consider changing doctors.

4. Creating a Durable Power of Attorney for Health Care

Even after you have specified your wishes in a health care directive regarding life-prolonging and comfort care medical treatment, certain matters may still be difficult to resolve. They include:

- when, exactly, to administer or withhold certain medical treatments
- whether or not to provide, withhold or continue antibiotic or pain medication, and
- whether to pursue complex, painful and expensive surgeries which may serve to prolong life but cannot reverse the medical condition.

To deal with these situations, you can create a power of attorney for health care or health care proxy to appoint someone who understands your wishes and whose judgment you trust to make these decisions in accordance with your wishes and in your best interest. To help the appointed person make and carry out these decisions, the power of attorney or proxy form may include specific authorizations:

- to give, withhold or withdraw consent to medical or surgical procedures
- to consent to appropriate care for the end of life, including pain relief
- to hire and fire medical personnel
- to visit you in the hospital or other facility even when other visiting is restricted
- to have access to medical records and other personal information, and
- to get any court authorization required to obtain or withhold medical treatment if, for any reason, a hospital or doctor does not honor the document.

a. Choosing a Health Care Attorney-in-Fact or Proxy

There are a number of things to consider when choosing a health care attorney-in-fact or proxy. Some are obvious: You should choose someone who understands your wishes and will follow them.

But you also want to make sure the person you appoint:

- is likely to be present when decisions need to be made—most often, this means someone who lives nearby or who is willing to travel to be at your side during your hospitalization
- would not easily be bullied or intimidated by doctors or family members who disagree with your wishes, and
- is capable of understanding your medical condition and the proposed life-prolonging measures.

It is also a good idea to appoint a second person to act as a backup or replacement attorney-in-fact or proxy if your first choice is unable or unwilling to serve. Make it clear, however, that the second person is only a backup. It is not wise to appoint co-proxies: two decision-makers can only complicate the process.

DO NOT APPOINT YOUR DOCTOR

Although your attorney-in-fact or proxy should consult your doctor concerning all health care decisions, you should not appoint your doctor to act as attorney-in-fact or proxy. The laws in most states specifically forbid treating physicians from acting in this role—to avoid the possibility or appearance that they may have their own interests at heart and so may not be able to act purely according to your wishes.

---

5. Legal Rules and Conditions

As mentioned, each state makes its own rules concerning medical directives. Here are some of the rules and conditions of which you should be aware.

Required form. In some states, the document you use must contain language specifically required by special provisions in state law. (See Section 7, below.)

Signing, witnessing, notarizing. Every state requires that you sign your documents—or direct another person to sign them for you—to verify that you understand them and that they contain your true wishes.

Most state laws also require that you sign your documents in the presence of witnesses. The purpose of this additional formality is so that at least one other person can attest that you were the person that signed the document, and that you were of sound mind and of legal age when you did so.

QUALIFICATIONS FOR WITNESSES

Many states require that two witnesses see you sign your health care documents and that they verify, in writing, that you appeared to be of sound mind and signed the documents without anyone else influencing your decision.

Each state's qualifications for these witnesses are slightly different. In many states, for example, a spouse, other close relative or any person who would inherit property from you is not allowed to act as a witness for the document directing health care. And many states prohibit your attending physician from being a witness. In others, the person named as attorney-in-fact or proxy cannot also serve as a witness to the document.

The purpose of the laws is to avoid any appearance or possibility that another person was acting against your wishes in encouraging specific medical choices.

In addition to the requirement that witnesses sign your medical directives, some states also require that you and the witnesses appear before a notary public and swear that the circumstances of your signing, as described on the documents, are true. In some states, you have the option of having a notary sign your document instead of having it witnessed.

6. Changing Your Mind—and Documents

You can change your medical care documents at any time, as long as you are legally competent to do so. Therefore, neither your decisions about health care nor about the proxy you have named are necessarily final decisions. Any time you wish to change the terms or the proxy, however, you must prepare a new document and date, sign and have it witnessed and possibly notarized again—depending on the formalities that must be followed in your state. You should also make sure that all copies of the document you made earlier are destroyed.

7. Obtaining the Right Medical Directive Form

In most instances, you do not need to consult a lawyer to prepare medical care forms. The forms for use in your state are usually quite simple and can be completed without a lawyer's help. You can obtain these documents free or for a nominal fee, from a number of sources, such as:

- **Senior referral & information.** The white pages in most telephone directories have a listing for Senior Referral & Information. This number refers people to various agencies, groups and other sources of assistance for seniors. Call your local Senior Referral & Information number and ask where you can obtain your state's official health care directive form.

- **Local senior center.** Often, your local senior center will have copies of your state's medical directive form. If it does not have a copy, it may be able to obtain one for you.

- **Consumer organization.** The national nonprofit organization Partnership for Caring (formerly the Society for the Right to Die) is one of the nation's oldest patients' advocacy groups. You can order health care forms from Partnership for Caring for a small fee, or you can download them for free from the organization's website.

Partnership for Caring
1620 Eye Street #202, NW
Washington, DC 20006
800-989-9455
www.partnershipforcaring.org

- **Computer program.** *Quicken® Lawyer Personal* (Nolo) is an easy-to-use software program that helps you prepare and update a medical directive for any state (except Louisiana)—as well as a regular legal will, durable power of attorney for finances (see Section B) and final arrangements document describing your wishes about body donation, cremation or burial and funeral.

8. What to Do With Your Completed Documents

Once you have completed the documents directing your medical care, there are several additional steps you should take.

Make and distribute copies. Keep your signed, original health care documents where your attorney-in-fact or health care proxy can easily find them if the need arises. Also, give copies to:

- your attorney-in-fact or health care proxy
- any physician with whom you consult regularly
- the office of the hospital or other care facility in which you are likely to receive treatment
- the patient representative of your HMO or insurance plan
- close relatives, particularly immediate family members—a spouse, children or siblings
- trusted friends, and
- clergy or lawyer, particularly if you do not have a family member who lives nearby.

Keep your documents up-to-date. Review your health care documents occasionally—at least once a year—to make sure they still accurately reflect your wishes for your medical care. Advances in technology and changes in medical treatments prompt many people to change their minds about the kind of care they want.

In addition, you should consider making new documents if:

- you move to another state
- you made and finalized a health care directive many years ago, or
- the proxy or representative you named becomes unable to serve or you wish to change your proxy or representative.

KEEPING TRACK OF COPIES

Keep a list of all the people and places that have copies of your medical directive. If you later decide to change the terms of the directive, you will be able to retrieve each of the old copies or have them destroyed.

B. Financial Decisions

Wills and probate will take care of distributing your income and assets after you're gone, but they do not kick in until your death. If you are incapacitated and unable to make financial decisions, you will need another document, called a durable power of attorney for finances, to make sure your finances are handled as you wish.

A durable power of attorney for finances allows you to name someone (called you attorney-in-fact) to handle your finances if you become incapacitated. Every state recognizes this type of document. Preparing a durable power of attorney is simple and inexpensive—and will help those closest to you figure out how you want them to handle your financial affairs, should the need ever arise. If you don't prepare a power of attorney before you become incapacitated, your loved ones will have to ask a court to grant them authority over your financial affairs in a conservatorship or guardianship proceeding—which can be a time-consuming and expensive process. (See Section C for more on conservatorships and guardianships).

1. Granting Authority to Your Attorney-In-Fact

The success of any power of attorney arrangement depends on the trust and understanding between you and the person you appoint as your attorney-in-fact. You can help make this relationship work by putting specific instructions in your document about the particular financial actions you do and do not want the attorney-in-fact to take. Your attorney-in-fact has only the financial authority you grant in your document. You can tailor the document to your specific financial situation, granting your attorney-in-fact the authority to pay routine bills, make bank deposits, handle Social Security, insurance and other paperwork, make investments, operate your business or even sell your home.

You may want to define and limit your attorney-in-fact's authority over certain financial matters. But keep in mind that you can't predict every financial issue that might arise in the future. To make sure that even unexpected financial matters are handled as you would want them to be, you must choose someone you trust, and who has sound financial judgment, to be your attorney-in-fact. It usually makes sense to name the same person you choose as your attorney-in-fact for healthcare decisions, unless that person isn't good with money. If you name two different people for these jobs, make sure they can—and will—work together.

HOW TO FIND THE FORMS YOU NEED

You can use *Quicken® WillMaker Plus* software from Nolo to prepare a durable power of attorney for finances that is valid in your state. If you live in California, you can also use the book *Medical Directives & Powers of Attorney for California*, by Shae Irving (Nolo).

---

2. Deciding When Your Durable Power of Attorney Should Take Effect

There are two types of durable powers of attorney for finances: those that take effect immediately, and those that don't go into effect unless and until a doctor certifies that you are incapacitated. Which one you should use depends on when you want your attorney-in-fact to start handling your financial affairs—and on the relationship you have with your attorney-in-fact.

If you want someone to take over some or all of your financial tasks now, you should make your document effective as soon as you sign it. Your attorney-in-fact can start helping you right away, and can continue to do so if you later are unable to make decisions for yourself.

If you want to make all of your own financial decisions unless and until you become incapacitated, you have two options. If you trust your attorney-in-fact not to take over until it's absolutely necessary, you can make your power of attorney effective immediately. This gives your attorney-in-fact the legal authority to act on your behalf should the need arise, but you can still handle your finances yourself.

If you don't want to make your document effective immediately, you can execute a "springing" power of attorney—a document that gives your attorney-in-fact the power to act only if you are declared incapacitated, in writing, by a doctor.

Springing powers of attorney are attractive to many people—they allow you to keep maximum authority over your own affairs, and permit someone else to step in only if absolutely necessary. However, there are a few drawbacks to springing powers of attorney. First, your attorney-in-fact will have to go through the potentially time-consuming and complicated process of getting a doctor to declare you incapacitated. Second, some people and institutions are reluctant to accept a springing power of attorney, even though the document is perfectly legal. An institution might insist on proof that you are really incapacitated, for example, or might hold up a transaction while it satisfies itself that the document is valid. Although these hassles don't come up very often, they can cause delays and disruptions.

3. Finalizing and Changing Your Documents

After you've completed your durable power of attorney for finances, you must observe a few formalities to make it legal. You must sign your power of attorney in the presence of a notary public for your state. In some states, notarization is legally required to make the document valid. But even if it isn't legally required, signing before a notary will make life easier for your attorney-in-fact. People and institutions often expect to see a notarized document—and may not accept one that isn't notarized, even though it's valid.

Some states also require you to sign your document in front of witnesses. Your witnesses must be mentally competent adults, and your attorney-in-fact may not act as a witness. A few states impose additional witness requirements—and some require your attorney-in-fact to sign the power of attorney or a separate consent form before taking action on your behalf.

If your document grants your attorney-in-fact power over real estate, you must file a copy of your document with the land records office of any county where you own real estate. This process is called "recording" or "registration." In two states, North Carolina and South Carolina, you must record your durable power of attorney in order for it to remain in effect if you become incapacitated.

Once you have finalized your document, you should give the original to your attorney-in-fact, if the document takes effect immediately. If you created a springing power of attorney, keep the original yourself, in a safe, convenient place that your attorney-in-fact can reach quickly, if necessary. Your attorney-in-fact will need the original document to act on your behalf. You may also want to give copies of the document to the people and institutions your attorney-in-fact will have to deal with—banks, government offices or insurance companies, for example.

As with a durable power of attorney for health care, you can change the attorney in fact or other terms of the document at any time, as long as you are legally competent.

POWERS OF ATTORNEY AND MEDICAID

As explained in Chapter 8, there are several ways to protect your assets from the reach of a long-term care facility while still qualifying for Medicaid. Several of these methods, however, might require you to transfer assets after you are no longer capable of doing so. If you create a durable power of attorney for finances, you may want to include the power to transfer title of property and other assets to a spouse, children or other specifically named people—the same people to whom you would want the property to pass after your death.

C. Guardianships and Conservatorships

Much of the advice so far in this chapter may not apply to you if the elder you are concerned about is already incapacitated and unable to make decisions. At that point, the elder can no longer enter into legal arrangements or delegate responsibility for decisions to others. Yet there is a danger that without these prior legal arrangements, financial institutions, government agencies, health care providers and bureaucrats of every variety will either refuse to take action regarding the elder's affairs or will take actions without regard for your wishes or for what you know the elder would want.

In this situation, you may have to go to court and ask a judge to appoint you or another friend or relative to act on the elder's behalf. There are procedures in every state to do this. Some states have only one legal category, usually called guardianship, while others have a second category, usually called conservatorship and often limited to financial matters.

In general guardianship proceedings, the legal question is whether or not the elder has become "incompetent" to handle any of his or her own affairs. In about half the states, you will have to present medical evidence of incompetence to the court. In more limited proceedings to establish a financial conservatorship or guardianship only (see below), the court can act if it finds that the elder is unable to handle financial affairs, even though he or she is not completely legally incompetent.

In conservatorship or guardianship proceedings, an elder has a right to appear in court with an attorney and to consent or object to the proposed arrangement. In many states, if the elder does not have an attorney, the court may appoint one. Similarly, changing the conservator or guardian's authority requires an additional court order to which the elder can consent or object. The conservator or guardian is held responsible for any mismanagement of the elder's property.

In some states, you can handle conservatorship proceedings without the assistance of a lawyer if no one challenges the need for the conservatorship and its scope. More complicated guardianship procedures, however, will require a lawyer's help, particularly if the elder or anyone else does not agree that the guardianship is necessary or that the person seeking to be guardian is the right person for the job.

1. Financial Conservatorship or Guardianship

A conservator or guardian can be appointed by a court solely to protect an elder's property—savings, real estate and investments, for example. He or she can also conduct daily financial affairs, such as paying bills, or arrange for services when the elder is unable to do so. This type of limited management assistance is appropriate when the elder is still capable of caring for himself or herself, but is unable to carry out personal business affairs efficiently because of disorientation or disability. In this situation, the conservator or guardian does not have power over the elder's personal conduct, but has authority over financial or other affairs as the court orders.

One advantage of a limited conservatorship or guardianship is that it leaves an elder free to make many important decisions independently: where to live, with whom to associate, what medical care to receive and how to handle property, for example. Nonetheless, it is still a court process in which a judge makes a ruling, occasionally against the elder's will, that gives another person authority over some parts of the elder's life. It is therefore a procedure to be used only if no other solution seems feasible.

2. Full Guardianship

Full guardianship is an extreme measure that severely restricts the legal rights of an elder based on a court's finding of legal incompetence. It reduces one's legal status to that of a minor, with no control over one's own money or property, decisions about medical care or institutionalization. A person under guardianship even loses the right to vote.

If an elder retains some degree of orientation and capability, a court's decision that he or she is incompetent can be emotionally devastating and, in fact, self-fulfilling. The person deemed legally incompetent may well give up the will to care for himself or herself and become much less competent than before. Obviously, full guardianship is a very serious step, to be taken only when a person's mental condition leaves no other choice.

CONSERVATORSHIPS, GUARDIANSHIPS AND MEDICAID

A conservator or guardian is under a legal obligation to act only in the best interests of the elder. There are times when those best interests may require transferring assets to a spouse, child or other person so the elder can qualify for Medicaid. Taken at face value, giving away someone's property does not appear to be in that person's best interests. Therefore, a conservator or guardian who wants to transfer an elder's property for Medicaid purposes should first go to court, explain the proposed transfer and get the court's approval.

Estate Planning: Controlling Your Money and Property

E state planning refers to actions you can take while living to determine what happens to your property when you die. It can include:

- deciding who will get your property when you die
- setting up procedures and devices to make sure your property passes to others free from probate, or that your estate owes the least amount possible in probate fees
- particularly if your estate is a large one, setting up ways to pass your property to others while reducing or avoiding taxes, and
- setting up a structure to give property to others who might need outside help in managing it—including minors, an older or unhealthy spouse or companion or a person who is unreliable with money.

Some people leave estate planning to lawyers, although the basic steps are easy enough to do yourself if you are willing to spend some time wading through rules. This chapter is not a comprehensive guide to estate planning, but it can help you learn about your options.

A. Drafting A Will

Despite their own best interests, and often despite their own best intentions, many people do not have a will—the legal document that directs how to parcel out a person's property after death. And others may have drawn up a will so long ago that it no longer accurately reflects the will-maker's wishes, assets or family circumstances.

If you die without leaving a will, you are said to die "intestate." Your property will then be distributed to your spouse, children or other relatives if you have no spouse or children, according to the statutory formula or "intestate succession laws" in your state.

Even if you opt to transfer your property to others using other techniques (such as a probate-avoiding living trust), preparing a simple will is an essential step to planning any estate. In a will, you spell out who you want to get your property and name a personal representative (executor) to round up and distribute that property and to wind up your business and financial affairs after your death. And a will is the only estate planning device that you can use to name a personal guardian for your own minor children and to name someone to manage property you leave to any minor or young adult child—until they reach an age you believe they will be capable of managing it alone.

Note that a "living will," discussed in Chapter 9, is a completely different document from the will discussed here. Living wills, more commonly called health care directives or something similar, let you express your wishes about medical treatment in case you become ill or incapacitated; they are not devices to transfer property after death.

It comes as a surprise to many people that it isn't really that hard to create your own, perfectly valid will. There are a few technical requirements, of course, but they aren't too complicated. Ultimately, you may find it more difficult to decide whom to leave your property to than to comply with the legal niceties.

You must be a mentally competent adult to make a valid will. In addition, your will must meet these basic requirements:

- It must state that it is your will.
- You must leave property to at least one beneficiary and/or appoint a personal guardian for your minor children.
- You must sign and date the will.
- At least two witnesses (three are required in Vermont) must watch you sign your will, then sign it themselves.

CREATING YOUR OWN WILL

Nolo has a number of helpful products you can use to create a legally valid will. *Quicken® WillMaker Plus* (Nolo) is a software program that lets you create a will, healthcare directive, durable power of attorney for finances and other documents. *Nolo's Simple Will Book* (Nolo) gives you all the forms and instructions you need (on paper and on CD) to create a legally valid will, with clauses you can use to tailor your will to your needs. *The Quick & Legal Will Book* (Nolo) also allows you to create a simple will on your own. Both books are by Denis Clifford.

B. Avoiding Probate

Probate is the legal process by which a person's property, called an "estate," is distributed after death. It involves filing a will, if there is one, with the local probate court and proving that the will is authentic and valid; identifying and appraising all the person's property; paying debts and estate taxes; and distributing what's left of the property according to the instructions in the will or according to state law if there is no will—all with the approval of the court.

Most states have adopted special procedures for small estates. The definition of a "small estate" varies from state to state—it can range anywhere from $10,000 to $200,000. And many states don't count certain types of property as part of your estate—this means that your estate may qualify as "small" even if the value of all of your property exceeds your state's limit. If you have a small estate under your state's requirements, your estate may be eligible for a simplified probate procedure that is much less complicated and time-consuming than the standard variety. Or, your beneficiaries may be able to skip court altogether—some states allow beneficiaries of small estates to prepare an affidavit stating that they are entitled to certain property under a will or state law. These affidavits are then given directly to the person or institution holding the property, which must release it to the beneficiary.

There are many good reasons to avoid probate. Probate is expensive—fees for lawyers, appraisers, accountants and the probate court often total about 5% of the deceased person's estate, which reduces the property that ultimately goes to beneficiaries. Probate is time-consuming—it usually takes about a year to complete the process, and the executor has to spend time gathering and distributing your property. And probate is public—your will becomes a public record that anyone can examine. To avoid these drawbacks, many people arrange to distribute their property through legal devices that avoid probate. Several of these methods—joint tenancy, pay-on-death accounts, life insurance, living trusts and retirement accounts—are discussed briefly below, with special attention to their estate planning implications for older people.

1. Joint Tenancy

Joint tenancy is one of the most popular probate avoidance devices. For many, joint tenancy is also an easy way to prepare to handle simple finances—maintaining bank accounts and paying household bills, for example—when the elder is no longer capable of doing so.

a. How Joint Tenancy Works

In a joint tenancy, two or more people own the same property equally. Joint tenancy carries with it the "right of survivorship." This means that when one joint tenant dies, his or her share of the joint tenancy property automatically passes to, and becomes owned by, the surviving joint tenants. They need not go through probate or other legal gyrations to get full ownership of the property. The same is true for "tenancy by the entirety," a slightly different form of joint tenancy that is available to married couples in some states, and "community property with right of survivorship," which married couples can use in a handful of states.

Joint tenancy is particularly useful as a management device for relatively small assets such as joint bank accounts. And, for older people, it may offer some convenience. If an elder becomes ill and is unable to get to the bank, or becomes unable to manage his or her affairs, for example, a joint tenant on the account can take care of the finances without having to go through complicated bank or court procedures.

In most states, joint tenancy is easy to set up. You can do it free without an attorney, by filling out a simple form available at the bank, stock brokerage or other financial institution that holds the assets. Some states require that you use the term "right of survivorship" on the form.

b. Drawbacks to Using Joint Tenancy

Although joint tenancy offers some benefits, it can be a poor estate planning choice, if your only goal is to avoid probate. There are several potential drawbacks to creating a joint tenancy:

Surrendering Control Over Your Property

If you make someone else a joint tenant of property, you are giving up half of your ownership in the property. The new owner could sell or mortgage his or her share—or lose it to creditors. And because each joint tenant has equal access to funds held in joint tenancy, there is always the danger that one joint tenant will misuse them, especially if large amounts of money are involved. Therefore, you should only consider joint tenancy if you have complete trust in the person to whom you give your property. Older people, many of whom are vulnerable to those eager to rip them off, should be on the look-out for anyone who tries to pressure them into changing ownership of their property.

In some states, you can protect again possible misuse by opening a joint tenancy bank account that requires the signatures of both tenants before withdrawals can be made. The problem with this arrangement, however, is that much of the convenience of joint tenancy is lost. If both signatures are required, joint tenancy funds won't be easily available to the other joint tenant if one becomes incapacitated.

CONSIDER USING A DURABLE POWER OF ATTORNEY FOR FINANCES

If your main goal in establishing a joint tenancy is to make sure that someone has access to your funds to handle financial transactions, you might want to use a durable power of attorney for finances instead. This device allows you to give someone you trust the authority to handle your finances if you are unable to do so. For more on durable powers of attorney for finances, see Chapter 9B.

Tax Consequences

If you create a joint tenancy by making another person a co-owner, the IRS may consider this transfer a taxable gift. If you give more than $11,000 per year to any one person (other than your spouse), you will have to file a gift tax return with the IRS. For real estate, the gift is made, for tax purposes, when the new joint tenant is listed on the deed and it is recorded with the county land records office. For bank accounts, however, the gift is not made until the other joint tenant removes some of the money—until then, the person who contributed the money could still withdraw it.

You could also deprive your spouse of an income tax break for property held in joint tenancy. Unless you live in a community property state (Arizona, California, Idaho, Louisiana, Nevada, New Mexico, Texas, Washington or Wisconsin), the IRS won't step up the tax basis on property that passes to your spouse through joint tenancy when you die. Ordinarily, you must pay tax on your profit when you sell property; your profit is the amount you sold it for, less your tax basis (which is generally what you paid for it, with a few adjustments). If you leave property to a spouse at death, his or her tax basis is "stepped up" to the value of the property at the time of inheritance—and this is a good thing if the property has increased in value, because a higher tax basis means lower taxes. If your property passes through joint tenancy, however, the tax basis of your portion of the property remains the same—it isn't stepped up.

Medicaid Eligibility Isn't Affected

Placing property in joint tenancy does not prevent Medicaid from considering that asset in determining whether you meet its eligibility rules. As covered in Chapter 7, these rules force an elder to spend most of his or her assets before Medicaid will begin to pay anything for long-term care or a residential facility. Medicaid will consider any property you hold in joint tenancy to be your asset when it makes its calculations.

2. Pay-on-Death Accounts, Stocks and Bonds

Setting up a pay-on-death bank account is an easy way to transfer funds at your death, without probate. All you have to do is name one or more persons to receive the funds when you die. You keep sole control of the account during your lifetime, but whatever is in the account then passes to the beneficiary upon your death.

However, this arrangement is not helpful if you become incompetent, since no one else can have access to that account during your lifetime. A durable power of attorney solves this problem by naming another person to handle financial matters which gives him or her legal access to the account in the event you become incompetent. (See the discussion of durable powers of attorney in Chapter 9.)

The Uniform Transfer-On-Death Securities Act, which has been adopted in almost all states, allows you to designate a beneficiary for your securities or security accounts. Whether or not you can make a pay-on-death designation depends on the state in which you live, the type of stock or security and the broker who handles the account. If you want a pay-on-death designation for your stocks, for example, but your broker cannot or will not set it up for you, consider hiring a different broker who will find a way to get the job done.

TRANSFER-ON-DEATH CAR REGISTRATION

In California, Connecticut, Missouri and Ohio, you can designate someone to receive ownership of your car when you die. If you live in one of these states, check with your local DMV to find out what procedures you'll have to follow to set this up.

---

3. Life Insurance

Life insurance is another way to transfer money outside of probate. This is because you name the beneficiary of the policy in the policy itself, not in your will. The only way the proceeds will be subject to probate is if you name your estate as the beneficiary on the policy. Some people do this if the estate will need immediate cash to pay debts and taxes, but it is fairly uncommon. (See Section C2 for a discussion of making a gift of life insurance while you are still alive to save on estate taxes.)

4. Retirement Accounts

Retirement accounts such as IRAs, 401(k) plans and Keogh accounts were not originally intended to be probate-avoidance devices, but they can easily be used that way. All you have to do is name a beneficiary to receive the funds still in your pension plan or retirement account at your death, and the funds will not pass through probate.

After you reach age 70½, however, federal law requires you to withdraw a minimum amount every year or face a monetary penalty. The amount you must withdraw is recomputed every year, based on your life expectancy.

5. Living Trusts

A revocable living trust performs the same basic function as a will—that is, you can use a living trust to leave your property to whomever you choose—but the property you leave won't have to go through probate. Living trusts are a very popular estate planning device not only because of this probate-avoidance feature, but also because they are relatively easy to set up and offer tremendous flexibility.

A revocable living trust gets its name from two of its primary features: It's a living trust because it goes into effect during your lifetime (unlike a will). And it's revocable because, as trustee, you can revoke—undo—the trust at anytime. These trusts are sometimes also referred to as "inter vivos" trusts.

a. How a Living Trust Works

You create a revocable living trust by preparing and signing a document called a Declaration (or Instrument) of Trust. In this document, you list the property in the trust, name the beneficiaries whom you wish to receive each item of property when you die and designate yourself (or yourself and your spouse, if you create a trust together) as the trustee. You must also designate a successor trustee—the person who will distribute your property under the terms of the trust when you die.

Once you've signed the trust document, you transfer your property into your name as trustee. However, for all practical purposes, this will have no day-to-day effect on how you use the property during your lifetime. In your role as trustee, you have complete control over the property in the trust. You can transfer property in and out of the trust, change the trust beneficiaries or even revoke the trust entirely. You will still have to pay taxes on the property, and creditors can still come after that property for your unpaid debts. In essence, the trust is kind of a legal fiction during your lifetime, but turns into a powerful estate planning tool when you're gone.

After your death, the successor trustee will gather up all of the trust property and distribute it directly to your beneficiaries, according to the trust's terms. The trust will then cease to exist.

Example. *Tony wants to leave his valuable painting collection to his son and his home to his daughter, but wants to enjoy his paintings and live in his home during his lifetime. He also does not want the value of his extensive collection and his home, which are worth nearly $1 million combined, to be subject to probate. So Tony establishes a living trust, with the paintings and house as trust assets. He names himself trustee while he lives, names his trusted friend Mavis as successor trustee and designates his son as the beneficiary of his paintings and his daughter as the beneficiary of his house. When Tony dies, Mavis will transfer the paintings and house to Tony's children, outside of probate. Then the trust will expire.*

b. Tax Issues

A basic living trust has no effect on estate taxes. Although the property you place in trust will not go through probate, the government will still consider it part of your estate when you die—and will tax you accordingly.

During your lifetime, the IRS treats property in a living trust just like any other property you own for purposes of income tax. You must report trust income on your own tax return, and you can take tax deductions for trust property just as if you still owned it outright. For example, if you put your home in trust, you can still deduct your mortgage interest on your tax return.

REVOCABLE LIVING TRUSTS AND MEDICAID

If a living trust is revocable, the assets you put into it are not exempt from Medicaid eligibility limits—that is, Medicaid will count them when it decides whether you are eligible for benefits. However, it is possible to create a revocable living trust with specific instructions to the trustee to transfer assets in a way that will get the most Medicaid eligibility and require the least in payment to a residential facility. Those instructions must be very carefully written to take advantage of the asset protection methods that may be available to you (as described in Chapter 8). Consult with a lawyer if you're thinking about creating this type of trust.

C. Saving on Estate Taxes

Unless you, or you and your spouse combined, have a substantial estate, you will not likely be affected by federal estate tax concerns. However, if your estate, or the combined estate of you and your spouse, is worth more than a million dollars, you may face a hefty estate tax liability. Marginal tax rates begin at 39% for the first non-exempt dollar and go up fairly rapidly from there.

Estate tax liability needn't concern many of us. The federal estate tax law provides a personal exemption of $1 million in 2003, rising to $3.5 million in 2009. In 2010, no estate tax will be assessed on estates of any size. However, in 2011, the estate tax is scheduled to return—and the exemption will diminish once again to $1 million (for exact exemption amounts, see chart below). Before that happens, however, it's very likely that Congress will revisit the politically charged issue of estate tax. If it concerns you, keep an eye out for law changes.

No estate tax will be assessed on the exempt amount of your estate. Taxes will be owed only on the amount by which your estate's value exceeds the exemption.

THE PERSONAL ESTATE TAX EXEMPTION

Year	Estate tax exemption	Highest estate and gift tax rate
2003	$1 million	49%
2004	$1.5 million	48%
2005	$1.5 million	47%
2006	$2 million	46%
2007	$2 million	45%
2008	$2 million	45%
2009	$3.5 million	45%
2010	Estate tax repealed	top individual income tax rate (gift tax only)
2011	$1 million unless Congress extends repeal	55% unless Congress extends repeal

Fortunately, in addition to the basic exemption, there are several other important estate tax exemptions. The most significant exemption is for property left to a surviving spouse. Quite simply, all property left to a surviving spouse who is a U.S. citizen is exempt from federal estate taxes. But beware: For very large estates, the fact that no federal estate tax is assessed may lead to a substantial tax liability when the second spouse dies. (See Section 1, below, for a discussion of how a marital trust can help deal with this.)

The other main exemptions from estate tax are:

- all property left to a tax-exempt charity
- some or all of the value of a family business left as part of an estate
- the expenses of a last illness
- burial costs
- probate fees and expenses, and
- certain debts, including a credit for state death taxes and death taxes imposed by foreign countries on property the deceased person owned there.

1. Marital Trusts

An AB trust (also called a marital life estate trust) is one of the simplest ways to save money on estate taxes while retaining control over your property.

An AB trust works like this: Each spouse sets up a trust and transfers all or most of his or property into that trust. As long as both spouses are alive, the couple's property is in a living trust, which can be revoked or changed. However, instead of leaving property directly to the surviving spouse, each spouse leaves the trust property to a trust, called "Trust A." When the first spouse dies, the living trust property (that is, the combined property of both spouses) is split into two trusts: Trust A, the deceased spouse's trust, which is now irrevocable, and Trust B, the surviving spouse's living trust. The surviving spouse does not receive the property in Trust A outright, but has the right to use and receive income from the trust property during his or her lifetime (this legal right is called a "life estate.") When the surviving spouse dies, all of the property left in each trust will pass to the final beneficiaries.

The primary benefit of an AB trust is that it allows couples whose combined assets are over the estate tax threshold to minimize their combined tax burden. Without an AB trust, if a prosperous spouse leaves all or more of his property to the surviving spouse, that money will not be taxed (because the spouse is the beneficiary). However, this may push the survivor's total estate well above the estate tax threshold. An AB trust allows each member of a married couple to use his or her entire state tax exemption—and prevents the surviving spouse's estate from getting taxed for all of the couple's combined property.

Example 1: Without an AB Trust. *Tim and Annette have a combined estate of $4 million, which they own equally. Each names the other as beneficiary. Eventually, when both of them are gone, they want their daughter Clara to inherit everything. When Tim dies in 2006, his estate is not taxed, because he left his property to his wife.*

After Tim's death, Annette's estate is worth $4 million. If Annette dies in 2007, she will allow estate tax on the entire estate, less the $2 million personal exemption for that year.

Example 2: With an AB Trust. *Same as above, only Tim and Annette create an AB trust. When Tim dies, his share of the property goes into Trust A. Because his property is worth $2 million—the personal exemption for that year—no estate tax is assessed. When Annette dies in 2007, her estate is also worth $2 million—and, again, is not subject to estate tax. The property in each spouse's trust is passed on to the final beneficiaries free of estate taxes.*

2. Gifts

One way to reduce your estate tax liability is to reduce the size of your estate by giving your property, during your lifetime, to the same people you would leave it to after your death. Recognizing that people might use this strategy to get out of paying any estate taxes at all, Congress imposes a tax on substantial gifts made during the lifetime of the giver. Gift tax rates are the same as estate tax rates, to eliminate any incentive for making large gifts. Here's how it works:

No taxes are imposed for gifts that fall within the gift tax exemption—currently $11,000. Each year, you may give up to $11,000 to as many people as you want, completely tax free. It is a particularly good idea to give property that is likely to go up in value—that way, you won't have to pay any taxes on the initial gift, and the increase in value won't be added to the net worth of your estate. If you make a gift that exceeds the gift tax exemption, you will not have to actually pay any tax when you make the gift. However, the taxable amount of the gift will be deducted from your total estate tax exemption.

Example: *Lydia gives Maria $150,000 in a single calendar year. $11,000 of the gift is not taxable, because it falls within the gift tax exemption. However, the remaining $139,000 is subject to the gift tax. Lydia cannot pay this tax now; instead, it is deducted from her personal estate tax exemption when she dies. Lydia dies in 2003. Her personal exemption is $1 million (the estate tax exemption for 2003) less the $139,000 taxable gift to Maria, or $861,000.*

In addition to gifts that fall within the $11,000 exemption, the following types of gifts are also tax-exempt (that is, you do not have to pay gift taxes on them, and they are not deducted from your federal estate tax exemption):

- Payments for someone else's medical bills or school tuition. If you pay this money directly to the school or provider of medical service, it is not taxed. However, if you pay the money to the ill person or student, or if you reimburse someone who has already paid a medical or tuition bill, the gift is taxable. Also, payments for a student's expenses other than tuition are taxable.

- Payments to your spouse. You can make a gift of any amount to your spouse, as long as she is a U.S. citizen, without gift tax liability. You may give a noncitizen spouse up to $110,000 per year, tax-free.
- Gifts to tax-exempt charities.

Congress has limited the total amount of gifts you can give, tax-free, during your lifetime. For now, this limit is the same as the estate tax threshold. However, the estate tax is scheduled to go up, while the gift tax will remain at $1 million. Once the estate tax threshold exceeds the gift tax threshold, you may have to pay tax on gifts that, had you kept them in your estate, would have passed to your beneficiaries tax-free.

Example: *Riley owns property and assets worth about $3.5 million. In the year before he dies, Riley gives his home (worth $1 million) and his collection of antiques (worth about $500,000) to his daughter. These gifts reduce the value of his estate to $2 million.*

Riley dies in 2009, when the estate tax threshold is $3.5 million and the gift tax threshold is $1 million. The $1.5 million Riley gave away (less the $11,000 he can give tax-free) will be deducted from his estate tax exemption, so that about $2 million (his entire estate) will be exempt from estate tax. However, because Riley's gifts exceed the gift tax threshold, his estate will have to pay tax on half a million dollars.

Had Riley hung onto his antiques, his entire estate ($2.5 million) would still be exempt from estate tax. And because his gift does not exceed the $1 million threshold, he would not owe any gift tax either. By making his daughter wait to inherit his antiques, Riley could have avoided paying taxes on half a million dollars.

GIFTS OF INSURANCE

If you own life insurance, the proceeds of that policy are included in your estate for federal estate tax purposes. If you think your estate will be liable for federal estate taxes at your death, you can reduce the tax bill by transferring ownership of the policy before your death. Although gift tax liability is imposed on the cash value of the policy at the time it is given, that amount will be substantially less than its pay-off value at death. Once you have transferred ownership of the policy, the proceeds will not be counted as part of your taxable estate.

To satisfy the Internal Revenue Service that you have authentically transferred ownership of a life insurance policy, you must verify that you have entirely given up your interest in the policy; you cannot keep the right to name beneficiaries, cancel coverage, borrow against the policy or make payments on it.

One final twist: You must transfer ownership of the policy—usually by completing a few simple forms you can get from your insurance company—at least three years before your death, or the IRS will count it as part of your taxable estate.

3. State Death Taxes

A handful of states impose death taxes on:

- all real estate owned in the state, no matter where the deceased person lived, and
- all other property of residents of the state, no matter where the property is located.

Most states don't impose any death taxes. But estate taxes imposed by states are becoming a greater concern to many people. It used to be that in most states, if someone left an estate large enough to owe federal estate tax, the state just took a share of that tax. But because Congress changed the tax rules, estates may now have to pay state tax even if they aren't large enough to pay federal estate tax.

Here's how it works. States can now claim a smaller share of the federal estate tax each year until 2005, when the amount falls to zero. To make up for this loss of revenue, some states have enacted their own estate taxes, which are no longer connected to the federal system.

If you're concerned about state taxes, see a tax lawyer in your state (and, if you own real estate elsewhere, in that state, too) who can bring you up to date on this rapidly changing area of the law.

Home is where the tax is. Your taxability will be assessed in the state deemed your "legal residence." To establish a legal residence in a particular state, register your vehicles there, keep bank accounts there and vote in that state.

If you live in a state that does not impose death taxes and you do not own real property in any state that imposes them, you don't need to worry about them. But if you spend different parts of the year in different states, your inheritors will take your personal property free of state inheritance tax only if you establish your permanent legal residence in a state that does not have the taxes.

Example. *Harry and Margot, an elderly married couple, spend their winters in Florida and summers in New Hampshire. Florida has no death taxes. New Hampshire does. It probably makes sense for Harry and Margot to make Florida their legal residence. To do this, they should register to vote in Florida and conduct as many business transactions there as possible—for example, using Florida banks and registering vehicles in Florida. It might also make sense for them to sell any real property they own in New Hampshire and simply rent when they are in that state.*

D. Managing Property

You can use ongoing trusts to manage and control property that you don't want to turn over to the beneficiary outright. Some beneficiaries, such as minors or people who have been declared legally incompetent, are not permitted to control substantial amounts of property on their own. Or the beneficiary may be seriously disabled, be a spendthrift, have drug or alcohol abuse problems or just not be "good with money"—all situations that may make it feasible for another person to manage the property and dole out money to the beneficiary on a periodic basis.

Property management trusts are a good option for an older person who wishes to pass property to someone who fits into one of these categories. With managerial trusts, it is particularly important to select a responsible trustee, someone who is attuned to the beneficiaries' needs. The trustee will have an ongoing relationship with the beneficiaries and will have to make important decisions on their behalf, such as how to invest trust money and whether to spend part of the trust principal to meet special needs of the beneficiary.

SPECIAL CONCERNS FOR SUBSEQUENT MARRIAGES

People who marry more than once may face problems reconciling their desires for their present spouse and family with their wishes to pass property to the children from their prior marriages. Individual situations vary drastically, and you must carefully tailor your estate plan to meet your concerns.

Example. *Gertrude, a widow, has three grown children. She owns a house and has other substantial assets. In her 70s, Gertrude marries Ted, also in his 70s. Ted has very little property. He has two children from a prior marriage whom Gertrude feels are both spoiled and ungrateful. As she plans her estate, Gertrude realizes that she wants to allow Ted to remain in the house if she dies before he does, but does not want him to be able to lease the property to his pushy kids. Understandably, Gertrude's own children share her concerns.*

Gertrude decides to give some of her property outright to her children. She also decides to create a trust for the house and to leave enough money in that trust to pay for the mortgage and upkeep on the house. The trust will specify that Ted has the right to live in the house for his lifetime, then the house will go to Gertrude's kids at Ted's death. If you want to set up one of these more complicated trusts, consult with a lawyer who specializes in estate planning.

ESTATE PLANNING RESOURCES FROM NOLO

Nolo publishes many products that can help you with estate planning. You may conclude that our recommendation is a bit prejudiced, but we think these are the best books and software available. And we offer a money-back guarantee if you don't agree.

- *Quicken® WillMaker Plus* (Nolo) is a comprehensive software package that allows you to create your own will, living trust, healthcare directive, durable power of attorney and other important documents.
- *Plan Your Estate*, by Denis Clifford and Cora Jordan (Nolo), is a comprehensive guide to estate planning goals and techniques.
- *Estate Planning Basics,* by Denis Clifford (Nolo), gives you the essentials about the most common estate planning tools.
- *Make Your Own Living Trust,* by Denis Clifford (Nolo), provides the forms and instructions you need to set up a basic living trust and a more complicated AB trust.
- *Nolo's Simple Will Book,* by Denis Clifford (Nolo), provides all the forms, instructions and sample clauses you need to create a legally valid will that meets your needs.
- *The Quick and Legal Will Book,* by Denis Clifford (Nolo), allows you to create a simple will on your own.
- *8 Ways to Avoid Probate*, by Mary Randolph (Nolo), is a guide to eight easy and inexpensive methods of transferring your assets outside of probate.
- *9 Ways to Avoid Estate Taxes,* by Denis Clifford and Mary Randolph (Nolo), explains the nine basic ways people can avoid or reduce federal estate taxes.

- *Medical Directives & Powers of Attorney for California*, by Shae Irving (Nolo), gives California residents the forms and information they need to create these important documents.
- *How to Probate an Estate in California*, by Julia Nissley (Nolo),
- *The Conservatorship Book*, by Goldoftas and Farren (Nolo), explains how and when to seek a conservatorship.
- *Living Together*, by Ralph Warner, Toni Ihara & Frederick Hertz (Nolo) provides comprehensive legal and practical advice—including estate planning tips for unmarried straight couples.
- *A Legal Guide for Lesbian & Gay Couples*, by Hayden Curry, Denis Clifford, Robin Leonard & Frederick Hertz (Nolo), provides comprehensive legal and practical advice—including estate planning tips—for lesbian and gay couples.

Long-Term Care Insurance

Over the past decade, people have become increasingly aware of how easily long-term care can wipe out a lifetime's savings—and insurance companies have been quick to capitalize on that fear. Long-term care insurance, also called nursing home insurance, has been widely advertised as protection against the costs of long-term care, particularly nursing facilities. But this kind of insurance is expensive. And it often provides only limited benefits—with many restrictions and conditions—that may cover only a small percentage, or nothing at all, of your total long-term care costs.

A. Risks and Benefits

Insurance companies market long-term care (LTC) insurance by suggesting to people that they are likely to wind up spending years in a nursing facility—a prospect that would wipe out their life's savings and perhaps leave them without a roof over their heads. The actual odds of such a long nursing facility stay, however, are considerably lower than the insurance industry would like you to imagine. And with the protection afforded by Medicaid laws, there is virtually no risk of being thrown out of a nursing facility and into the street. (See Chapters 4 and 7.)

When you consider the true odds of a long nursing facility stay along with the high cost of LTC insurance and the other things you could do with that premium money, you may find that for you—as for the 95% of the population over age 65 that has not invested in it—LTC insurance is not a good bet.

Nonetheless, there are some people—for example, those who have assets of between $300,000 and $500,000 beyond the value of their homes—for whom LTC insurance may be a sound idea. This is particularly true if LTC is viewed as a safety net rather than a financial investment—and if your policy includes coverage for assisted living facilities. (See Chapter 3.) Those who do buy LTC insurance make the purchase at a median age of 65. Before that age, most people's financial and health future is too unpredictable for this insurance to make sense; by the time they reach their 80s, the premiums are usually unaffordable.

1. The Odds of a Long Nursing Facility Stay

The true figures about how much time a person is likely to spend in a nursing facility present a rather different picture than the one painted in dark and somber tones by the insurance industry.

- Two-thirds of all men, and one-third of all women, age 65 and older will never spend a day in a nursing facility.
- Most nursing facility stays are brief. Of people age 65 and over, only about 10% of men and 25% of women spend more than a year in a nursing facility.
- Only 7-8% of all nursing facility residents will stay longer than three years.
- More than half of all nursing facility stays last six months or less. Of people who do enter a custodial care nursing facility, the average stay is about 18 to 20 months.

2. The Performance of Long-Term Care Insurance

The relatively slight chance that an elder will need three or more years of nursing facility care means that the insurance industry has not had to pay out on its policies to nearly the extent that it suggested when they were sold. And when the policies' conditions, exclusions and benefit limits are figured in, the performance of these policies—at least in the decade up to the mid 1990s, for which complete statistics are available—has been quite poor.

- About 50% of all policies lapsed before any benefits were paid; people were unable or unwilling to continue paying their premiums.
- Of those people who bought the insurance and later entered a nursing facility, about half never collected a dollar from their LTC policies.
- No benefits were ever paid to the many who bought nursing facility coverage but instead received home care or entered a residential facility, not covered by the insurance.
- When benefits were paid, they were far below the actual cost of care.
- For many of the longest-term residents, benefits were used up before the nursing facility stay ended.

In all of these situations, the LTC insurance failed to live up to its promise to help people avoid using up their savings, or relying on Medicaid, to pay for long-term care. In other words, it was a lousy investment.

3. Improvements in LTC Insurance

In response to pressure from consumer groups, embarrassing media exposure and increased competition from other insurers joining the market, new LTC policies improved somewhat in the second half of the 1990s. Those improvements included clearer terms and conditions, so that people are better informed about what they can expect for their money.

Also, many policies extended coverage to include some types of assisted living residences, not just nursing facilities. (See Chapter 3.) Many policies now permit elders to use a pool of benefit funds for either home care or residential care, rather than only one or the other. The requirements to qualify for benefits also have been loosened somewhat. And policies now routinely permit the policy holder to "step down" to lower levels of coverage, for a lower premium, if continuing to pay for the higher benefits becomes too financially burdensome.

If you are considering long-term care insurance, be a very careful consumer. Comparison shop among several policies and check each policy carefully for the exclusions and limitations discussed in this chapter. If you find one or two policies that sound good, remind yourself that you may never need long-term care at all, or you might not need enough care to collect much in the way of insurance benefits. Before making a final decision, check with an accountant or financial advisor about whether some other types of secure long-term investments might give you as much money as these particular insurance policies would pay—then you can spend some or all of that money on long-term care only if you need it.

The only way you can determine whether long-term care insurance is a good value for you is to gauge how much you are likely to pay in premiums before requiring home care or entering a facility, based on your age and general health. Remember, if you are buying a policy when you are in your 60s, you are likely to be paying premiums for 20 years or more before you might need long-term care. Measure that amount against the benefits you are likely to collect and the costs of care that would not be paid by the policy. Since you are protecting against the cost of substantial long-term care, base your calculations on estimates for your geographic area. Estimate the costs in 10, 20 and 30 years from now of a three-year and six-year period of home care and a one-year, two-year and three-year residence in a nursing facility. Consider, too, that you might never need extensive long-term care—in that case the policy will pay you little or no benefits.

4. The 5% of Income Rule

Consumer and financial experts generally agree that long-term care insurance is a bad investment—unless you can pay the monthly premium with no more than 5% of your income. When calculating this 5% figure for future years, bear in mind that your premiums are likely to rise, while at some point your income will probably drop. (See Sections E1 and E2.)

In general, if, in addition to your home, you expect to have substantial assets and income—over $300,000 in assets and over $50,000 per year in income (in today's dollars)—when you reach your 80s, then a long-term care policy with high benefits and compounded inflation protection might be a reasonable investment while you are in your 50s to early 70s.

However, even if you do expect to have sizable assets, a financial advisor may show you more profitable ways of investing the same money you would put into insurance premiums. And those investments plus permissible transfers of assets under Medicaid rules may combine to provide better protection and liquidity for your money than a long-term care insurance policy.

In any event, do not base your decision solely on advice from an insurance agent or broker who is trying to sell you a long-term care policy. Check the latest analysis of long-term care policies done by *Consumer Reports*, a consumer information magazine. The magazine regularly does comprehensive studies of specific long-term care policies and may be a valuable reference for you. *Consumer Reports* can be found at any local library.

LONG-TERM CARE INSURANCE NOW TAX-DEDUCTIBLE

As of January 1, 1997, a certain amount of long-term care insurance premiums may be deductible as medical expenses—if your total medical deductions exceed 7.5% of your gross adjusted income. And benefits under a long-term care insurance policy are no longer treated like income.

However, these tax advantages apply only to policies that constitute Qualified Long Term Care Insurance (QLTCI), under guidelines established by the federal government.

If you enrolled in your policy before 1997, it is automatically considered a QLTCI for tax purposes. If you enrolled after January 1, 1997, the policy must meet the federal requirements.

The maximum amount per year of QLTCI policy premiums that can be deducted as a medical expense depends on your age.

The amounts change every year—check the instructions on your federal tax return for the current figures.

LONG-TERM CARE INSURANCE FOR FEDERAL EMPLOYEES/RETIREES

Beginning in 2002, the Office of Personnel Management of the federal government, in partnership with private insurance companies, has begun sponsoring long-term insurance at group rates. The insurance policies under this "Long-Term Care Partners" program are available to federal employees, retirees and certain immediate family members. The premiums may be slightly less expensive than for similar retail policies. However, the insurance itself operates just like any other private policy, with all the risks and limitations described in this chapter.

To find out about these policies, look at the website of the Office of Personnel Management (www.opm.gov/insure) or the insurance partnership (www.ltcfeds.com).

STATE POLICIES HELP PROTECT ASSETS

California, Connecticut, Indiana and New York Medicaid programs allow Medicaid and private insurance companies to work together to offer long-term care policies that protect a greater measure of assets than Medicaid normally allows. The asset-protection aspects of these special long-term care policies are described in Chapter 8B.

However, the mere fact that these policies might protect some assets does not automatically make them a good investment. Don't purchase one of these policies unless it also meets other requirements for a good long-term care policy, as explained in this chapter.

B. Warnings About Insurance Practices

Shopping for any kind of insurance can be a daunting task. You have to read the fine print, compare the rates and benefits of different policies and figure out which policy will best meet your individual needs. If you're searching for long-term care insurance, you'll need to keep a few additional issues in mind.

1. Beware of Pretty Promises

Don't be blinded by the first numbers you get from insurance advertisements, agents or brokers. And don't be fooled by the boldface promises of a glossy brochure. Too often, a company flashes what seem like high benefits for low premiums, plus a promise that the premiums will never rise. Unfortunately, the fine print always permits the insurance companies to increase premiums one way or another—

and they will. (See Section E, below.) And what seem like high benefits today may be far from adequate when you finally need them. (See Section F, below.)

2. Beware of Brochures and Agents

Insurance brochures and advertisements are often misleading and always incomplete. These devices are intended to get you interested in insurance policies and to convince you how great they are—not to explain their pitfalls or even to accurately explain how they work. And brochures are generally not detailed enough to bind an insurance company to anything in particular, so you cannot rely on their glossy promises.

Insurance agents, too, are in the business of selling policies—not of warning you why you should not buy one. Although most agents are conscientious about not selling a policy they know is not right for a customer, some will say almost anything to make a sale. Other agents may not intentionally mislead you, but will sell you a bad policy simply because they do not know better. Long-term care insurance is relatively new and policies change rapidly, so many agents simply do not have much experience with particular policies and coverages.

In general, an insurance agent—as opposed to an insurance broker—represents only one company or group of companies. He or she may know that company's policies fairly well, but cannot compare their premiums and coverage to those offered by another company's policies. If you have received information from one company's agent, even if the agent has shown you all of that company's policies, be sure to investigate several other companies' policies as well. Also, do not rely on what an agent tells you about how a policy works. If you are going to rely on something the agent tells you, insist that you see the promise in writing on the policy itself or from the agent or another company representative in official company correspondence addressed to you.

An insurance broker, as opposed to an agent, works independently and can offer policies from a number of different companies. A broker can probably show you a somewhat wider selection of long-term care policies than could an agent who works for only one company. A broker may not know very well how the different policies operate, however. And a broker cannot make binding promises on behalf of the insurance company. If the broker contends that a policy operates in a certain way, be sure you see it in writing on the policy or in official correspondence from the insurance company to you.

3. Beware of Mail-Order and Limited-Time-Only Policies

You have probably seen these advertising catch-phrases before: Limited Offer! Once-in-a-Lifetime! When this offer expires, you'll never get the same chance again! One Month Only!

These one-time-only offers are usually misleading nonsense. The best advice may simply be to avoid buying any policy touted in an advertisement that uses an exclamation point. If it is a reputable insurance company with a legitimate policy to offer, the same or similar terms will be available to you at any time (except for premium increases as you grow older). No matter what the advertising says, don't be rushed into buying anything.

4. Check the Company's Reliability Rating

Even the best-sounding insurance policy won't do you any good if the company who issued it has gone bankrupt by the time you try to collect your benefits. An independent insurance industry guide called

Best's Insurance Reports rates the general reliability and financial health of individual insurance companies. Consider buying a policy only from an insurance company with a Best's rating of A+ or A. Best's is available at many local libraries, but if you have trouble finding a recent copy, the insurance agent or broker you deal with should be able to get you a written statement of the company's Best's rating.

Remember, however, that even a high *Best's* rating is no guarantee. If you buy now, you may not need to collect benefits under the policy for 15, 20 or 25 years. And there is no way anyone can predict the financial health of a particular insurance company over that period. This uncertainty is yet another reason to consider other forms of long-term investment instead of long-term care insurance.

5. Examine the Policy

When you consider a particular long-term care insurance policy, don't be content to just look at a summary of it. Examine the entire policy—and not in the insurance agent or broker's office. Take it home so that you can study it carefully and have family, friends or a financial advisor check it with you.

After reading the policy carefully, ask the agent or broker any questions you have about any aspect of the policy—premiums, coverage, exclusions or benefits—and request responses in writing, signed, either directly from the company or from the agent stating that he or she is responding on behalf of the company. Get these responses from someone who officially represents the insurance company. Ask for some evidence that the person who is giving you the explanation is authorized to speak on behalf of the company. If you choose to purchase a policy based on such an extra written explanation, make sure that the written explanation is attached to and made an official part of your policy.

GROUP LONG-TERM CARE INSURANCE

Your employer, union, trade association or professional organization may offer you the chance to buy group long-term care insurance, rather than buying an individual policy. In a group insurance policy, the group (called the "master policyholder"), rather than the individual, has the direct contractual relationship with the insurance company. Policy terms are established by the group and the insurance company. As a result, you may have fewer options to choose from than you might get in an individual policy.

Group policies usually offer an advantage over individual policies: because of the group's greater purchasing power, the initial policy premiums are generally lower than they would be for an individual policy.

But group policies also carry their own hidden risks. Over the years, the group will be free to decide—in negotiations with the insurance company—how much premiums will rise. The group may make decisions that favor newer or younger members over older ones—or may even decide to terminate the policy altogether. And the insurance company is free to cancel group coverage, something it cannot do to an individual policy. Depending on the policy's terms, those covered by the group policy may then have to continue as individual policyholders at much higher premiums—or may have no right to convert to individual coverage, which means they would no longer have any long-term care insurance at all.

If you are considering a group long-term care policy, study its terms very carefully. Pay special attention to what rights you have if the group or the insurance company cancels the policy altogether.

C. Extent of Coverage

The long-term care you or a loved one may one day need could take one of several forms—and over time, even more than one form. Initially, you might need regular but not daily help at home with some of the routine activities of daily living (ADLs). You may require 24-hour monitoring and care in a nursing facility. Or you might need any level of at-home or residential care in between.

Some LTC policies cover nursing facility care, but not home care. Others cover home care only. And some comprehensive policies cover not only those two types of care, but also assisted living or custodial care in non-nursing facilities. When you consider LTC insurance, look for policies covering the broadest types of care that might be useful to you. And be sure to determine what benefits will be provided, and for how long, for each type of care.

1. Custodial Care Nursing Facilities

Unless you are interested in a policy that only covers home care (see Section C3, below), your primary concern will be finding a policy that will pay for a long stay in a nursing facility or other residential care facility.

Look for a policy that covers as many different types of facilities as possible. A policy should specifically state that it will pay for "custodial care." A good policy should also state that it will pay benefits if you live in any facility—regardless of what it is called—that is licensed by the state as a custodial care facility. Don't purchase a policy that pays benefits only for stays in "nursing facilities." And avoid any policy that will pay for care only in facilities that are certified by Medicare or Medicaid. Many custodial care facilities do not provide skilled nursing care—and so do not need (or bother to get) Medicare certification. And some high-end custodial care facilities do not seek Medicaid certification because they do not want to accept the lower payments of Medicaid-supported residents.

Beware of any policy requirement regarding the size of the facility. Some policies will not cover care in a facility with less than a certain number of beds, usually 20 or 30. But there is no reason a smaller facility cannot provide excellent care, and a smaller residence might be better able to meet your needs.

2. Assisted Living Facilities

One of the most important recent developments in long-term care has been the rise of assisted living residences as an alternative to nursing facilities. They provide part-time personal assistance and monitoring for people who need some help with the activities of daily life but do not need the intensive care and monitoring of a nursing facility. (See Chapter 3B for more on assisted living facilities) And now LTC insurance, which before had covered only long-term custodial care facilities and home care, is beginning to recognize this change.

One of the first things to investigate about any policy is whether (and under what terms) it covers assisted living residences. Find out the specific conditions under which a policyholder may qualify for coverage. (The events that trigger coverage are explained in Section D, below.) The policy should use the same triggers for assisted living as it does for a nursing facility. Your decision about whether to move to an assisted living facility or a more restrictive, institutional and expensive nursing facility should be based on your personal needs and preferences, not on whether an insurance policy will cover you.

3. Home and Community Care

Many insurance companies provide coverage for certain types of long-term home care and care provided at nonresident community care facilities, either in the same policy as residential facility coverage or as a separate home-care-only policy. Because home care and community care are becoming available in more places, with broader and more innovative services, it makes good sense for most people to look for a policy that covers these services.

a. Home and Community Care Coverage Only

Some people may want to consider home and community care coverage only, without any residential facility coverage.

You may want to consider doing without the more expensive residential nursing facility coverage if:

- you are considerably older or more physically limited than your spouse, and she or he is capable of caring for you at home if the need should arise; your spouse should have residential care coverage, however

- you have other supportive family who live nearby and would help with care, or

- you have adult children who will take you into their homes to care for you if the need should arise, and you prefer that arrangement to living in a residential facility; you live in an area with good home and community care services available; and you do not have large assets (over $300,000) other than your home which you seek to protect from long-term care facility home costs. (See Chapter 8.)

Remember, though, that you are insuring for a need that may not arise for 10, 15 or 20 years—and it is difficult to predict what your situation will be at that time. If you choose to purchase home and community care coverage only, be sure to also protect your assets from nursing home costs under Medicaid rules. (See Chapter 8.)

RESIDENTIAL COVERAGE WITHOUT HOME CARE

Some people may want a policy that provides residential facility coverage, but not home care. If you are unmarried, do not have younger family members close by who will help you if you stay at home and live in an area with few home or community care services available, home care might not be a realistic alternative for you. There probably seems little point in paying extra for its coverage.

However, if the cost of adding home care is not too great, the extra coverage might be worth the expense. By the time you need long-term care—10, 15, 20 years from now—home and community care may have become a much more viable alternative for you than it would be now.

b. Broadest Possible Coverage

As discussed in Chapter 2, home care covers a wide variety of services, including fairly intensive nursing and physical or speech therapy; help with activities of daily living (ADLs) such as bathing, eating or moving about; and homemaker services such as housecleaning, shopping and laundry. If you seek long-term home care insurance, try to get the widest variety of coverage possible. There are a number of conditions and restrictions of which you should be aware:

- A few policies cover skilled nursing care and physical therapy in the home but not custodial care. Such coverage is far too limited, and you should reject it.
- Most home care policies cover skilled nursing care, other professional medical services and nonmedical personal care, provided by a licensed home care agency. Personal care includes help with the Activities of Daily Living (ADLs), such as eating, bathing, dressing,

using the toilet and moving around. It may also cover what are sometimes called "instrumental" ADLs, such as monitoring medications, going outside, light shopping, helping with meals and clean-up, laundry and household telephone calls and paperwork.

• A few policies also provide limited coverage of some homemaker services—such as regular house cleaning, grocery shopping and meal preparation—if an agency home health aide also does other personal assistance duties.

• Good policies cover care provided not only in the home, but also in licensed community care facilities such as adult daycare centers.

• Good home care policies also provide for respite care and hospice care (see Chapter 2J).

c. Coverage for Independent Home Care Providers

You can get high-quality, flexible and less costly personal care at home from independent aides who do not work for a home care agency. (See Chapter 2D for more on independent home care aides). Therefore, you should look for home care coverage that pays for independent aides as well as agency care.

There are two types of coverage that might pay for independent home care aides. If your policy requires only minimal qualifications, such as state or county certification as a home care aide, for coverage, independent aides will probably fall within the policy's guidelines.

However, the best policies will pay home care benefits no matter who provides the care. These policies pay up to the policy's maximum daily home care benefit for home care provided by *anyone*, as long as the care is part of a formal Plan of Care developed by your physician or by a home care agency under the direction of a physician. Once you qualify for home care benefits under this type of policy, the money is paid directly to you—and you can use it to hire whomever you choose as a personal care aide, even if that aide doesn't have formal qualifications for the job. Some states require any home care policy sold in that state to offer this type of coverage.

D. Coverage Conditions and Exclusions

The biggest risk you take on by purchasing a long-term care insurance policy is the great likelihood that you will pay premiums for many years but never require care for a long enough period to collect substantial insurance benefits. However, these policies also present other barriers to collecting benefits. The many terms, conditions and exclusions in long-term care policies sometimes eliminate coverage for the very people who need it most. You must consider these conditions—particularly the most common ones discussed below— very carefully when shopping for a policy.

1. Prior Hospital or Skilled Nursing Facility Stay

One of the insurance industry's cruelest tricks during the early days of long-term care coverage was to hide in the small print of a policy the condition that benefits would be paid only if the long-term care began within a short time—usually 7 to 30 days—after the insured spent at least three days in a hospital or skilled nursing facility (SNF). Sometimes, custodial care does immediately follow a hospital or SNF stay. However, most long-term custodial care is for chronic illness, frailty, Alzheimer's Disease or other physical or mental impairment, and does not follow an acute medical episode requiring a three-day or longer stay in a hospital or SNF.

Most states have now banned this condition. However, in about a quarter of the states, such provisions are still legal. It is up to you as a consumer to spot such a provision in any policy that is offered to you.

Ask the insurance agent or broker whether such a provision exists in any policy you are considering— and don't buy any policy that requires a prior hospital or skilled nursing facility stay.

 BEWARE OF PERMANENT EXCLUSIONS

A few policies permanently exclude coverage if you enter a nursing facility or begin receiving home or community care as a result of specified illnesses or medical conditions. This means that you receive no benefits, no matter how long you received care, if you need care for one of the listed conditions.

Conditions commonly excluded are mental illness, HIV-related illness, nervous disorders, alcohol or chemical dependency, certain heart diseases, certain forms of cancer and diabetes. If your need for long-term care arises from any excluded condition, your policy will not pay any benefits toward the cost of that care.

If you already know that you have suffered from one of the excluded conditions listed in a particular policy, this policy obviously won't work for you. But you should also avoid any policy that has a long list of exclusions even if you have never had any of the listed illnesses or conditions. You may not need the policy coverage for many years—and in those intervening years, you may develop an excluded illness or condition.

2. Pre-Existing Condition Exclusion

Like other health-related insurance policies, some long-term care policies don't cover care required by an illness or condition that was diagnosed or treated within a certain period of time—usually six months to two years—before the start of the policy.

The exclusion may work in any of several ways. Some policies exclude coverage for a certain time after you begin receiving long-term care. During that exclusion period, the insurance company pays no benefits for your care. If this period is relatively short—one to three months—it may not restrict your coverage too much. If the exclusion is for a longer period—more than six months, for example—you may never receive any benefits under the policy. Look for a policy with no exclusion at all. If you must accept an exclusion, look for a combination of the shortest pre-care period and the shortest exclusion period.

3. Qualifying for Benefits: Benefit "Triggers"

Your policy won't automatically begin paying benefits on the day you start receiving covered care. Instead, most policies require you to first meet a certain standard—often called a "benefit trigger"—as certified by a physician. What the benefit trigger is, and which physician decides whether you meet it, plays a large role in determining whether you actually receive benefits.

a. Performing Activities of Daily Living (ADLs)

The benefit trigger most commonly used in long-term care policies is "inability to perform without assistance" some specified number of the activities of daily living (ADLs). Each insurance policy includes its own list of five to seven ADLs, including:

- bathing
- eating
- dressing
- using the toilet ("toileting")
- walking ("ambulating")

- getting in and out of bed or a chair ("transferring")
- taking medication ("medicating"), and
- continence.

These policies will pay benefits only when you need assistance with a specified number of the ADLs on their lists.

When considering a policy that uses your inability to perform ADLs as a trigger, consider these tips:

- Some policies pay benefits if you need assistance with only two ADLs; other policies require three. Some policies will pay for home care once you need assistance with two ADLs, but won't pay for residential facility care until you need assistance with three. Obviously, the fewer ADLs necessary to qualify, the better for the insured.
- Consider a policy that requires you to need assistance with three ADLs only if there are at least seven ADLs on the total list.
- Bathing is almost always one of the first ADLs with which people need help—so make sure that bathing is included on the list of qualifying ADLs. Ditto for dressing.
- Make sure that you will be considered unable to perform an ADL without assistance if you are able to perform the ADL sometimes, but not without supervision.
- A policy should state that benefits will be paid if you have a "cognitive impairment" (diminished mental capabilities) that prevents you from regularly performing the requisite number of ADLs, even though you are physically capable of performing them. This is a crucial policy term because so many people end up needing long-term care because of Alzheimer's Disease or some other type of dementia, not for physical disability.
- Do not buy a policy in which benefit payments are triggered only by "severe" cognitive impairment. This is a tough standard to meet.

b. Medically Necessary Due to Illness or Injury

In some policies, benefits are triggered only if you need care that is "medically necessary due to an illness or injury." "Medically necessary" is sometimes defined to mean that your medical condition will deteriorate if you do not receive the recommended level of care.

You should avoid these standards if possible, for several reasons. First, the policy may not define "illness or injury" in a manner that includes many common ailments. Simple frailty, sometimes combined with some disorientation or memory loss, is the most common reason elders require long-term care. But you may not be able to pinpoint a specific "illness" that has caused your condition. Second, your inability to perform several ADLs may make your life miserable without causing your medical condition to deteriorate—and therefore, without triggering coverage. Third, it is often difficult to determine when an illness or injury ends. Even if you originally need care because of an illness or injury, the insurance company might eventually claim that the injury or illness has ended—and, therefore, that your care is no longer covered. Because of these serious problems for the consumer, some states have gone so far as to outlaw policies that contain this "medically necessary due to illness or injury" trigger.

c. As Determined by a Physician

Some policies will pay benefits only after a physician certifies, in writing, that the insured cannot perform the specified number of ADLs without assistance. Other policies require a physician or licensed home care agency to prepare a Plan of Care that describes the patient's needs and prescribes the type and amount of care needed. In either case, the policy should permit your personal physician, rather than a doctor appointed by the insurance company, to make the initial determination that you qualify for care. However, almost all policies include a provision that allows for a second opinion by a doctor appointed by the company.

SPECIAL RULES FOR ALZHEIMER'S DISEASE

Most states now require all long-term care policies to provide benefits to those who require care for Alzheimer's Disease, as diagnosed by a physician. This sounds like a valuable consumer protection—except that there is no clear medical test to determine when someone has Alzheimer's Disease rather than some other form of mental disorientation. Therefore, regardless of whether Alzheimer's is specifically mentioned, a good policy must include the inability to perform a number of ADLs because of physical limitations or "cognitive impairment" as a benefit trigger (See Section 3, above).

E. Premiums

When you consider any long-term care policy, remember that the terms under which premiums may be raised are as important as the initial premium cost.

1. Initial Premium Cost

The cost of initial premiums depends on your age and overall health as well as the quality, amounts and length of coverage provided. If you are in your 50s, you may be able to get a long-term policy with small benefits over a limited period for less than $1,000 per year. If you are over 70 and want broad coverage and sizable benefits payable for several years, a new policy may cost $7,000 per year.

If your purpose in purchasing long-term care insurance is to protect your income and assets from the high cost of long-term care, it only makes sense to buy coverage if it will be comprehensive enough, and last long enough, to defray a lot of those costs. If your benefits cover only a small percentage of your long-term care costs, those costs will eat up all your savings anyway—and you will have spent money on years of premiums for nothing. So, as a rule, policies with small benefits (under $100 day for residence facility care) and a limited coverage period (less than two years) are of questionable value, particularly as to nursing facility costs.

In addition to your age and the benefits offered, less obvious things like the number of conditions and exclusions, levels of care, benefit flexibility, inflation protection, waiver of premiums, terms of renewal or premium hikes and premature death refunds will all affect the amount of premiums you pay for any specific policy.

2. Premium Hikes

No matter what an advertising brochure seems to indicate, an insurance company always retains the right to raise premiums in one way or another. And, one way or another, they are sure to do so. There are two common ways policies allow for premium increases.

a. Avoid "Attained-Age" Provisions.

One of the ways insurance companies entice customers to a particular policy is to offer very low initial premiums while burying in the fine print the fact that the premiums will rise automatically when the insured attains certain age levels—usually 70, 75, 80 and 85. These policies make no guarantees about how much the premium will increase when you reach these ages. And a premium rise might be so high that you would be forced to drop your coverage—wasting all the money you've paid in premiums up to that point—just when you are most likely to need its benefits.

b. "Level" Premiums Are Better

With what are called "level" premiums, insurance companies promise that your premiums will be raised only if they are raised by the same percentage for all other holders of the same policy. Unlike attained-age increases, an insurance company must get the approval of each state's insurance commission.to raise level premums. But insurance commissions routinely grant such across-the-board increases, so you must plan to pay higher premiums in future years even with a level premium policy.

"NON-CANCELABLE" GROUP POLICIES ARE

NOT AS GOOD AS THEY SOUND

Some insurance companies advertise their group long-term care insurance policies as "non-cancelable," meaning that the insurance company cannot raise premiums—and cannot cancel an individual's coverage unless he or she fails to pay those premiums. While this sounds like a great deal, the reality isn't nearly so terrific. Despite these limitations, insurance companies always retain the right to terminate an entire group policy whenever they see fit. And this is exactly what they do when premiums no longer earn them enough profit. When the insurance company terminates a group policy, people who were covered under the policy are allowed to convert to individual policies offering identical or equivalent coverage. But the new policy premiums are then calculated on an individual basis, not at the previous group rate. And the insurance company then has the same right to raise those premiums as it has regarding any other individual policy.

READ THE FINE PRINT

Many insurance companies engage in sneaky advertising about long-term care premiums. Their brochures often state in large, bold letters that Premiums Do Not Increase With Age—which suggests that, if you buy a policy, your rates will not go up as you get older. But all it really means is that your rates will not *automatically* go up as you get older. The insurance company can still raise your rates—a lot—if they also raise premiums for all other policyholders in your state.

Another underhanded insurance advertising practice is to promise in bold letters in advertisements and brochures that Rates Will Never Change, only to follow that in fine print with the words "on your individual policy unless they are changed for all similar policies in your state." People tend to read the bold statement but not the fine print. And even if they read the fine print, the printing set-up suggests that such statewide changes are unlikely.

The truth, however, is that across-the-board rate increases are inevitable, and often large. In the late 1990s, several companies with many long-term care customers increased their premiums on some policies by as much as 40% in a single year. Others increased rates by smaller amounts per year, but did so for three years in a row. Before buying a policy, compare rate increases by different companies over the previous five years. (If you ask, an insurance broker or agent can and should provide you with such information.) A company that offers lower opening premiums but has a history of frequently or greatly raising rates may be a worse bet than a company that has higher initial premiums but fewer and smaller rate increases.

STEP-DOWN PROVISIONS: GOOD EXTRA PROTECTION

One of the major problems with long-term care insurance is that policyholders may have trouble making their premium payments, especially if they don't need benefits for 20 or 30 years. Premiums rise over time, incomes drop and other expenses may take over most of an elder's expendable income. Because of this slow deterioration in many older people's finances, over half of those holding LTC policies written in the mid 1980s to the early 1990s were forced to allow their coverage to lapse.

To help reduce the odds of this happening to you, look for a policy that allows you to "step down" your coverage. In a step-down policy, the amount of the daily benefit the policy will pay, the level of care it will cover or the length of coverage is reduced from the amount for which you originally signed up. In exchange, the insurance company lowers your premium by a certain percentage. This may make it possible for you to keep the policy in effect—although for a diminished benefit—if you have trouble meeting the more expensive original premium.

Policies with step-down provisions sometimes permit you to "step up" as well—to increase potential benefits in exchange for a higher premium. However, many policies require a step-up to be underwritten—meaning that you must still be in good health to move to higher benefits. A step-up provision may be of particular interest to someone who is young and doesn't want to take on high premiums until he or she is sure that the financial future will be rosy enough to pay for them, but who wants to leave open the option to pay for higher benefit protection.

3. Waiver of Premiums

A waiver of premiums provision allows you to stop paying premiums after you have been collecting benefits for a certain period of time. Without this important provision, most of the benefits you receive may just go back to the insurance company in the form of premiums

Waiver of premiums often applies to residential care benefits only, not to home care. A few policies offer premium waivers as soon as benefits begin, although most require that you continue paying premiums for the first 30 to 90 days you receive benefits. As with most other policy terms, the better the waiver of premiums provision, the higher your initial premiums will be.

F. Benefit Amounts

Almost all long-term care policies will only pay a fixed dollar amount of benefits for covered care—usually well below the actual cost of services. Maximum benefits vary from $50 to $300 a day. Generally, a policy's maximum benefit for residential facility care is about twice the maximum for home care, with maximum benefits for assisted living somewhere in between. Of course, the amount of benefits a policy pays depends on how high its premiums are. But the actual amount you wind up receiving will also depend on whether your policy has benefit flexibility, a limited "elimination" or waiting period and inflation protection.

1. Flexible Benefit Pay-Out

Long-term care policies have a limit on the total dollar value of benefits they will pay over the life of a policy. This limit is the amount paid for daily benefits multiplied by the length of coverage you purchase. For example, $100/day for three years of residence facility care or $50/day for six years of home care = $109,500 in total benefits. If you have coverage for both residential facility care and home care or for long-term care facility, assisted living and home care, it is a great advantage to have a policy that will pay its maximum benefits in any combination, sometimes called a "pool of coverage." This policy term allows you to use your benefits for one level of care, then switch to another level and use whatever total amount of benefits remains unpaid. Do not get a policy that forces you to choose between one level of care or another, or one that will not pay for a different level of care if you later need it.

Take, for example, a policy with a maximum benefit of $109,500—$50/day for six years of home care, $100/day for three years of residential facility care. You would want flexible benefit terms in that policy so you can use three years of home care benefits amounting to $54,750 ($50/day for 1,095 days) and leave the remaining amount (another $54,750) for use in a long-term care facility ($100/day for 547 days).

You will also want a policy that is flexible regarding the time period by which it measures home care benefit amounts—that is, a policy that will pay by the week, month or year, not merely by the day. This provision will save you money if the daily cost of your home care exceeds your daily benefit amount, but you don't get the care every day. For example, if you receive $100 per day worth of home care three days a week, a policy that only pays $75 per day would leave you with $25 per day unpaid for each of the three days of care. On the other hand, if your policy was flexible and paid either by the day or week—$75 per day or $525 per week (7 days x $75/day = $525)—then the policy would cover the full amount of your $300 per week home care costs.

2. Elimination or Waiting Period

Almost all long-term care policies have an initial waiting period immediately after you file a claim for benefits. During this elimination or deductible period, no benefits are paid—you are responsible for paying all your long-term care costs. Elimination periods range from ten days to a full year. Generally, the longer the elimination period, the lower your premiums. An elimination period of six months to one year may reduce your premiums by as much as one-third.

In many instances, an elder only needs care—either at home or in a nursing facility—for a short period of time. A long elimination period means you might not receive any benefits at all in this situation. However, the real purpose of a long-term care policy is not to cover the costs of a short period of care, but to prevent the impoverishing costs of a long period of expensive care. Therefore, purchasing a policy with a longer elimination period—90 days to six months— probably makes good sense if it results in substantial premium savings. This is particularly true if you are buying the policy when you are in your 50s or 60s and therefore will probably be paying the premiums for a long time.

3. Inflation Protection

A benefit of $100 per day for residential care probably seems reasonable, given today's average residential facility costs $40,000 to $50,000 per year. But you are not buying a policy to protect yourself against today's long-term care costs. You are buying a policy to protect against the costs of care 10, 20 or even 30 years from now, when you are far more likely to need its coverage. Because the cost of medical care widely outpaces the overall cost of living, custodial care in a long-term care facility could easily cost $300 per day 10 years from now; in 20 years who knows how high the cost will be? If your benefits then are still only $100 daily, the uncovered costs would eat up your personal assets at lightning speed, and the insurance premiums you've paid for years would be wasted.

The only way to protect yourself from such skyrocketing costs is to make sure your long-term care policy has good inflation protection built into it. Note the emphasis on *good* inflation protection—it comes in several different forms, and some are better than others.

- *Added coverage purchase.* This type of provision permits you to purchase added coverage every few years with higher benefits. The problem is that the added coverage will also come with new premiums—based on your increased age plus any other rate increases—that you may not be able to afford. You may find yourself with benefits too low to be useful and no way to buy added coverage, which means you may wind up dropping the insurance just as you reach an age when you might need coverage.

- *Simple automatic increase.* Many policies offer benefits which increase by a fixed percentage—usually 5%—or by each year's national cost-of-living increase. However, these policies always use the original benefit amount to calculate the percentage increase. These policies are better than the added coverage purchase option because your benefits go up automatically without requiring higher premiums.

- *Compounded automatic increase.* These policies automatically increase benefit amounts each year by a set percentage or by the cost-of-living increase. These policies compound the increases each year rather than always using the original benefit amount as a base figure. Over 10 to 20 years, this compounding might increase your benefits substantially. Of course, because automatic compounded inflation protection is so much better for the insured, the premiums for such coverage are usually considerably higher from the beginning.

• *Time limited protection.* Most policies put a time limit on the yearly inflation benefit increase. The limit is usually 10 to 25 years from the date the policy begins, or when the insured reaches a certain age, usually 80 or 85. If you buy the policy when you are in your 50s or 60s, make sure you get the longest possible period of inflation protection.

Good inflation protection may raise the initial cost of a policy by 25% to 50%. But without good inflation protection, the lower premiums may be a total waste of money.

G. Refund Provisions

There are several reasons why you might end your long-term care policy before you receive all or any of its benefits—a change in your financial picture, a sharp increase in premiums, a change in health or death. If you end your policy, what happens to all those years of premiums you paid?

As with life insurance, a few long-term care policies provide that some of your premiums will be refunded if your coverage ends before full benefits have been paid. These provisions are only offered in some policies—most often in group policies—and do not provide any great financial protection. Therefore, they should not be major considerations when you choose a policy. But if you are trying to decide between two policies that are close in most important respects, the existence of one or another of these refund provisions might tip the balance.

1. Nonforfeiture Provisions

If you drop your coverage before you have collected benefits, a non-forfeiture provision requires some percentage of your equity in the policy—that is, the total amount of premiums you have paid—to be returned to you. The amount refunded is usually quite small—and the provision often applies only if the policy has been in effect for a certain period of time—10, 15 or 20 years. For example, a non-forfeiture provision probably offers the most benefits to someone young, who is more likely to pay premiums for many years before requiring care.

2. Reduced Paid-Up Provisions

Reduced paid-up provisions allow you to drop your coverage—that is, stop paying premiums—but still collect reduced benefit amounts when you qualify, once you have paid premiums for a set number of years (usually 20 or 25).

3. Death Refunds

Death refunds provide that a small percentage of the premiums paid (less any benefits paid) will be returned to the insured's estate, if an insured dies before a certain age (usually 65 or 70).

4. Survivorship Provisions

Survivorship provisions give some protection to a surviving spouse when both spouses have purchased LTC policies. With a survivorship clause, if one insured spouse dies, the surviving spouse may stop paying premiums after a set number of years, but the insurance will remain in effect. This can be very important if the death of one spouse drastically reduces the couple's income. ■

Appendix

Resource Directory

Aging, State Agencies

These are the central offices in each state, run by the state government, that provide general information and referrals to all agencies within the state that provide services for elders. To find out about the services these agencies offer, check the website of the Federal Administration on Aging at www.aoa.dhhs.gov.

ALABAMA

Alabama Department of Senior
Services
RSA Plaza, Suite 470
Montgomery, AL 36130
334-242-5743

ALASKA

Alaska Commission on Aging
Division of Senior Services
Department of Administration
P.O. Box 110209
Juneau, AK 99811-0209
907-465-3250

ARIZONA

Aging & Adult Administration
Department of Economic
Security
1789 West Jefferson, Suite
950A
Phoenix, AZ 85007
602-542-4446

ARKANSAS

Division of Aging and Adult
Services
Arkansas Dept. of Human
Services
P.O. Box 1437, Slot S-53
1417 Donaghey Plaza South
Little Rock, AR 72203
501-682-2441

CALIFORNIA

Department on Aging
1600 K Street
Sacramento, CA 95814
916-322-5290

COLORADO

Aging and Adult Services
Colorado Dept. of Human
Services
1575 Sherman Street, Ground
Floor
Denver, CO 80203
303-866-2800

CONNECTICUT

Division of Elderly Services
25 Sigourney Street, 10th Floor
Hartford, CT 06106
860-424-5298

DELAWARE

Delaware Division of Services
for Aging and Adults with
Physical Disabilities
Department of Health and
Social Services
1901 North Dupont Highway
New Castle, DE 19720
302-577-4791

DISTRICT OF COLUMBIA

Office on Aging
One Judiciary Square – 9th
Floor
441 Fourth Street, NW
Washington, DC 20001
202-724-5622

FLORIDA

Department of Elder Affairs
Building B – Suite 152
4040 Esplanade Way
Tallahassee, FL 32399-7000
904-414-2000

GEORGIA

Division of Aging Services
Dept. of Human Resources
Two Peachtree Street, N.E., 36th
Floor
Atlanta, GA 30303
404-657-5258

HAWAII

Executive Office on Aging
250 South Hotel Street, Suite
109
Honolulu, HI 96813
808-586-0100

IDAHO

Idaho Commission on Aging
P.O. Box 83720
Boise, ID 83720
208-334-3833

ILLINOIS

Department on Aging
421 East Capitol Avenue, Suite
100
Springfield, IL 62701
217-785-3356
Toll-free Senior HelpLine (for
calls within the state): 800-
252-8966

INDIANA

Bureau of Aging and In-Home
Services
Division of Disability, Aging
and Rehabilitative Services
Family and Social Services
Administration
402 West Washington St.,
#W454
Indianapolis, IN 46207
317-232-7020

IOWA

Department of Elder Affairs
Clemens Building, 3d Floor
200 Tenth Street
Des Moines, IA 50309-3609
515-242-3333

KANSAS

Department on Aging
New England Building
503 South Kansas
Topeka, KS 66603-3404
785-296-4986

KENTUCKY

Office of Aging Services
Cabinet for Families and
Children
Commonwealth of Kentucky
CHR Building, 6th Floor
275 East Main Street
Frankfort, KY 40621
502-564-6930

LOUISIANA

Governor's Office of Elder
Affairs
P.O. Box 80374
Baton Rouge, LA 70898-0374
225-342-7100

MAINE

Bureau of Elder and Adult
Services
Department of Human Services
State House, Station #11
35 Anthony Avenue
Augusta, ME 04333
207-624-5335

MARYLAND

Department of Aging
State Office Building
301 West Preston Street, Room
1007
Baltimore, MD 21201
410-767-1100

MASSACHUSETTS

Executive Office of Elder Affairs
One Ashburton Place, 5th Floor
Boston, MA 02108
617-727-7750

MICHIGAN

Office of Services to the Aging
611 West Ottawa Street
N. Ottawa Tower, 3rd Floor
P.O. Box 30676
Lansing, MI 48909
517-373-8230

MINNESOTA

Board on Aging
444 Lafayette Road
St. Paul, MN 55155-3843
612-296-2770
TTY: 800-627-3529

MISSISSIPPI

Division of Aging and Adult
Services
750 North State Street
Jackson, MS 39202
601-359-4925

MISSOURI

Division of Senior Services
Department of Health and
Senior Services
P.O. Box 1337
615 Howerton Court
Jefferson City, MO 65102-
1337
573-751-3082

MONTANA

Senior and Long Term Care
Division
Department of Public Health
and Human Services
P.O. Box 4210
111 Sanders, Room 211
Helena, MT 59620
406-444-4077

NEBRASKA

Division on Aging
1343 M Street
P.O. Box 95044
Lincoln, NE 68509
402-471-2307

NEVADA

Division on Aging
Department of Human
Resources
State Mail Room Complex
3416 Goni Road, Building D-
132
Carson City, NV 89706
775-687-4210

NEW HAMPSHIRE

Division of Elderly and Adult
  Services
State Office Park South
129 Pleasant Street
Brown Building #1
Concord, NH 03301
603-271-4680

NEW JERSEY

Division of Senior Affairs
Department of Health and
  Senior Affairs
P.O. Box 807
Trenton, NJ 08625-0807
609-588-3141
800-792-8820

NEW MEXICO

State Agency on Aging
224 East Palace Avenue,
  Ground Floor
La Villa Rivera Building
Santa Fe, NM 87501
505-827-7640

NEW YORK

Office for the Aging
2 Empire State Plaza
Albany, NY 12223
518-474-5731
800-342-9871

NORTH CAROLINA

Dept. of Health and Human
  Services
Division on Aging
2101 Mail Service Center
Raleigh, NC 27699
919-733-3983

NORTH DAKOTA

Dept. of Human Services
Aging Services Division
600 South 2nd St., Suite 1C
Bismarck, ND 58504
701-328-8910
800-451-8693

OHIO

Department on Aging
50 West Broad Street, 9th Floor
Columbus, OH 43215-5928
614-466-5500

OKLAHOMA

Aging Services Division
Department of Human Services
P.O. Box 25352
312 N.E. 28th Street
Oklahoma City, OK 73125
405-521-2327

OREGON

Senior and Disabled Services
  Division
500 Summer St., NE, 3rd Floor
Salem, OR 97301
503-945-5811

PENNSYLVANIA

Department of Aging
Commonwealth of Pennsylvania
Forum Place
555 Walnut Street, 5th Floor
Harrisburg, PA 17101-1919
717-783-1550

PUERTO RICO

Governor's Office of Elderly
  Affairs
Call Box 50063
Old San Juan Station, PR
  00902
787-721-5710
787-721-4560
787-721-6121

RHODE ISLAND

Department of Elderly Affairs
160 Pine Street
Providence, RI 02903
401-277-2858

SOUTH CAROLINA

Office of Senior and Long Term
  Care Services
Dept. of Health and Human
  Services
P.O. Box 8206
Columbia, SC 29202
803-898-2501

SOUTH DAKOTA

Office of Adult Services and
  Aging
Richard F. Kneip Building
700 Governors Drive
Pierre, SD 57501-2291
605-773-3656

TENNESSEE

Commission on Aging and
  Disability
Andrew Jackson Building, 9th
  Floor
500 Deaderick Street
Nashville, TN 37243-0860
615-741-2056

TEXAS

Department on Aging
4900 North Lamar, 4th Floor
Austin, TX 78751
512-424-6840

UTAH

Division of Aging and Adult
  Services
Box 45500
120 North 200 West
Salt Lake City, UT 84145
801-538-3910

VERMONT

Aging and Disabilities Department
Waterbury Complex
103 South Main Street
Waterbury, VT 05671
802-241-2400

VIRGINIA

Department for the Aging
1600 Forest Avenue, Suite 102
Richmond, VA 23229
804-662-9333

WASHINGTON

Aging and Adult Services
Administration
Department of Social and
Health Services
P.O. Box 45050
Olympia, WA 98504-5050
360-725-2310

WEST VIRGINIA

Bureau of Senior Services
Holly Grove, Building 10
1900 Kanawha Boulevard East
Charleston, WV 25305-0160
304-558-3317

WISCONSIN

Bureau of Aging and Long Term
Care Resources
Dept. of Health and Family
Services
1 West Wilson St., Room 450
Madison, WI 53707
608-266-2536

WYOMING

Division on Aging
Wyoming Dept. of Health
6101 Yellowstone Rd., Suite
259B
117 Hathaway Building
Cheyenne, WY 82002
307-777-7986

Alzheimer's Disease Organizations

Two national organizations focus exclusively on Alzheimer's Disease.
Both provide information on the disease, on medical and nonmedical care and on assistance for those who provide care to those
with Alzheimer's.

Alzheimer's Association
919 North Michigan Ave., Suite 1100
Chicago, IL 60611-1676
800-272-3900
www.alz.org

Alzheimer's Disease Education & Referral Center
P.O. Box 8250
Silver Spring, MD 20907-8250
800-438-4380
www.alzheimers.org

Caregiver Support Groups

Children of Aging Parents
1609 Woodbourne Road, #302A
Levittown, PA 19057
800-227-7294
www.caps4caregivers.org

A nonprofit organization that provides support and information to the families and friends of the dependent elderly. It maintains a directory of self-help support groups for family caregivers, publishes a number of pamphlets for caregivers and puts out a newsletter that provides information on programs for the elderly and their families. Enclose $1 and a self-addressed, stamped envelope with any request for information.

National Family Caregivers Association
10400 Connecticut Ave. #500
Kensington, MD 20895-3944
800-896-3650
www.nfcacares.org

A membership group that publishes a newsletter for family caregivers, provides referrals and conducts a caregiver-to-caregiver support network. Also publishes a caregiver resources guide, available through the organization.

Home Care, Community Programs and Senior Residences

The following organizations provide information about home care agencies, community senior services and non-nursing home senior residences. Some provide referrals to specific providers and facilities. They can also put you in touch with state and local organizations, which can in turn provide you with even more detailed information and referrals.

Following this list of national organizations is a list of state associations that provide information on home care.

National Organizations

Alliance for Children and Families
11700 West Lake Park Drive
Milwaukee, WI 53224
414-359-1040
www.alliance1.org

Offers senior referrals as well as other family services.

The Eldercare Locator
800-677-1116

Open Monday through Friday, 9 a.m. to 11 p.m. (EST), this hotline refers people to eldercare services in communities across the country.

National Association for Home Care
228 Seventh Street, SE
Washington, DC 20003
202-547-7424
www.nahc.org

Maintains a list of home care agencies and offers a guide on choosing the right one.

National Association of
Professional Geriatric Care Managers
1604 North Country Club Road
Tucson, AZ 85716
520-881-8008
www.caremanager.org

National Council on the Aging
409 3rd Street SW, Suite 200
Washington, DC 20024
202-479-1200
800-424-9046
www.ncoa.org

National Health Information Center
Dept. of Health and Human Services
P.O. Box 1133
Washington, DC 20013
800-336-4797
www.health.gov/nhic

National Hispanic Council on Aging
2713 Ontario Road, NW
Washington, DC 20009
202-265-1288
www.nhcoa.org

Provides information on topics related to Hispanics and aging, and
provides assistance for Spanish-speaking seniors.

National Parkinson Foundation
1501 NW 9th Avenue
Miami, FL 33136-1494
305-547-6666
800-327-4545
www.parkinson.org

Visiting Nurse Associations of America
11 Beacon Street, #910
Boston, MA 02108
617-523-4042
www.vnaa.com

State Associations

ALABAMA

Alabama Association of Home
Health Agencies
P.O. Box 40
Montgomery, AL 36101
334-395-9949
800-934-4312
www.aahha.org

ALASKA

Alaska Home Care Association
Geneva Woods Home Health
Care
501 W. International Airport
Rd., Suite 1A
Anchorage, AK 99518

ARIZONA

Arizona Association for Home
Care
2334 McClintock Drive
Tempe, AZ 85282
602-967-2624

ARKANSAS

Home Care Association of
Arkansas
411 S. Victory, Suite 205
Little Rock, AR 72201
501-376-2273

CALIFORNIA

California Association for
Health Services at Home
723 S Street
Sacramento, CA 95814
916-443-8055
www.cahsah.org

COLORADO

Home Care Association of
Colorado
7853 East Arapahoe Road, Suite
2100
Englewood, CO 80112
303-694-4728
www.hcaconline.org

CONNECTICUT

Connecticut Association for
Home Care
110 Barnes Road
P.O. Box 90
Wallingford, CT 06492-0090
203-265-9931
www.cthomecare.org

DELAWARE

Delaware Association of Home
  Care and Community Care
Veale Road Professional Center
309 Veale Road
Wilmington, DE 19810
302-529-3000

DISTRICT OF COLUMBIA

Capitol Home Health Association
5151 Wisconsin Avenue, NW,
  Suite 400
Washington, DC 20016-4124
202-686-8728

FLORIDA

Associated Home Health
  Industries of Florida
512 North Calhoun St.
Tallahassee, FL 32301-2600
850-222-8967
www.ahhif.org

GEORGIA

Georgia Association for
  Comprehensive Home Care,
  Inc.
2100 Roswell Road
Suite 200 C – PMB 407
Marietta, GA 30062
770-565-4531

HAWAII

Home Care and Hospice
  Division
Healthcare Association of
  Hawaii
932 Ward Ave., Suite 430
Honolulu, HI 96814
808-521-8961
www.hahc.org

IDAHO

Idaho Association of Home
  Health Agencies
P.O. Box 6508
Boise, ID 83707
208-362-8190

ILLINOIS

Illinois Home Care Council
1926 Waukegan Rd., Suite 1
Chicago, IL 60025
847-657-6960

INDIANA

Indiana Association of Home
  and Hospice Care, Inc.
8604 Allisonville Rd., Suite 260
Indianapolis, IN 46250
317-844-6630
www.ind-homecare.org

IOWA

Iowa Association for Home
  Care
1520 High Street, Suite 203-B
Des Moines, IA 50309
515-282-3965
www.iowahomecare.org

KANSAS

Kansas Home Care Association
1512 B Legend Trail Drive
Lawrence, KS 66047
785-841-8611
www.kshomecare.org

KENTUCKY

Kentucky Home Health
  Association
154 Patchen Drive, Suite 90
Lexington, KY 40517
606-268-2574
www.khha.org

LOUISIANA

Home Care Association of
  Louisiana
233-A East Main Street
New Iberia, LA 70562
318-560-9610
www.hcla2000.org

MAINE

Home Care Alliance of Maine
20 Middle Street
Augusta, ME 04330
207-623-0345
www.homecarealliance.org

MARYLAND

Maryland National Capital
  Homecare Association
625 Slaters Lane, Suite 200
Alexandria, VA 22314
703-535-1885

MASSACHUSETTS

Home & Health Care Association of Massachusetts
31 James Ave., Suite 780
Boston, MA 02116
617-482-8830
www.mass-homehealth.org

MICHIGAN

Michigan Home Health
  Association
2140 University Park Drive,
  Suite 220
Okemos, MI 48864
517-349-8089
www.mhha.org

MINNESOTA

Minnesota Home Care
  Association
1711 West County Road B,
  Suite 211S
St. Paul, MN 55113-4036
612-635-0607
www.mnhomecare.org

MISSISSIPPI

Mississippi Association for
Home Care
P.O. Box 1468
Ridgeland, MS 39158
601-853-7533
www.mahc.org

MISSOURI

Missouri Alliance for Home
Care
2420 Hyde Park Road, Suite A
Jefferson City, MO 65109
314-634-7772
www.homecaremissouri.org

MONTANA

Montana Association of Home
Health Agencies
1905 River Road
Missoula, MT 59801
406-721-4035
www.mahha.org

NEBRASKA

Nebraska Association of Home
and Community Health
Agencies
7421 Forbes Drive
Lincoln, NE 68516
402-489-1117

NEVADA

Home Health Care Association
of Nevada
P.O. Box 186298
Reno, NV 89511

NEW HAMPSHIRE

Home Health Care Association
of New Hampshire
8 Green Street
Concord, NH 03301
603-225-5597
www.homecarenh.org

NEW JERSEY

Home Health Assembly of New
Jersey, Inc.
14 Washington Rd., Suite 211
Princeton Junction, NJ 08550
609-275-6100
www.homecarenj.org

NEW MEXICO

New Mexico Association for
Home Care
3200 Carlisle Boulevard, NE,
Suite 117
Albuquerque, NM 87110
505-889-4556
www.nmahc.org

NEW YORK

Home Care Association of New
York State
194 Washington Ave., Suite
400
Albany, NY 12210
518-426-8764
www.hcanys.org

NORTH CAROLINA

North Carolina Association for
Home & Hospice Care
226 West Millbrook Road
Raleigh, NC 27609
919-848-3450
www.homeandhospicecare.org

NORTH DAKOTA

North Dakota Association of
Home Health Services
c/o APT, Inc.
P.O. Box 2175
Bismarck, ND 58502-2175
701-224-1815
www.aptnd.com/ndahc

OHIO

Ohio Council for Home Care
1395 East Dublin Granville Rd.,
Suite 350
Columbus, OH 43229-1826
614-885-0434
www.homecareohio.org

OKLAHOMA

Oklahoma Association for
Home Care
8108 NW Tenth, Suite C3
Oklahoma City, OK 73127
405-495-5995
www.oahc.com

OREGON

Oregon Association for Home
Care
1249 Commercial St., SE
Salem, Oregon 97302
503-364-2733
www.oahc.org

PENNSYLVANIA

Pennsylvania Association of
Home Health Agencies
20 Erford Road, Suite 115
Lemoyne, PA 17043
717-975-9448
www.pahha.org

PUERTO RICO

Puerto Rico Home Health
Agencies and Hospices
Association
c/o Arecibo Medical Home Care
P.O. Box 141597
Arecibo, PR 00614
787-879-2955
787-878-7672

RHODE ISLAND

Rhode Island Partnership for
Home Care
P.O. Box 603309
Providence, RI 02906
401-751-2487

SOUTH CAROLINA

South Carolina Home Care
Association
P.O. Box 1763
Columbia, SC 29202
803-254-7355

SOUTH DAKOTA

South Dakota Association of
Health Care Organizations
3708 Brooks Place
Sioux Falls, SD 57106
605-361-2281
www.sdaho.org

TENNESSEE

Tennessee Association for
Home Care
131 Donelson Pike
Nashville, TN 37214-2901
615-885-3399
www.tahc-net.org

TEXAS

Texas Association for Home
Care
3737 Executive Center Drive,
Suite 268
Austin, TX 78731
512-338-9293
www.tahc.org

UTAH

Utah Association of Home
Health Agencies
6949 South High Tech Drive,
Suite 150
Midvale, UT 84047
801-255-5888

VERMONT

Vermont Assembly of Home
Health Agencies
10 Main Street
Montpelier, VT 05602
802-229-0579
vnavt.com

VIRGINIA

Virginia Association for Home
Care
5407 Patterson Avenue, Suite
200B
Richmond, VA 23226
804-285-8636
800-755-8636
www.vahc.org

WASHINGTON

Home Care Association of
Washington
P.O. Box 2016
Edmonds, WA 98020
425-775-8120
www.hcaw.org

WEST VIRGINIA

West Virginia Council of Home
Health Agencies, Inc.
Route 1, Box 190
Elk Fork Road
Middlebourne, WV 26149
304-758-4312

WISCONSIN

Wisconsin Homecare Organization
5610 Medical Circle, Suite 33
Madison, WI 53719
608-278-1115
www.wishomecare.org

WYOMING

Home Health Care Alliance of
Wyoming
1515 S. Spruce St.
Cheyenne, WY 82001
307-237-7042

Insurance — Long-Term Care

The following groups can tell you about long-term care insurance policies available in your state.

American Association of Health Plans
1129 20th Street, NW, Suite 600
Washington, DC 20036
202-778-3200
www.aahp.org

Health Insurance Association of America
1201 F Street NW, #500
Washington, DC 20004
202-824-1600
www.hiaa.org

State Departments of Insurance

Each state has a government agency that regulates the sale of insurance. There should be a listing for an insurance department in the Government Section of the telephone directory. These agencies can provide you with a list of companies authorized to sell long-term insurance in your state.

State Agencies on Aging

Like the Departments of Insurance, the Office on Aging in your state should have a current list of long-term care policies authorized for sale in your state. The Offices on Aging are listed earlier in this Resource Directory.

Legal Assistance

The following groups either provide, or give referrals for, legal assistance for elders. Some provide information on government programs and legislation affecting the elderly. Others will refer you to lawyers in your area who specialize in legal matters affecting elders, such as reviewing the terms of a reverse mortgage, preparing powers of attorney and planning your estate.

American Bar Association
Commission on Legal Problems for the Elderly
740 Fifteenth Street, NW
Washington, DC 20005-1022
202-662-8690
www.abanet.org/elderly

National Academy of Elder Law Attorneys
1604 North Country Club Road
Tucson, AZ 85716
520-881-4005
www.naela.com

National Caucus and Center on Black Aged
1220 L St., NW #800
Washington, DC 20005
202-637-8400
www.ncba-aged.org

National Senior Citizens Law Center
1101 14th Street, NW, #400
Washington, DC 20005
202-289-6976
www.nsclc.org

Licensing and Certification

Nursing Facility License and Certification Offices

These offices are the government agencies in each state that inspect nursing facilities and issue state licenses and Medicare and Medicaid certifications. You can check the record of any nursing facility in the state through this office.

ALABAMA

Dept. of Health Care Facilities
Alabama Department of Public
  Health
Div. Health Care Facilities
P.O. Box 303017
Montgomery, AL 36130
334-206-5077

ALASKA

Health Facilities Licensing and
  Certification
4730 Business Park Boulevard,
  Building H, Suite 18
Anchorage, AK 99503
907-561-8081

ARIZONA

Department of Health Services
Assurance and Licensure
1647 East Morten Ave., Suite 220
Phoenix, AZ 85020
602-674-4200

ARKANSAS

Office of Long-Term Care
Dept. of Human Services
Medical Services
P.O. Box 8059, Slot 402
Little Rock, AR 72203
501-682-8486

CALIFORNIA

California Dept. of Health
  Services
Licensure and Certification
1800 3rd St., Suite 210
P.O. Box 942732
Sacramento, CA 94234
916-445-3054

COLORADO

Colorado Department of Health
  and Environment
Health Facilities Division
4300 Cherry Creek Drive South
Denver, CO 80222
303-692-2819
www.cdphe.state.co.us/hf/
  hfd.asp

CONNECTICUT

Connecticut Department of
  Public Health
Division of Health Systems
  Regulation
410 Capitol Ave., MS#12HSR
Hartford, CT 06134
860-509-7400

DELAWARE

Health Care Facilities Administrator
Office of Health Facilities L & C
2055 Limestone Rd., Suite 200
Wilmington, DE 19808
302-995-8521

DISTRICT OF COLUMBIA

Health Regulation Administration
825 North Capitol St., NE, 2nd
  Floor
Washington, DC 20002
202-442-5888

FLORIDA

Licensing and Certification
Agency for Health Care
  Administration
Division for Health Quality
  Assurance
2727 Mahan Drive, Room 200
Tallahassee, FL 32308
904-487-2527

GEORGIA

Licensing and Certification
Georgia Dept. of Human
  Resources
Office of Regulatory Services
Two Peachtree Street, NW, 31st
  Floor, Suite 31-325
Atlanta, GA 30303
404-657-5700

HAWAII

Licensing and Certification
Hawaii Dept. of Health
Office of Health Care Assurance
601 Kamokila Blvd., Room 395
Kapolei, HI 96707
808-692-7420

IDAHO

Idaho Department of Health
    and Welfare
Facility Standards Bureau
3380 Americana Terrace #260
P.O. Box 83720
Boise, ID 83720-0036
208-334-1864

ILLINOIS

Illinois Department of Public
    Health
Office of Health Care Regula-
    tion
525 West Jefferson, 5th Floor
Springfield, IL 62761
217-782-2913

INDIANA

Licensing and Certification
Indiana State Dept. of Health
Consumer Health Services
    Comm.
2 North Meridian Street,
    Section 3B
Indianapolis, IN 46206-1964
317-233-7022

IOWA

State Department of Inspections
    & Appeals
Division of Health Facilities
Lucas State Office Building, 3rd
    Floor
Des Moines, IA 50319
515-281-4233

KANSAS

Kansas Department of Health
    and Environment
Division of Health
Landon State Office Building
900 SW Jackson, Suite 1001
Topeka, KS 66612-1290
913-296-1240

KENTUCKY

Kentucky Cabinet for Health
    Services
Div. of Long Term Care
275 East Main Street, 5E-B
Frankfort, KY 40621-0001
502-564-2800

LOUISIANA

Division of Licensure &
    Certification
Louisiana Department of Health
    and Hospitals
Health Standards Section
P.O. Box 3767
Baton Rouge, LA 70821-3767
504-342-0415

MAINE

Maine Dept. of Human Services
    - BMS
Division of Licensing and
    Certification
35 Anthony Avenue
State House Station 11
Augusta, ME 04333
207-624-5443
www.state.me.us/bms/licensing/
    division

MARYLAND

MD Dept. of Health and Mental
    Hygiene
Office of Health Care Quality
Spring Grove Hosp. Center
Bland Bryant Building
55 Wade Ave.
Baltimore, MD 21228
410-402-8001

MASSACHUSETTS

Licensing and Certification
Department of Public Health
Division of Health Care Quality
10 West St., 5th Floor
Boston, MA 02111
617-753-8100

MICHIGAN

Division of Operations
MI Dept. of Consumer &
    Industry Svc.
525 West Ottawa, 5th Floor
Lansing, MI 48909
517-241-4154

MINNESOTA

Licensing and Certification
Minnesota Dept. of Health
Facility & Provider Compliance
85 East 7th Place, Suite 300
P.O. Box 64900
St. Paul, MN 55164-0900
651-215-8715

MISSISSIPPI

Mississippi Dept. of Health
Health Facilities L&C
P.O. Box 1700
Jackson, MS 39215-1700
601-354-7300

MISSOURI

Missouri Department of Health
    and Senior Services
Section for LTC Regulation
P.O. Box 1337
615 Howerton Court
Jefferson City, MO 65102
573-526-0721

MONTANA

MT Dept. of Health & Human
    Services
2401 Colonial Drive, 2nd Floor
P.O. Box 202953
Helena, MT 59620
406-444-2099

NEBRASKA

Nebraska Dept. of Health &
  Human Services
Health Facility Licensure and
  Inspection
Credentialing Division
P.O. Box 95007
Lincoln, NE 68509
402-471-0179

NEVADA

Dept. of Human Resources
Bureau of Licensure and
  Certification
1550 College Parkway, Suite
  158
Carson City, NV 89710
702-687-4475

NEW HAMPSHIRE

Department of Health and
  Human Services
Bureau of Health Facilities
  Administration
Licensing and Certification
129 Pleasant St.
Brown Building
Concord, NH 03301
603-271-4966

NEW JERSEY

N.J. State Dept. of Health &
  Senior Services
120 South Stockton St.
P.O. Box 367
Trenton, NJ 08625
609-633-8980
www.state.nj.us/health/

NEW MEXICO

New Mexico Dept. of Health
Licensing & Certification
2040 S. Pachecho, 2nd Floor,
  Room 413
Santa Fe, NM 87505
505-476-9025

NEW YORK

New York State Department of
  Health
Bureau of Long Term Care
  Services
Hedley Park Place
443 River St., Suite 303
Troy, NY 12180
518-402-1045

NORTH CAROLINA

NC Dept. of Human Services
Certification Section, Facility
  Services
2711 Mail Service Ctr.
P.O. Box 29530
Raleigh, NC 27699
919-733-7461

NORTH DAKOTA

State Department of Health
Health Resources Section
600 East Boulevard Avenue
Bismarck, ND 58505
701-328-2352

OHIO

Ohio Department of Health
Division of Quality Assurance
246 North High Street
Box 118
Columbus, OH 43266-0118
614-466-7857

OKLAHOMA

Oklahoma Department of
  Health
Special Health Services
1000 NE Tenth St.
Oklahoma City, OK 73117
405-271-4200

OREGON

Nursing Facility Program Unit
Health Care Licensure &
  Certification
Or Dept. of Human Services
500 Summer St., NE, E-13
Salem, OR 97301
503-945-6456

PENNSYLVANIA

Pennsylvania Dept. of Health
Bureau of Facility L & C
P.O. Box 90
Health & Welfare Building
  #932
Harrisburg, PA 17120
717-787-8015

RHODE ISLAND

Rhode Island Department of
  Health
Facilities Regulation
3 Capitol Hill, Room 306
Providence, RI 02908-5097
401-277-2566

SOUTH CAROLINA

Nursing Home Licensure Office
Division of Health Facilities and
  Services
Department of Health Licensing
2600 Bull Street
Columbia, SC 29201
803-737-7370

SOUTH DAKOTA

Department of Health
Division of Licensure and
  Certification
Office of Health Care Facilities
615 East 4th St.
Pierre, SD 57501-3182
605-773-3356

TENNESSEE

Department of Health
Division of Health Care
  Facilities
425 Fifth Avenue, North
First Floor, Cordell Hull
  Building
Nashville, TN 37247-0530
615-741-7221

TEXAS

Texas Dept. of Human Services
Long Term Care Regulatory
P.O. Box 149030
701 West 51st St.
Austin, TX 78751
512-438-2625
www.dhs.state.tx.us

UTAH

Medicare/Medicaid Program
  Cert./Resident Assessmt.
Health Systems Improvement
P.O. Box 144103
Salt Lake City, UT 84114
801-538-6559

VERMONT

Department of Aging &
  Disabilities
Licensing and Protection
Ladd Hall
103 South Main Street
Waterbury, VT 05671-2306
802-241-2345

VIRGINIA

Department of Health
Center for Quality Health Care
Services & Consumer Protection
3600 West Broad Street, Suire
  216
Richmond, VA 23230
804-367-2102

WASHINGTON

Facilities and Services Licensing
P.O. Box 47852
Olympia, WA 98504
360-705-6652

WEST VIRGINIA

WV Dept. of Health
Health Facility Licensure
1900 Kanawha Boulevard East
Building 3, Suite 550
Charleston, WV 25304
304-558-0050

WISCONSIN

Dept. of Health & Family
  Services
Bureau of Quality Assurance
P.O. Box 2969
Madison, WI 53701
608-267-7185

WYOMING

Department of Health
Health Facilities Program
First Bank Building, 8th Floor
Cheyenne, WY 82002
307-777-7121

Medicaid Assistance

Qualifying for Medicaid coverage can be complicated and confusing. However, there is a national nonprofit organization that can help. The Health Insurance Counseling and Advocacy Program (HICAP) provides free assistance to older people seeking Medicaid coverage. HICAP has offices in almost all metropolitan areas. For the number of the HICAP office nearest you, call the toll-free number for your state's central HICAP office, listed below.

Alabama	800-243-5463	Nebraska	800-234-7119
Alaska	800-478-6065	Nevada	800-307-4444
Arizona	800-432-4040	New Hampshire	800-852-3388
Arkansas	800-224-6330	New Jersey	800-792-8820
California	800-434-0222	New Mexico	800-432-2080
Colorado	800-544-9181	New York	800-333-4114
Connecticut	800-994-9422	(NY City only)	212-869-3850
Delaware	800-336-9500	North Carolina	800-443-9354
District of		North Dakota	800-247-0560
Columbia	202-676-3900	Ohio	800-686-1578
Florida	800-963-5337	Oklahoma	800-763-2828
Georgia	800-669-8387	Oregon	800-722-4134
Hawaii	808-586-7299	Pennsylvania	800-783-7067
Idaho	800-247-4422	Puerto Rico	800-981-4355
Illinois	800-548-9034	Rhode Island	800-322-2880
Indiana	800-452-4800	South Carolina	800-868-9095
Iowa	800-351-4664	South Dakota	800-822-8804
Kansas	800-860-5260	Tennessee	800-525-2816
Kentucky	502-564-7372	Texas	800-252-9240
Louisiana	800-259-5301	Utah	800-541-7735
Maine	800-262-2232	Vermont	800-642-5119
Maryland	800-243-3425	Virginia	800-552-3402
Massachusetts	800-882-2003	Virgin	
Michigan	800-803-7174	Islands	809-778-6311
Minnesota	800-333-2433	Washington	800-397-4422
Mississippi	800-948-3090	West Virginia	800-642-9004
Missouri	800-390-3330	Wisconsin	800-242-1060
Montana	800-332-2272	Wyoming	800-856-4398

Nursing Facility and Alternative Residence Organizations

American Association of Homes and Services for the Aging
2519 Connecticut Ave., NW
Washington, DC 20008-1520
202-783-2242
www.aahsa.org

A nonprofit national association of nursing facilities and senior independent living and assisted living residences. It will provide a list of all member facilities in your state, including level of facility, type of sponsorship, number of living units or beds and services offered.

American Health Care Association
12301 L Street, NW
Washington, DC 20005
202-842-4444
www.ahca.org

A national association of accredited nursing facilities. It will provide a list of its member facilities in your state.

National Citizens' Coalition for Nursing Home Reform
1424 16th Street, NW, #202
Washington, DC 20036-2211
202-332-2275
www.nccnhr.org

Monitors enforcement of state and federal laws regarding conditions and practices in nursing facilities and other facilities for the elderly. Although it does not provide referrals to nursing facilities or other residences, it can refer you to local organizations that have information about specific facilities.

Ombudsman Offices

Each state has a central office that can refer you to the long-term care ombudsman responsible for any nursing facility that you are considering or in which you already reside. Long-term care ombudsmen respond to complaints about long-term care facilities and mediate disputes between residents and the facilities. They are in a unique position to know whether a facility has frequent complaints, and whether the facility responds well to them. There is no charge for their services.

ALABAMA

State LTC Ombudsman
Department of Senior Services
770 Washington Avenue, RSA
  Plaza, Suite 470
Montgomery, AL 36130-1851
334-242-5743

ALASKA

Deputy State LTC Ombudsman
Office of the State Ombudsman
AK Mental Health Trust
  Authority
550 West 7th Ave., Suite 1830
Anchorage, AK 99501

ARIZONA

State LTC Ombudsman
Aging and Adult Administration
1789 West Jefferson 25 W 950
  A
Phoenix, AZ 85007
602-542-6454

ARKANSAS

State LTC Ombudsman
Division of Aging and Adult
  Services
P.O. Box 1437, Slot 1412
Little Rock, AR 72201
501-682-8952

CALIFORNIA

State LTC Ombudsman
California Department on
  Aging
1600 K Street
Sacramento, CA 95814
916-323-6679

COLORADO

State LTC Ombudsman
The Legal Center
455 Sherman St., Suite 130
Denver, CO 80203
800-288-1376
www.thelegalcenter.org/
  services_older.html

CONNECTICUT

State LTC Ombudsman Office
CT Dept. of Social Services
25 Sigourney St., 10th Floor
Hartford, CT 06106
860-424-5200

DELAWARE

State LTC Ombudsman
Division of Services for Aging &
  Adults
1901 North Dupont Highway
Main Admin. Bldg. Annex
New Castle, DE 19720
302-577-4791

DISTRICT OF COLUMBIA

State LTC Ombudsman
Legal Counsel for the Elderly
601 E St., N.W. A4-315
Washington, DC 20049
202-434-2140

FLORIDA

Florida State LTC Ombudsman
Council
600 South Calhoun St., Suite
270
Tallahassee, FL 32301
888-831-0404
http://myflorida.com/ombuds-
man

GEORGIA

Office of the State LTC
Ombudsman
Two Peachtree Street, NW, 9th
Floor
Atlanta, GA 30303
888-454-5826
www2.state.ga.us/departments/
dhr/aging.html

HAWAII

State LTC Ombudsman
Executive Office on Aging
250 South Hotel Street, Suite
406
Honolulu, HI 96813
808-586-0100

IDAHO

State LTC Ombudsman
Idaho Commission on Aging
3380 Americana Terrace, Suite
120
P.O. Box 83720
Boise, ID 83720
208-334-2220

ILLINOIS

State LTC Ombudsman
Department on Aging
421 East Capitol Avenue, Suite
100
Springfield, IL 62701-1789
217-785-3143

INDIANA

State LTC Ombudsman
Indiana Division
Disabilities\Rehab Services
402 West Washington St.,
Room W 454
P.O. Box 7083
Indianapolis, IN 46207-7083
800-545-7763

IOWA

State LTC Ombudsman
Department of Elder Affairs
Clemens Building
200 10th Street, 3rd Floor
Des Moines, IA 50309
515-242-3327

KANSAS

Office of the State LTC
Ombudsman

610 SW 10th St., 2nd Floor
Topeka, KS 66612
785-296-3017

KENTUCKY

State LTC Ombudsman
Office of Aging Services
5C-D
275 East Main Street
Frankfort, KY 40621
502-564-4595

LOUISIANA

State LTC Ombudsman
Office of Elderly Affairs
421 North Fourth Street, 3rd
Floor
P.O. Box 80374
Baton Rouge, LA 70898
225-342-7100

MAINE

Maine LTC Ombudsman
Program
1 Weston Court
P.O. Box 128
Augusta, ME 04333
207-621-1079
www.maineombudsman.org

MARYLAND

State LTC Ombudsman
Maryland Dept. of Aging
301 West Preston Street, Room
1007
Baltimore, MD 21201
410-767-1100

MASSACHUSETTS

State LTC Ombudsman
Massachusetts Executive Office
of Elder Affairs
One Ashburton Place, 5th Floor
Boston, MA 02108
617-727-7750

MICHIGAN

State LTC Ombudsman
Elderlaw of Michigan
221 N. Pine
Lansing, MI 48933
866-485-9393

MINNESOTA

Office of Ombudsman for
Older Minnesotans
121 East Seventh Place, Suite
410
St. Paul, MN 55101
800-657-3591

MISSISSIPPI

State LTC Ombudsman
MS Dept. of Human Services,
Division of Aging
750 North State Street
Jackson, MS 39202
601-359-4927

MISSOURI

State LTC Ombudsman
Dept. of Health & Senior
   Services
P.O. Box 570
615 Howerton Court
Jefferson City, MO 65102
800-309-3282
www.dss.state.mo.us/da/
   ombud/htm

MONTANA

State LTC Ombudsman
Department of Health &
   Human Services
P.O. Box 4210
111 N. Sanders
Helena, MT 59604
406-444-4676

NEBRASKA

State LTC Ombudsman
Division of Aging Services
P.O. Box 95044
Lincoln, NE 68509
402-471-2307
www.hhs.state.ne.us/ags/
   ltcombud.htm

NEVADA

State LTC Ombudsman
Division of Aging Services
445 Apple St., # 104
Reno, NV 89502
775-688-2964

NEW HAMPSHIRE

NH LTS Ombudsman Program
129 Pleasant Street
Concord, NH 03301
603-271-4375

NEW JERSEY

Office of Ombudsman for
   Institutional Elderly
P.O. Box 807
Trenton, NJ 08625-0807
609-943-4026

NEW MEXICO

State LTC Ombudsman
State Agency on Aging
1410 San Pedro, NE
Albuquerque, NM 87501
505-255-0971

NEW YORK

State LTC Ombudsman
Office for the Aging
Agency Building #2
2 Empire State Plaza
Albany, NY 12223
518-474-7329

NORTH CAROLINA

State LTC Ombudsman
Division of Aging
2101 Mail Service Center
Raleigh, NC 27603
919-733-8395

NORTH DAKOTA

State LTC Ombudsman
Aging Services Division
600 South 2nd St., Suite 1C
Bismarck, ND 58504
800-451-8693

OHIO

State LTC Ombudsman
Ohio Department of Aging
50 West Broad Street, 9th Floor
Columbus, OH 43215
614-466-1221

OKLAHOMA

State LTC Ombudsman
Aging Services Division
312 NE 28th St.
Oklahoma City, OK 73105
405-521-6734

OREGON

Oregon Office of the LTC
   Ombudsman
3855 Wolverine NE, Suite 6
Salem, OR 97305
503-378-6533
www.teleport.com/~ombud/

PENNSYLVANIA

State LTC Ombudsman
Department of Aging
555 Walnut St., 5th Floor
P.O. Box 1089
Harrisburg, PA 17101-2301
717-783-7247

PUERTO RICO

State LTC Ombudsman
Puerto Rico Governor's Office
   Elder Affairs
Call Box 50063
Old San Juan Station
San Juan, PR 00902
787-725-1515

RHODE ISLAND

State LTC Ombudsman
Alliance for Better Long Term
   Care
422 Post Road, Suite 204
Warwick, RI 02888
401-785-3340

SOUTH CAROLINA

State LTC Ombudsman
SC DHHS, Office on Aging
P.O. Box 8206
Columbia, SC 29202
803-898-2850

SOUTH DAKOTA

State LTC Ombudsman
Office of Adult Services and
  Aging
Department of Social Services
700 Governor's Drive
Pierre, SD 57501-2291
605-773-3656

TENNESSEE

State LTC Ombudsman
Commission on Aging and
  Disability
Andrew Jackson Bldg.
500 Deaderick Street, 9th Floor
Nashville, TN 37243-0860
615-741-2056

TEXAS

State LTC Ombudsman
Texas Department on Aging
4900 N. Lamar Blvd., 4th Floor
P.O. Box 12786
Austin, TX 78711
512-424-6875
www.tdoa.state.tx.us

UTAH

State LTC Ombudsman
Dept. of Human Services
Division of Aging and Adult
  Services
120 North, 200 West, Room
  401
Salt Lake City, UT 84103
801-538-3924

VERMONT

State LTC Ombudsman
Vermont Legal Aid, Inc.
264 N. Winooski
P.O. Box 1367
Burlington, VT 05402
802-863-5620

VIRGINIA

State LTC Ombudsman
Virginia Assn. Area Agencies on
  Aging
530 East Main St., Suite 800
Richmond, VA 23219
804-644-2804
www.vaaaa.org

WASHINGTON

State LTC Ombudsman
South King County Multi-
  Service Center
1200 South 336th St.
P.O. Box 23699
Federal Way, WA 98093
253-838-6810
www.ltcop.org/index.htm

WEST VIRGINIA

State LTC Ombudsman
West Virginia Bureau of Senior
  Services
1900 Kanawha Blvd. E
Holly Grove Bldg., #10
Charleston, WV 25302
304-348-3317

WISCONSIN

State LTC Ombudsman
Board on Aging and Long-Term
  Care
214 North Hamilton St.
Madison, WI 53703
608-266-8945

WYOMING

State LTC Ombudsman
Wyoming Senior Citizens, Inc.
756 Gilchrist
P.O. Box 94
Wheatland, WY 822201
307-322-5553

Reverse Mortgage and Home Equity Conversion Assistance

The following organizations can provide information on reverse mortgages and various other types of home equity conversions that might be available to help you finance home care. Remember, though, that these are referrals only. You should examine any plan offered with a personal financial advisor.

National Center for Home Equity Conversion
360 N. Robert # 403
St. Paul, MN 55101
651-222-6775
www.reverse.org

American Association of Retired Persons (AARP)
601 E. St., NW
Washington, DC 20049
800-424-3410
www.aarp.org.revmort

Ask for the pamphlet "Home Made Money: A Consumer's Guide to Reverse Mortgages."

American Bar Association
Commission on Legal Problems for the Elderly
740 15th St., NW
Washington, DC 20005-1002
202-662-8690
www.abanet.org/elderly

Ask for the "Attorney's Guide to Home Equity Conversion."

HUD USER
U.S. Department of Housing & Urban Development
451 7th St., NW
Washington, DC 20410
202-708-1112
www.hud.gov/buying/rvrsmort.cfm

Viatical Settlement Assistance

The following organizations may give you leads to reputable viatical settlement companies in your area. They may also provide you with some general information about the terms offered in viatical settlement plans. However, they do not answer specific questions about the advisability of entering into a viatical settlement or about the terms of any specific settlement offer. That is still entirely up to you, with the help of an accountant, lawyer or other financial advisor.

Viatical and Life Settlement Association of America
800 Mayfair Circle
Orlando, FL 32803
800-842-9811
www.viatical.org

Your state's Department of Insurance
    Look in the "Government Listings" section of the white pages of your telephone book. ■

Index

M

CATALOG

...more from nolo

	PRICE	CODE
Nondisclosure Agreements	$39.95	NAG
The Small Business Start-up Kit (Book w/CD-ROM)	$29.99	SMBU
The Small Business Start-up Kit for California (Book w/CD-ROM)	$34.99	OPEN
The Partnership Book: How to Write a Partnership Agreement (Book w/CD-ROM)	$39.95	PART
Sexual Harassment on the Job	$24.95	HARS
Starting & Running a Successful Newsletter or Magazine	$29.99	MAG
Take Charge of Your Workers' Compensation Claim	$34.99	WORK
Tax Savvy for Small Business	$36.99	SAVVY
Working for Yourself: Law & Taxes for the Self-Employed	$39.99	WAGE
Your Crafts Business: A Legal Guide	$26.99	VART
Your Limited Liability Company: An Operating Manual (Book w/CD-ROM)	$49.99	LOP
Your Rights in the Workplace	$29.99	YRW

CONSUMER

	PRICE	CODE
How to Win Your Personal Injury Claim	$29.99	PICL
Nolo's Encyclopedia of Everyday Law	$29.99	EVL
Nolo's Guide to California Law	$24.95	CLAW
Trouble-Free Travel...And What to Do When Things Go Wrong	$14.95	TRAV

ESTATE PLANNING & PROBATE

	PRICE	CODE
8 Ways to Avoid Probate	$19.99	PRO8
9 Ways to Avoid Estate Taxes	$29.95	ESTX
Estate Planning Basics	$21.99	ESPN
How to Probate an Estate in California	$49.99	PAE
Make Your Own Living Trust (Book w/CD-ROM)	$39.99	LITR
Nolo's Simple Will Book (Book w/CD-ROM)	$36.99	SWIL
Plan Your Estate	$44.99	NEST
Quick & Legal Will Book	$16.99	QUIC

FAMILY MATTERS

	PRICE	CODE
Child Custody: Building Parenting Agreements That Work	$29.99	CUST
The Complete IEP Guide	$24.99	IEP
Divorce & Money: How to Make the Best Financial Decisions During Divorce	$34.99	DIMO
Do Your Own California Adoption: Nolo's Guide for Stepparents and Domestic Partners (Book w/CD-ROM)	$34.99	ADOP
Get a Life: You Don't Need a Million to Retire Well	$24.99	LIFE
The Guardianship Book for California	$39.99	GB
A Legal Guide for Lesbian and Gay Couples	$29.99	LG

	PRICE	CODE
Living Together: A Legal Guide (Book w/CD-ROM)	$34.99	LTK
Medical Directives and Powers of Attorney in California	$19.99	CPOA
Using Divorce Mediation: Save Your Money & Your Sanity	$29.95	UDMD

GOING TO COURT

	PRICE	CODE
Beat Your Ticket: Go To Court and Win! (National Edition)	$19.99	BEYT
The Criminal Law Handbook: Know Your Rights, Survive the System	$34.99	KYR
Everybody's Guide to Small Claims Court (National Edition)	$26.99	NSCC
Everybody's Guide to Small Claims Court in California	$26.99	CSCC
Fight Your Ticket ... and Win! (California Edition)	$29.99	FYT
How to Change Your Name in California	$34.95	NAME
How to Collect When You Win a Lawsuit (California Edition)	$29.99	JUDG
How to Seal Your Juvenile & Criminal Records (California Edition)	$34.95	CRIM
The Lawsuit Survival Guide	$29.99	UNCL
Nolo's Deposition Handbook	$29.99	DEP
Represent Yourself in Court: How to Prepare & Try a Winning Case	$34.99	RYC
Sue in California Without a Lawyer	$34.99	SLWY

HOMEOWNERS, LANDLORDS & TENANTS

	PRICE	CODE
California Tenants' Rights	$27.99	CTEN
Deeds for California Real Estate	$24.99	DEED
Dog Law	$21.95	DOG
Every Landlord's Legal Guide (National Edition, Book w/CD-ROM)	$44.99	ELLI
Every Tenant's Legal Guide	$29.99	EVTEN
For Sale by Owner in California	$29.99	FSBO
How to Buy a House in California	$34.99	BHCA
The California Landlord's Law Book: Rights & Responsibilities (Book w/CD-ROM)	$44.99	LBRT
The California Landlord's Law Book: Evictions (Book w/CD-ROM)	$44.99	LBEV
Leases & Rental Agreements	$29.99	LEAR
Neighbor Law: Fences, Trees, Boundaries & Noise	$26.99	NEI
The New York Landlord's Law Book (Book w/CD-ROM)	$39.99	NYLL
New York Tenants' Rights	$27.99	NYTEN
Renters' Rights (National Edition)	$24.99	RENT
Stop Foreclosure Now in California	$29.95	CLOS

HUMOR

	PRICE	CODE
Poetic Justice	$9.95	PJ

	PRICE	CODE

IMMIGRATION

	PRICE	CODE
Becoming a U.S. Citizen: A Guide to the Law, Exam and Interview	$24.99	USCIT
Fiancé & Marriage Visas	$44.95	IMAR
How to Get a Green Card	$29.99	GRN
Student & Tourist Visas	$29.99	ISTU
U.S. Immigration Made Easy	$44.99	IMEZ

MONEY MATTERS

	PRICE	CODE
101 Law Forms for Personal Use (Book w/CD-ROM)	$29.99	SPOT
Bankruptcy: Is It the Right Solution to Your Debt Problems?	$19.99	BRS
Chapter 13 Bankruptcy: Repay Your Debts	$34.99	CH13
Creating Your Own Retirement Plan	$29.99	YROP
Credit Repair (Book w/CD-ROM)	$24.99	CREP
Getting Paid: How to Collect from Bankrupt Debtors	$24.99	CRBNK
How to File for Chapter 7 Bankruptcy	$34.99	HFB
IRAs, 401(k)s & Other Retirement Plans: Taking Your Money Out	$34.99	RET
Money Troubles: Legal Strategies to Cope With Your Debts	$29.99	MT
Stand Up to the IRS	$24.99	SIRS
Surviving an IRS Tax Audit	$24.95	SAUD
Take Control of Your Student Loan Debt	$26.95	SLOAN

PATENTS AND COPYRIGHTS

	PRICE	CODE
The Copyright Handbook: How to Protect and Use Written Works (Book w/CD-ROM)	$39.99	COHA
Copyright Your Software	$34.95	CYS
Domain Names	$26.95	DOM
Getting Permission: How to License and Clear Copyrighted Materials Online and Off (Book w/CD-ROM)	$34.99	RIPER
How to Make Patent Drawings Yourself	$29.99	DRAW
Inventor's Guide to Law, Business and Taxes	$34.99	ILAX
The Inventor's Notebook	$24.99	INOT
Nolo's Patents for Beginners	$29.99	QPAT
License Your Invention (Book w/CD-ROM)	$39.99	LICE
Patent, Copyright & Trademark	$39.99	PCTM
Patent It Yourself	$49.99	PAT
Patent Pending in 24 Hours	$29.99	PEND

	PRICE	CODE
Patent Searching Made Easy	$29.95	PATSE
The Public Domain	$34.95	PUBL
Trademark: Legal Care for Your Business and Product Name	$39.95	TRD
Web and Software Development: A Legal Guide (Book w/ CD-ROM)	$44.95	SFT

RESEARCH & REFERENCE

| Legal Research: How to Find & Understand the Law .... | $39.99 | LRES |

SENIORS

Choose the Right Long-Term Care: Home Care, Assisted Living & Nursing Homes	$21.99	ELD
The Conservatorship Book for California	$44.99	CNSV
Social Security, Medicare & Goverment Pensions	$29.99	SOA

SOFTWARE

Call or check our website at www.nolo.com
for special discounts on Software!

LeaseWriter CD—Windows	$129.95	LWD1
LLC Maker—Windows	$89.95	LLP1
PatentPro Plus—Windows	$399.99	PAPL
Personal RecordKeeper 5.0 CD—Windows	$59.95	RKD5
Quicken Legal Business Pro 2004—Windows	$79.95	SBQB4
Quicken WillMaker Plus 2004—Windows	$79.95	WQP4

Special Upgrade Offer

Get 35% off the latest edition off your Nolo book

It's important to have the most current legal information. Because laws and legal procedures change often, we update our books regularly. To help keep you up-to-date we are extending this special upgrade offer. Cut out and mail the title portion of the cover of your old Nolo book and we'll give you 35% off the retail price of the NEW EDITION of that book when you purchase directly from us. For more information call us at 1-800-728-3555. This offer is to individuals only.

Order Form

Name

Address

City

State, Zip

Daytime Phone

E-mail

Our "No-Hassle" Guarantee

Return anything you buy directly from Nolo for any reason and we'll cheerfully refund your purchase price. No ifs, ands or buts.

☐ Check here if you do not wish to receive mailings from other companies

Item Code	Quantity	Item	Unit Price	Total Price

Method of payment

☐ Check   ☐ VISA   ☐ MasterCard
☐ Discover Card   ☐ American Express

Subtotal	
Add your local sales tax (California only)	
Shipping: RUSH $9, Basic $5 (See below)	
"I bought 3, ship it to me FREE!"(Ground shipping only)	
TOTAL	

Account Number

Expiration Date

Signature

Shipping and Handling

Rush Delivery—Only $9

We'll ship any order to any street address in the U.S. by UPS 2nd Day Air* for only $9!

* Order by noon Pacific Time and get your order in 2 business days. Orders placed after noon Pacific Time will arrive in 3 business days. P.O. boxes and S.F. Bay Area use basic shipping. Alaska and Hawaii use 2nd Day Air or Priority Mail.

Basic Shipping—$5

Use for P.O. Boxes, Northern California and Ground Service.

Allow 1-2 weeks for delivery. U.S. addresses only.

For faster service, use your credit card and our toll-free numbers

**Call our customer service group
Monday thru Friday 7am to 7pm PST**

Phone	1-800-728-3555
Fax	1-800-645-0895
Mail	Nolo
950 Parker St.
Berkeley, CA 94710

Order 24 hours a day @
www.nolo.com

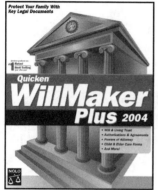

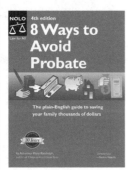

Remember:

Little publishers have big ears.
We really listen to you.

Take 2 Minutes & Give Us Your 2 cents

Your comments make a big difference in the development and revision of Nolo books and software. Please take a few minutes and register your Nolo product—and your comments—with us. Not only will your input make a difference, you'll receive special offers available only to registered owners of Nolo products on our newest books and software. Register now by:

PHONE
1-800-728-3555

FAX
1-800-645-0895

EMAIL
cs@nolo.com

or **MAIL** us
this registration card

fold here

Registration Card

NAME _____ DATE _____

ADDRESS _____

_____

CITY _____ STATE _____ ZIP _____

PHONE _____ EMAIL _____

WHERE DID YOU HEAR ABOUT THIS PRODUCT? _____

WHERE DID YOU PURCHASE THIS PRODUCT? _____

DID YOU CONSULT A LAWYER? (PLEASE CIRCLE ONE)   YES   NO   NOT APPLICABLE

DID YOU FIND THIS BOOK HELPFUL?   (VERY)   5   4   3   2   1   (NOT AT ALL)

COMMENTS _____

_____

_____

WAS IT EASY TO USE?   (VERY EASY)   5   4   3   2   1   (VERY DIFFICULT)

We occasionally make our mailing list available to carefully selected companies whose products may be of interest to you.

❑ If you do not wish to receive mailings from these companies, please check this box.

❑ You can quote me in future Nolo promotional materials.
   Daytime phone number _____.

ELD 4.2

Nolo in the NEWS

"Nolo helps lay people perform legal tasks without the aid—or fees—of lawyers."

—USA TODAY

Nolo books are ..."written in plain language, free of legal mumbo jumbo, and spiced with witty personal observations."

—ASSOCIATED PRESS

"...Nolo publications...guide people simply through the how, when, where and why of law."

—WASHINGTON POST

"Increasingly, people who are not lawyers are performing tasks usually regarded as legal work... And consumers, using books like Nolo's, do routine legal work themselves."

—NEW YORK TIMES

"...All of [Nolo's] books are easy-to-understand, are updated regularly, provide pull-out forms...and are often quite moving in their sense of compassion for the struggles of the lay reader."

—SAN FRANCISCO CHRONICLE

fold here

- -

Place
stamp here

Nolo
950 Parker Street
Berkeley, CA 94710-9867

Attn: ELD 4.2